"*Racial Justice and Nonviolence Education* is a must read for any educator working to create a healthy culture in their classrooms, or for anyone working on peace building anywhere. Romano combines touching, real life stories along with theory to bring the philosophy of nonviolence to life. This book helps to keep Dr. King's legacy current and alive."

— **Kazu Haga**, *Kingian nonviolence trainer, Founder and Coordinator of East Point Peace Academy (Oakland, CA) and author of the book Healing Resistance: A Radically Different Response to Harm*

T0383686

Racial Justice and Nonviolence Education

This book examines the role that community-based educators in violence-affected cities play in advancing Dr. Martin Luther King Jr.'s radical nonviolent vision for racial and social justice.

This work argues that nonviolence education can help communities build capacity to disrupt and transform cycles of violence by recognizing that people impacted by violence are effective educators and vital knowledge producers who develop unique insights into racial oppression and other forms of systemic harm. This book focuses on informal education that takes place beyond school walls, a type of education that too often remains invisible and undervalued in both civil society and scholarly research. It draws on thousands of hours of work with the Connecticut Center for Nonviolence (CTCN), a grassroots organization that presents an ideal case study of the implementation of King's core principles of nonviolence in 21st-century urban communities. Stories of educators' life-changing educational encounters, their successes and failures and their understanding of the six principles of Kingian nonviolence animate the text. Each chapter delves into one of the six principles by introducing the reader to the lives of these educators, providing a rich analysis of how educators teach each principle and sharing academic resources for thinking more deeply about each principle. Against the backdrop of today's educational system, in which reductive and caricatured treatments of King are often presented within the formal classroom, CTCN's work outside of the classroom takes a fundamentally different approach, connecting King's thinking around nonviolence principles to working for racial justice in cities deeply impacted by violence.

This book will be of much interest to students of conflict resolution, race studies, politics and education studies, as well as to practitioners in the field.

Arthur Romano is Assistant Professor at the Jimmy and Rosalynn Carter School for Peace and Conflict Resolution at George Mason University, USA.

Routledge Studies in Peace and Conflict Resolution
Series Editors: Tom Woodhouse and Oliver Ramsbotham
University of Bradford

The field of peace and conflict research has grown enormously as an academic pursuit in recent years, gaining credibility and relevance amongst policy makers and in the international humanitarian and NGO sector. The Routledge Studies in Peace and Conflict Resolution series aims to provide an outlet for some of the most significant new work emerging from this academic community, and to establish itself as a leading platform for innovative work at the point where peace and conflict research impacts on International Relations theory and processes.

Theorising Civil Society Peacebuilding
The Practical Wisdom of Local Peace Practitioners in Northern Ireland, 1965–2015
Emily E. Stanton

Neighborhood Resilience and Urban Conflict
The Four Loops Model
Karina V. Korostelina

Reconciling Divided States
Peace Processes in Ireland and Korea
Edited by Dong Jin Kim and David Mitchell

Interactive Peacemaking
A People-Centered Approach
Susan H. Allen

Racial Justice and Nonviolence Education
Building the Beloved Community, One Block at a Time
Arthur Romano

For more information about this series, please visit: www.routledge.com/ Routledge-Studies-in-Peace-and-Conflict-Resolution/book-series/RSPCR

Racial Justice and Nonviolence Education

Building the Beloved Community, One Block at a Time

Arthur Romano

LONDON AND NEW YORK

Cover image: © Connecticut Center for Nonviolence

First published 2022
by Routledge
4 Park Square, Milton Park, Abingdon, Oxon OX14 4RN

and by Routledge
605 Third Avenue, New York, NY 10158

Routledge is an imprint of the Taylor & Francis Group, an informa business

British Library Cataloguing-in-Publication Data
A catalogue record for this book is available from the British Library

Library of Congress Cataloging-in-Publication Data
A catalog record for this book has been requested

ISBN: 978-1-032-15064-2 (hbk)
ISBN: 978-1-032-15062-8 (pbk)
ISBN: 978-1-003-24391-5 (ebk)

DOI: 10.4324/9781003243915

Typeset in Bembo
by Apex CoVantage, LLC

Dedicated in loving memory to Adeline Robustelli who taught me about MLK and the importance of lovingly fighting for justice, remaining curious, following my heart and speaking the truth even when it was inconvenient.

Contents

Illustrations

Acknowledgments

It is with great joy that I express gratitude to the many people who helped make this book a reality. I want to thank everyone involved with the Connecticut Center for Nonviolence (CTCN) who allowed me to work beside them and so generously shared pieces of their lives with me, inviting me into their homes and taking time to reflect amid many competing demands. I am particularly indebted to Victoria Christgau who introduced me Dr. Bernard LaFayette and to the Kingian nonviolence curriculum more than 15 years ago. She invited me to contribute to the development of CTCN and played a critical role in helping me build bridges with the wider community of peace practitioners in Hartford and New Haven and in expanding my understanding of nonviolence. I am so fortunate that Dr. Bernard LaFayette has so generously offered his mentorship, feedback and ideas on nonviolence education and peace pedagogy in the process of writing this book and provided first-hand accounts of his experiences with Dr. King and others in the civil rights movement.

In the writing of this book, I was privileged to have a very dedicated and talented group of people who offered critical and constructive feedback. Dr. Jacob Werblow worked meticulously through each of the chapters, offering insights based on his knowledge as an expert in urban education and his familiarity with education in Hartford and state-wide in Connecticut. He also played a critical role in helping me clarify the structure of this book and opened his home to me while I was conducting the most intensive phase of research. Dr. Patricia Parker and Dr. David Ragland offered their deep insights into liberatory education, Black history and the power dynamics of doing activist research in Black communities as a white male academic. Dr. Dorothy (Dot) Maver was one of the first people to work with me in outlining the overall themes of the book drawing on her years of experience as a national leader on issues of peacebuilding in helping me refine the scope of this work. Dr. Sara Diamond's comments and familiarity with CTCN and her many years of experience conducting participatory action research in Connecticut were also invaluable in contextualizing this work. Several nonviolence experts including Stellan Vintagarden, Daryn Cambridge and Sean Chabot offered their critical and creative perspectives on the theory and practice of nonviolence in ways that helped me refine some of the major themes of the book. Vikas Goras and his father took the time to video conference with me from India and discuss in depth the history of the Gandhian constructive project and its relevance today based on their work. I also owe a debt of gratitude to the peer reviewers who provided detailed and productive feedback to strengthen the final manuscript and to my colleagues at the Carter School for Peace and Conflict Resolution who were consistently supportive of the project and provided a vibrant intellectual atmosphere to come home to.

An international team of research assistants at the Carter School was instrumental in helping me substantiate this project. Ziad Achkar played a critical role in updating the research featured in the manuscript, helping finalize bibliographical information and talking through each of the chapters at length. In the earlier phases of the project, Farishta Sakhi, Kuldeep Niraula, Lauren Kinney and Singmila Shimrah conducted vital background research that made this project possible.

In addition to those featured in this book, numerous expert practitioners gave of their time. Andrew Clark from the Institute of Regional and Municipal Planning at Central Connecticut State University offered invaluable insight on the political context and policy landscape in Connecticut and provided me with a base in the city from which to conduct this research. Gabriel Boyd not only shared his deep insights about working with youth in Hartford on numerous occasions but also opened up his classes for me to observe. Diane Jones a long-time community advocate took time to introduce me to people doing re-entry and violence prevention work in Hartford and her son Dean Jones, a leader in his own right drove me through the city to see firsthand how relationship building and violence interrupters work in the city. Bishop Jonathan Selders offered his reflections on the movement for black lives in Connecticut and nationally.

Finally, I could have not done this without my family. My wife Dawoon Chung was a clear and consistent voice for the value of this project, even when I doubted my ability to carry it out. She helped me develop the central ideas highlighted in the book, reading through the manuscript several times and offering critical and honest feedback each time. She sacrificed a great deal so that I could share this work with others even while holding down a vibrant career of her own. I am also profoundly grateful for my in-laws, Myung Kyu Chung and Keumok (Kay) Kim, as I wrote the bulk of the book while we lived together and their support, love and intergenerational perspective grounded me and our whole family throughout this journey. My daughter EJ's love, curiosity and creativity bolstered my spirits daily and she along with my niece and nephew Tino and Mari reminded me of what is at stake in working for social justice. My sister Sabrina and brother-in-law Buell were key supports stepping up throughout this process of writing as we navigated my mother's terminal illness and walked her home. I am also grateful to my father, Arthur and my aunt Anne Marie and uncles Gino and Tony who have always been supportive of my intellectual work.

Introduction

It is a hot summer day, and I'm sitting in an empty high school classroom interviewing a 14-year-old girl named Tanisha. Tanisha identifies as Black and lives in Hartford, Connecticut. She is nearing the end of a two-week-long nonviolence workshop and summer jobs program, part of a community-based violence prevention effort hosted by the Connecticut Center for Nonviolence (CTCN). A nonprofit organization that has engaged people from across Hartford and neighboring New Haven, CTCN explores Dr. Martin Luther King, Jr.'s ideas of nonviolence as a way to uncover root causes of violence and build a grassroots educational movement in the city. This is the first time I've met Tanisha, and she is sincere and surprisingly candid in her responses to my questions. I begin by asking her what interests her about nonviolence, and why she chose this workshop.

Tanisha immediately explains that issues of violence are a big part of her life, and that, like many young people, she struggles to find answers to these problems through her education. It is no wonder that she is struggling. Tanisha lives in the richest state in the richest country in the world, yet in her home city of Hartford, over 90% of the students attending Hartford Public Schools are youth of color, and over 90% are living below the poverty line.[1]

She continues,

> I chose nonviolence because my uncle was recently, a year ago, killed [at] a basketball tournament. When he passed away, I just thought that violence is never the answer. Like I really felt heartbroken because he really, truly was my best friend and everything. And, like, I just felt like I- if I can make a change [now], I hope that way somewhere down the line it happens [for someone else]. So, I figure I need to start when I'm young.

Tanisha chose to attend CTCN's Youth Nonviolence Leadership Program because "I felt like if I could use this to help stop violence in the town that I live in or the city . . . it can make a [wider] difference".

Even though she hasn't entered high school yet, Tanisha has already started working to influence positive change in her community.

DOI: 10.4324/9781003243915-1

She wrote a book, she tells me, in order to make a difference in her school.

> It's for bullies – it's called *Dear Bullies* and is just talking about people that I've known or seen, that I've seen get bullied and stuff – what they get called when they're younger tends not to be something great. So, it's a book about people that get made fun of when they're younger and turn out to [achieve their own] greatness when they get older.

★★

Realities for kids in Hartford and New Haven often differ from the ending that Tanisha imagines in her book. Many youth and adults in these communities experience high levels of trauma because they've witnessed violence firsthand, face housing and food insecurity and end up behind bars[2] in one of America's most racially and economically divided states.[3] Far too many people are not given the opportunity to cultivate their greatness in the face of these obstacles. When outsiders look at Hartford, Tanisha's city, they often do not see potential there, just like the bullies she writes about. Media reports on Hartford often focus on gun violence with headlines such as: "Six Shot, Two Killed in Separate Hartford Shootings", "Community Mourns 15-year-old Gunned Down in Connecticut" or "Residents Concerned as Police Work to Solve Crimes".[4,5,6] Likewise, policymakers and researchers have much to say about the (apparently) intractable problems that urban communities such as Hartford face on a national scale. They often highlight violent crime, guns, drugs and "failing schools", while describing the spaces that Tanisha calls home in terms of urban "blight" and "decay".[7]

Indeed, people in America's most violence-affected cities face daunting problems. The list is a familiar one by now: The United States stands apart from other high-income countries with its significantly elevated rates of violence, particularly gun violence and homicide. According to the World Health Organization (WHO), the most violent cities in the US are some of the deadliest in the entire world. Consider, for example, Baltimore and St Louis, which have per capita homicide rates so high that they are in the top 50 most violent cities in the world.[8] In 2017, Hartford was the 22nd most violent city in America, with some of the highest per-capita homicide rates in the country.[9] In the most deeply impacted neighborhoods in these cities, one's chance of being killed can be higher than that of a US soldier sent to war in Afghanistan or Iraq.[10] This grim reality is not lost on residents; some Chicago citizens have nicknamed their city Chi-raq, a reference to the war-torn Middle Eastern country.

All of these problems are formidable, but media accounts and policy briefs almost always overlook the creative capacity of people within these communities to effect change. From Chicago to Newark to Milwaukee, people of color and especially Black people living in American cities are too often rendered either as passive victims or irredeemable perpetrators of violence. This narrative fails to portray how people living with these problems produce knowledge about the underlying causes of violence, proactively explore solutions and share information within their communities. Although leaders often call for *community engagement* or *culturally relevant approaches*, in reality, violence prevention and urban education often rely heavily on expert-driven approaches. For this reason, stories such as Tanisha's are essential to transforming the narrative about the problem of violence in America.

Is it possible for Tanisha's dream of a nonviolent society to become reality? What will it take to break deeply established cycles of violence in America's most vulnerable cities? Most of the young people that I interviewed for this book, including Tanisha, agree that education can play an important role in influencing change. Sadly, they also report rarely finding the space in school to talk through the tangled challenges of poverty, systemic racism and violence that they face every day in their neighborhoods. Accordingly, young people like Tanisha must find other avenues to make sense of their circumstances and get help. While it is widely cited that some urban youth in violence-affected cities turn to gangs to find support,[11] most turn to family and friends, engage with churches and religious organizations and join sports leagues or groups focused on music and arts, as well as community-based programs run by activists, not-for-profits and civic organizations.[12] They come in search of insight, skills and knowledge, but also to feel a sense of belonging, support and courage, not only to survive but also to heal and change their communities' violent dynamics.

These desires and goals led Tanisha and thousands of others to the CTCN. In Connecticut, community-led education allows people to pursue unfamiliar paths and explore stepping into the role of a community educator committed to nonviolence, but it also does something more – it brings people together to imagine and work toward what Dr. King called the beloved community. The beloved community envisions a society grounded in an ethics of love and solidarity and a steadfast commitment to racial justice. Community-based education provides a vital space in which to model and enact those values of the beloved community in the here and now and not only as a utopic goal for the future. Indeed, the beloved community is not so much a destination as an ongoing and continuous commitment to learning around a specific set of values.

This book is about the important and often overlooked role of community-based educators in advancing understanding of Dr. King's radical nonviolent vision for racial and social justice. It reveals how grassroots education grounded in the historical legacy of nonviolent resistance can help not only make King's lifework more relevant but also embolden hope, increase agency and amplify moral imagination as community members step more fully into the role of educators and peacebuilders. The educators profiled here, who are mostly people of color without formal teaching credentials, possess invaluable insights regarding the possibilities for teaching nonviolence outside classroom walls and within their own communities.

★★

The idea for the CTCN began in 2005 when Victoria Christgau, a long-time peace educator, artist and event organizer, attended a training with Dr. Bernard LaFayette, a world-renowned civil rights activist who had worked closely with Dr. Martin Luther King, Jr. Christgau had already worked for nearly two decades in her predominately White rural community in northwest Connecticut founding and producing an annual MLK celebration while she worked as an art educator focused on peace-related themes. After attending a number of nonviolence workshops and becoming a certified nonviolence trainer with Dr. LaFayette, Christgau and LaFayette discussed Dr. King's legacy and he asked her to begin a nonviolence training center in Connecticut and to employ an approach that would put community members at the forefront of this work. At Dr. LaFayette's request, Christgau began by leading workshops in several schools in Hartford and attending local *Stop the Violence* rallies while reaching out to people engaged in community work in Hartford. In the ensuing months, she met Pastor James Lane, Warren Hardy and several of the community leaders and educators featured in this book, who still work with the Center today.

Over the past 15 years, the CTCN has grown from a small local educational movement staffed entirely by a handful of volunteers with no funding to a not-for-profit organization with several hundred thousand dollars of annual project-based funding at its peak. Participants in CTCN's programs are diverse and include students, teachers, police officers, community-level violence prevention advocates, clergy, people of faith and other community members. CTCN has undertaken a very challenging kind of work in an extremely difficult context for its community-based educators, where participants experience violence, poverty and marginalization and often operate with limited state resources. CTCN's funding and volunteers come and go, and even their physical spaces – workshop spaces and offices – are donated by community members and groups, and therefore change frequently. Even so, CTCN has built and sustained its work for over a decade now, and in Hartford and New Haven has engaged over 10,000 people to consider Dr. King's nonviolent approach to uproot systemic racism and violence in their everyday lives. There are now over 100 nonviolence trainers across Connecticut certified by CTCN, many of whom have led workshops and helped anchor the citywide network of community-based educators.

The nonviolence educators featured in this book take an existing curriculum developed by one of King's closest associates and adapt it to their context. **And this is the first approach for creating a pedagogy that embodies the beloved community: understanding nonviolence as a living and principled philosophy practiced by King and others that needs to be adapted and experimented with to be relevant to issues of racial justice today**. While the curriculum centers on Dr. King and civil rights history, community-based educators explore their own struggles and dreams, inner conflicts and tensions. In the process, they re-articulate their identities in relation to nonviolence as a method for both personal and social transformation and strive to build communities grounded in this understanding.

The curriculum, created in 1995 by Dr. Bernard LaFayette and his colleague David Jensen, is available in *The Leaders Manual: An Introduction to Kingian Nonviolence*, which educators have used all over the world since its publication.[13] According to LaFayette, the night before King was assassinated, he and King were engrossed in a conversation about important challenges to sustaining and moving forward with their work. During this conversation, King explained to LaFayette that they would need to figure out a way both to "internationalize and institutionalize nonviolence".[14]

LaFayette was inspired by King's words – what he refers to as his marching orders – and wanted to make nonviolence more accessible to people from all walks of life. LaFayette and Jensen used participatory pedagogies that incorporate role plays, simulations, discussion-based models and other ways of building on the knowledge of local participants to explore King's work, the wider US civil rights movement and the philosophy and practice of nonviolence. Central to this model was the idea that there needed to be community ownership of Kingian nonviolence and that community members should be given opportunities to become trainers and facilitate this work themselves. CTCN has embraced and expanded this community engagement model. Their work reveals a **second approach to the pedagogy of the beloved community that is to involve the community and people affected by oppression as educators and leaders**. Connecticut residents do not have to have a college degree or prior experience as an educator to attend a "training of trainers" (TOT) leadership program and become a community nonviolence educator. Participants must commit to attending the introductory workshop and following and learning the TOT process, which includes working alongside senior nonviolence educators, most of who are from Hartford and New Haven.

Since the mid-1990s, tens of thousands of people around the world have participated in Kingian nonviolence workshops, briefings and trainings. From Lagos, Nigeria, to Medellin, Colombia, certified Kingian nonviolence trainers from local communities operate in over forty countries. In the 2010s, Kingian nonviolence education grew and became more visible in the US as well. The January 21, 2017 Women's March, the largest march in US history, adopted the six principles of nonviolence as key organizing tenets on the recommendation of Carmen Perez, one of the march leaders. Perez, who worked closely with LaFayette and entertainer and activist Harry Belafonte, said that she grounded her moral and strategic approach in "Kingian nonviolence" and emphasized the role of nonviolent action in transforming, rather than simply destroying and antagonizing existing structures.[15] Almost a year later, during the March for Our Lives in Washington, DC, Alex King and D'Angelo McDade, two teenagers from Chicago, illuminated Kingian nonviolence principles once more. They walked to the microphone in front of thousands of people and a national television audience and declared,

> the beloved community is the framework of the future. And what that means is how our community is now, it will be affected in the future if we

don't make a change . . . If we aren't acting like a family now, we won't act like a family in the future. If pain is in our community now, pain will forever be in our community in the future, if we don't make a change.[16]

These youth were part of the North Lawndale High School Peace Warriors program, structured by Kingian nonviolence and developed by Tiffany Childress, a science teacher at the school, Kazu Haga and Jonathan "Globe" Lewis, whom LaFayette had trained a few years earlier. In response to the 2018 mass shooting at Marjory Stoneman Douglas High School in Parkland, Florida, the Peace Warriors met with Parkland students and committed to working together as part of a larger national youth movement. Alex King expressed they joined forces "not only knowing that we would support one another, but also realizing that without the proper grassroots resources, this issue of violence will not be solved, and we will not stop until we are properly resourced in our communities".[17]

★★

As a university professor and scholar practitioner in the field of conflict resolution, I have long been interested in the transformative potential of grassroots educational work and the wider peacebuilding networks they help build and sustain. I have had the honor to collaborate with and learn alongside activists and educators across the country. This work has taken me to a variety of places – from rural towns in Appalachia to cities across the US; from teargas-filled protests to somber, quiet memorials constructed after a mass shooting. Time and again, I've observed community members coming together to respond to violence by developing participatory forms of education that meaningfully engage people, many of whom are at the margins of American society. I saw this in the cities of Ferguson and St Louis when I worked with local activists Pastor Cori Bush and Dr. David Ragland to bring together family members and friends who had lost loved ones to police violence, to support each other in healing and respond through grassroots truth-telling as part of the Ferguson St Louis Truthtelling Project. In North Carolina, Black feminist organizers – including Dr. Patricia Parker, Nia Wilson and Alexis Pauline Gumbs – the Ella Baker Women's Center and Spirit House led community explorations to create Harm Free Zones in their communities. These organizers put Black women and girls at the forefront of their movements and built on the resilience and brilliance already present in their communities. I saw this in the Bay area, where Kingian nonviolence trainer Kazu Haga developed a program in which incarcerated people in San Quentin prison became nonviolence trainers and experimented with these principles behind bars.

From the comfort of my high-rise office building that overlooks Washington, DC, in the suburbs of Northern Virginia, I often find myself searching through the many books, articles and reports written about violence prevention, conflict resolution, urban education and conflict analysis that fill my shelves and computer. These resources often cannot adequately explain or respond to the violence that people navigate in the cities where the educators featured in this book work and live. This is not to say that academic resources and my academic training are of no use or have nothing to contribute; in fact, community members are typically more eager than my traditional classroom students to learn about academic models and are adept at testing both the relevance and applicability of those theories. We frequently discuss the body of research on peace and conflict resolution, and I have brought together my master's and Ph.D. students from conflict-affected countries with community-based educators from Connecticut to share ideas.

However, I have seen consistently in my work over the past 20 years that people impacted by violence have forms of knowledge about it that *experts* and more professionalized service providers simply lack. They have insights about the causes of violence and understanding of discrete mechanisms that reproduce violence (which are seen most clearly from within systems of oppression) as well as familiarity with cultural practices to make sense of these causes and mechanisms. Victor Frankl and Paulo Freire's classic works highlight that knowledge and a desire to understand can powerfully drive people to take action and are not the domain of the professional class alone (or even primarily). Frankl pointed out in *Man's Search for Meaning*, which reflects on his experiences at Auschwitz, that this desire to make meaning in the midst of extreme injustice is so strong, and anchors people's sense of self-worth so profoundly, that not even the most heinous forms of violence can extinguish it. Freire insightfully noted in his seminal work, *Pedagogy of the Oppressed*, that people that are oppressed need the opportunity to frame and respond to the problems impacting their lives and to take control of their educational experience. Similarly, today, the drive to make sense of oppression and seek broader meaning is a vital source of energy for challenging injustice and envisioning and building more just societies that motivate community educators to work for racial justice.

As a White male and a newly class-privileged academic, my views are consistently challenged and expanded in this field work. Often, I underestimate the depth, complexity and impact of systemic racism in people's lives. I'm not alone with these blind spots: numerous studies demonstrate that White and Black people differ widely in their perceptions of racial discrimination and racism in American education and urban life.[18] Nonetheless, groups of *experts* – educated, class privileged, primarily White, academics and other professionals – often fail to seriously grapple with those who "do not understand" the problems as they do, even though Black people (and other marginalized groups) have the epistemic advantage: They are consistently subjected to harmful, racist practices.[19,20,21] Through community-led education centered on issues of peace and justice, people of color and other marginalized groups take more control of their educational experiences. This is one of the most interesting facets of CTCN's work, as it highlights knowledge production as a form of epistemic resistance that has a longstanding history in America especially in Black communities which have enacted what Jarvis Givens has aptly called Fugitive Pedagogy.[22] Educators are pushing back against powerful structural arrangements that shape what we think should be taught (curriculum), by whom, where and through what forms of instruction (pedagogy). **A third approach to the pedagogy of the beloved community is to foster peer learning and shared leadership so that people can step readily into leadership positions in a context of solidarity and ongoing learning.**

Much of the current research on violence prevention and urban education has a bias toward technocratic solutions and elite-led processes that disconnect education from people's lived experiences. Although the idea of "engagement" (the mutually beneficial exchange of knowledge and resources in a context of partnership and reciprocity) is *en vogue* in both the university and the non-profit world, power differences mean that subjects of this research are too often excluded and not positioned as key knowledge producers.[23,24] A shallow commitment to engagement can make it seem that people living with violence and racism are being paraded around for others' benefit in these programs, which ultimately leaves power structures unchallenged and community members exhausted.

At the same time, however, excellent work is taking place to creatively develop learning communities that draw on the historically overlooked expertise of community leaders and members and the ways they resist injustice. This book is informed by the wider literature on community-based, participatory and critical education. In the broadest terms, community-based education means that the community provides the vital energy for education and learning – student projects center on community needs and interests, and community members serve as resources and partners in all aspects of teaching and learning.[25] Scholars and practitioners in education are increasingly using rich sources of pedagogical innovation that emerge out of urban life. For example, they draw on barber shop pedagogy, hip-hop pedagogy and even more recently, the pedagogy of Ferguson.[26,27,28] Growing movements in my own field of peace and conflict resolution are also beginning to examine and recognize "everyday" peacebuilding, referring to local people who work with their own definitions, models, approaches and strategies for peace.[29,30] Many of these educators get no recognition for their efforts and might not fit preconceived images of teachers or change-makers. They operate without formal teaching credentials and often facilitate outside of formal school settings at YMCAs, libraries, community centers and other locations. Consequently, many experts, policymakers and funders have failed to support these efforts or to adequately understand the scope of the challenges of urban education. But scholars of peace and conflict resolution are coming to see that we must learn from these models to sustain a kind of peace that is responsive to people's everyday lives.

This book is the result of over a decade of engaged research during which I worked closely with, and learned from, the community educators at the

CTCN. I write as both a participant and an observer of these activities, as I am a nonviolence educator and, since the Center's founding, have assisted in facilitating nonviolence workshops and supporting their strategic planning and evaluation efforts. I have spent over 1,500 hours working with CTCN and have also conducted nearly 50 formal interviews with community educators, workshop participants, activists and government officials across both Hartford and New Haven, including both youth and adults. Their voices and experiences – as well as my own participation and research – form the basis of this book.

★★

The community-based educators at CTCN use Dr. Martin Luther King, Jr.'s life and work as a starting place to explore racial justice in urban America. They are certainly not alone in their interest. Dr. King is America's most well-known and beloved peacemaker, and most public schools mandate that students and teachers commemorate his life and study the civil rights movement. Hundreds of books have been written about King's life, which is honored with a national holiday and day of service. Thousands of events are held annually on MLK day in the US alone. However, we engage with King in ways that often leave educators with few resources for making sense of violence, systemic racism and social justice action today even as they experience oppression in their own lives.

Even worse, King can easily get put on a pedestal as a saint, with little explanation of how he developed his militant approach to social change and was pushed to the center of Black freedom struggles. Forgotten or erased is the analysis that drove him to champion radical social change to challenge White supremacy, militarism and economic exploitation, and how he developed courage over time and handled the violent resistance that he and others faced at every turn. Professor Michael Dyson says,

> we forget the fact that Martin Luther King Jr. was hated and harassed and resisted and opposed by many white Americans who felt him to be . . . the most dangerous Negro leader in America. Now, we want to remove those claws . . . His danger has been sweetened. His threat has been removed. There are only smiles and whispers and applause now without the kind of threat that he represented.[31,32]

By isolating King's leadership qualities and vision for civil rights, we lose sight of how King was part of a larger movement, overlooking the many thousands of people – women, queer folks, youth and others – who took risks alongside King and inspired him. Furthermore, by placing King on a pedestal, we can ignore his struggles and personal process of development to present a finished product that is too polished and unrealistic. As Marianne Wright Edelman vividly says, we need to understand Dr. King in human terms in order to learn from him:

> Most Americans remember Dr. King as a great leader. I do too. But I also remember him as someone able to admit how often he was afraid and unsure about his next step. But faith prevailed over fear and uncertainty and fatigue and depression. It was his human vulnerability and his ability to rise above it that I most remember. In this, he was not different from any black adults whose credo has been to make "a way out of no way".[33]

Uniquely at CTCN, educators go beyond the popular post-racial exultations of Dr. King, the peacemaker, and his "I Have a Dream" speech. Instead, community educators analyze how King's understanding of justice evolved and deepened over time, especially as a result of his involvement in the wider civil rights and, later, anti-war and labor movements. The six key principles of nonviolence that CTCN utilizes not only offer insight into King's method of struggle but also invite consideration of how they might apply today. These principles are not merely rules that prescribe "when X happens, do Y". Rather, each principle intentionally raises important and unsettling questions about taking risks in the face of oppression and violence, the possibilities for personal and social redemption and the emotional toll of sustaining resistance over the long term. These principles touch on the ethical and practical demands of using nonviolence in people's daily lives, and they also raise larger questions about the roots or underlying causes of violence. Conversations regularly explore ways to dismantle systemic racism and White supremacy, militarism and unrestrained capitalism – what Dr. King termed the "triple evils".[34]

Most of the heroes in this book are not singular charismatic leaders, nor do they fit the mode of leadership typically described in bestselling books about the role of courage in social change. For the most part, they are not educated in the most elite schools in America, nor are they White males who helm the most powerful institutions in the world. The people who teach Kingian nonviolence in Hartford and New Haven come from a wide range of educational backgrounds and are primarily working-class people and women and men of color that bring an innovative approach to teaching in the community. They remain on the margins of mainstream educational efforts, in part because they are attempting to address issues of violence and systemic racism in America today in ways that critique inequalities in education, criminal justice and even the economic system. These are issues that require deep self-reflection, not only for communities most affected by the fear of violent crime, housing insecurity and grinding poverty but also for those of us who have the privilege of living without these things. As one of Dr. LaFayette's teachers, the Reverend Lawson puts it, "In a nonviolent movement you need all kinds of people" to challenge the status quo.[35]

★★

The Kingian nonviolence method can be taught, applied and improved and does not belong to experts alone, all of which are key aspects of participatory education.[36] Nonviolent struggles for democracy and human rights have taken place in countries around the world over the past 80 years.[37,38,39]

And yet analysis of these nonviolent movements' success typically pays little or no attention to the role of education. This point became vividly clear to me when I interviewed Dr. James Lawson, one of the most influential nonviolence educators during the 1960s civil rights movement, and someone Dr. King knew well and had personally recruited to help with trainings. When I interviewed Lawson in Nashville, Tennessee, I wanted to hear about the inner workings of nonviolence education and asked if he would give me a play by play of how he designed his nonviolence education workshops. I assumed that given Lawson's well-known and respected work, which has been recounted in numerous popular books and films, he had gotten this question many times.

"I know you must have been asked about this so many times before and may be tired of these questions". I began to apologize before Lawson, at the time well into his 80s, stopped me short and replied:

> Not really. Because . . . no, not really. If you look at the books that talk about the Freedom Rides or the sit-in campaigns or Stride toward Freedom, Montgomery Boycotts . . . I haven't read all the works yet by any means, but I've read quite a number. If you look at those books, there's almost nowhere any curiosity about what nonviolence is, what its dynamics were, how it worked, almost none, no curiosity.

I was taken aback. He continued, "Well I think that preparation, which is educational- that includes strategy, planning, tactics, history- all of that is critical [for application] in the 21st century especially".

Despite the vital importance of this kind of nonviolence method and education, most of the attention in the media on nonviolence (and even in scholarly literature) goes either to iconic personalities discussed in isolation, such as King, or to highly visible and acute moments of resistance. Michael Nagler, a world-renowned researcher of nonviolence, refers to the preoccupation with dramatic moments of public resistance and protest as "nonviolence peak experiences", and much of the current research on nonviolence is, indeed, intently focused on the peak.[40] For example, think of the one man standing in front of the tank in Tiananmen Square, or the mass mobilization in Egypt's Tahrir Square during the Arab spring, or unarmed protestors in Ferguson, Missouri stared down by police armed with military weapons. These actions take courage in the extreme, and Louis Kireberg rightly highlights in his scholarship that nonviolent conflict escalation and dramatic, peak experiences can bring hidden issues to the surface and help change power dynamics for marginalized groups.[41] Yet focusing solely on these flashpoints can obscure the dedication, planning and subtle work required behind the scenes and in response to everyday challenges obscuring what lies behind "the peak".

King saw nonviolence education as a moral and pragmatic necessity and believed that movements focused solely on short-term political gain would lose vital sources of inspiration and a long-term view. Yet social movement research on nonviolence predominately considers large-scale mobilizations, and thus it can miss the process through which groups of people facing violence change their perceptions of conflict, sense of the available options and underlying ethics. Strategic and principled nonviolence are deeply intertwined. And while stories about the tactical organization of major nonviolent campaigns are extremely important, these stories, by their design, don't have enough to say about the everyday work of nonviolence education as a response to the equally daunting everyday challenges of systemic racism. Education in this context requires supporting learners in developing and refining conceptual frameworks, reflective inquiry and repertoires for effective political and moral action[42] that form the backbone of a democratic community committed to racial justice.

The concept of structural violence also pushes us to move beyond the dramatic flashpoints and analyze more deeply acts of direct physical violence in cities, such as gun or gang-involved violent crime. It challenges us to examine the larger social context that makes this violence seem acceptable or even necessary to those who engage in crime or self-defense. Peace researcher Johan Galtung coined the term "structural violence" to expand how we understand and define violence. The term describes forms of violence that are not immediate and direct; for example, when political, economic and cultural systems deprive people of their human needs, shorten their lives and strip them of their sense of dignity and worth in society.[43] Galtung, like other thinkers such as Hannah Arendt, James Baldwin, Franz Fanon and Bell Hooks, interprets violence as a phenomenon with multiple levels and causes, many of which are a result of structured inequalities in our society that often indirectly shorten, disfigure or end people's lives without the use of a gun or weapon.

As Gandhi noted, poverty is one the worst forms of violence.[44] Structural violence around race means that Black Americans contend with poverty and economic inequality that leads to more limited educational opportunities, poorer health, substandard housing options and a greater likelihood of being the victims of physical violence.[45,46,47,48,49,50]

Central to his concept of structural violence, Galtung observes that unjust social arrangements are often rendered invisible, especially to those who benefit from them. Ultimately, these inequalities are baked into the cake. They are an integral part of many overlapping institutions, reinforced in everyday life and engrained in our often-unstated assumptions about the relative value of human lives. As Galtung pointed out nearly 50 years ago – highlighted with the illustration below – structural violence can be invisible and exists everywhere, and we sometimes sincerely perceive it to be normal.

Nonviolence educators in violence-affected cities who want to teach King in ways that are relevant to contemporary life need to help people see, understand and respond to structural violence in order to disrupt it and devise alternatives. **And this is a fourth approach to the pedagogy of the beloved community: examining and exposing structures of violence and systemic injustices to change them.**

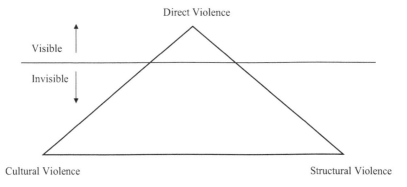

Figure 0.1 Galtung's "Violence Triangle"

Envisioning more peaceful and socially just communities goes beyond matters of physical safety and into an exploration of the psychological, emotional and everyday political dimensions. This requires what global peacemaker and author John Paul Lederach calls "moral imagination".[51] According to Lederach, the development of moral imagination requires that we muster the vulnerability and strength to envision a beloved community beyond the familiar landscape of violence and cultivate the creativity, motivation, outrage and resilience to work toward achieving it.

★★

I have found in my research over the past decade that community educators are interested in larger challenges than picking up discrete and specific skills sets in conflict resolution or violence prevention, although those skills are often desired as well. For community educators and participants featured in this book, envisioning and working for peace can be a radical act of care and commitment in a world where Black life is too often devalued. For anyone interested in urban education, especially in communities impacted by systemic racism and other forms of violence, we can learn a great deal from the work of nonviolence community educators. These educators explicitly engage in the difficult work of sustaining hope in the midst of violence and oppression.[52] Educators and community members featured here are often interested in personal and collective exploration of what a healthy and thriving community would and should look like; in other words, the desire to envision and model the beloved community animates their efforts to build local learning communities that they believe are fundamentally important to achieving racial justice. These small acts of resistance can be powerful, as we see in Tanisha's commitment to finding ways of drawing out the greatness in her community even while grieving the loss of her uncle. These same goals of focusing on a community's strengths and potential for the future animate community-led nonviolence education.

Each chapter of this book introduces the lives of these educators and demonstrates how they teach and explore one of the six specific principles of Kingian nonviolence:

- Nonviolence is a way of life for courageous people.
- The beloved community is the framework of the future.
- Attack forces of evil, not persons doing evil.
- Accept suffering without retaliation for the sake of the cause to achieve the goal.
- Avoid internal violence of the spirit as well as external physical violence.
- The universe is on the side of justice.

These chapters replicate the journey of CTCN participants as they explore the featured principle. It introduces basic tenets of that principle, key debates related to that principle and how people interpret, struggle with and attempt to apply the principle to their everyday lives and work. Through these chapters and descriptions, policymakers, researchers and community leaders can see how education plays a vital role in violence prevention and social justice efforts.

The interplay between these educators' life-changing educational encounters, their successes and failures and their understanding of the six principles of nonviolence shapes this book. Chapters move between theory and practice, as King is transformed from an iconic object of once-yearly commemoration into a living legacy relevant and connected to contemporary urban life in America. Chapters show how community-based educators use the arts, theater, storytelling, multi-media engagement and other pedagogical approaches to building bridges between King's legacy and communities today. **A fifth approach to the pedagogy of the beloved community is to use the arts and participatory pedagogy to give people many ways to make meaning about nonviolence and draw on their diverse experiences and ways of knowing**.

★★

When Dr. King persuaded educator Jim Lawson to come to Nashville and begin teaching workshops on nonviolence, he made one of the most important decisions for the success of the civil rights movement. So important was this kind of education to King that he made a point whenever he could of attending Lawson's talks and other educational events, always sitting in the front row.

Throughout this book, I argue that nonviolence education can effectively build capacity to disrupt and transform cycles of violence by recognizing that people impacted by violence can be, and already are, effective educators and vital knowledge producers. In fact, they have unique insight into racial oppression and issues of justice. This ongoing desire to make meaning about oppression, as Frankl and Freire's work describes, is a powerful driver of participation and a key aspect of solving these problems and building the beloved community.

Notes

1 Rich Scinto, "Thousands Rally for Education Equality; Vernon Among Lowest Perform-ing Schools," *CT Patch*, December 3, 2014, https://patch.com/connecticut/vernon/thousands-rally-education-equality-vernon-among-lowest-performing-schools-0.
2 Megan Kathleen, "Small Gains on State Test, but Troubling Achievement Gap Per-sists," *The CT Mirror*, September 9, 2019, https://ctmirror.org/2019/09/09/small-gains-on-state-test-but-troubling-achievement-gap-persists/.
3 Mary Buchanan and Mark Abraham, "Concentrated Wealth and Poverty in Con-necticut's Neighborhoods," *Data Haven*, August 8, 2015, https://datahaven.carto.com/viz/923322b6-e446-11e4-8d59-0e018d66dc29/embed_map.
4 Mattt Astin, "Community Mourns 15-year-old Gunned Down in Hartford," *NBC Connecticut*, March 20, 2017, https://www.nbcconnecticut.com/news/local/community-mourns-15-year-old-gunned-down-in-hartford/32590/
5 Rebecca Lurye, "Six Shot, Two Killed in Separate Hartford Shootings, Police Say," *Hartford Courant*, September 24, 2017. Breaking News, www.courant.com/breaking-news/hc-br-hartford-gunfight-20170923-story.html.
6 Nicholas Rondinone, "Amid Four Homicides This Week, Hartford Residents Concerned as Police Work to Solve Crimes, Stem Violence," *Hartford Courant*, February 23, 2019, www.courant.com/breaking-news/hc-br-hartford-fatal-stabbing-20190222-6c3bdx4bjvdipmnnytbx6q7eoq-story.html.
7 Brentin Mock, "What We Mean When We Talk About 'Blight,'" *Bloomberg*, Febru-ary 16, 2017, www.bloomberg.com/news/articles/2017-02-16/why-we-talk-about-urban-blight.
8 Christopher Woody, "These Were the 50 Most Violent Cities in the World in 2018," *Business Insider*, March 12, 2019, www.businessinsider.com/most-violent-cities-in-the-world-in-2018-2019-3.
9 Elisha Fieldstat, "The Most Dangerous Cities in America, Ranked," *CBS News*, Novem-ber 9, 2020, www.cbsnews.com/pictures/the-most-dangerous-cities-in-america/.
10 Niall McCarthy, "Homicides in Chicago Eclipse U.S. Death Toll in Afghani-stan and Iraq [Infographic]," *Forbes*, September 8, 2016, sec. Business, www.forbes.com/sites/niallmccarthy/2016/09/08/homicides-in-chicago-eclipse-u-s-death-toll-in-afghanistan-and-iraq-infographic/.
11 James C. Howell, "Youth Gang Structures and Collective Violence," in *Handbook on Crime and Deviance*, ed. Marvin D. Krohn, Nicole Hendrix, Gina Penly Hall, and Alan J. Lizotte. Handbooks of Sociology and Social Research (Cham: Springer International Publishing, 2019), 497–511, https://doi.org/10.1007/978-3-030-20779-3_25.
12 Soo Ah Kwon, *Uncivil Youth: Race, Activism, and Affirmative Governmentality* (Durham, NC: Duke University Press, 2013).
13 Bernard LaFayette and David C. Jehnsen, *The Briefing Booklet: An Orientation to the King-ian Nonviolence Conflict Reconciliation Program & The Leaders Manual – a Structured Guide and Introduction to Kingian Nonviolence: The Philosophy and Methodology* (IHRR Publica-tions, 1995).
14 Paul Bueno de Mesquita, *Kingian Nonviolence: Applications for International & Institutional Change* (Kingston, Rhode Island: Center for Nonviolence & Peace Studies, 2015).
15 Marie Berry and Erica Chenoweth, "Who Made the Women's March?" *The Resistance: The Dawn of the Anti-Trump Opposition Movement* (2018): 75–89.
16 Lucy Diavolo, "Alex King and D'Angelo McDade Had a Message for Their March for Our Lives Family," *Teen Vogue*, March 24, 2018, www.teenvogue.com/story/alex-king-dangelo-mccade-march-for-our-lives-washington-dc-speeches.
17 Ibid.
18 Joanna Piacenza, "Americans' Racial Disconnect on Fairness and Discrimination," *Public Religion Research Institute* 10 (2014).
19 Kristie Dotson, "Tracking Epistemic Violence, Tracking Practices of Silencing," *Hypatia* 26, no. 2 (ed 2011): 236–57, https://doi.org/10.1111/j.1527-2001.2011.01177.x.

20 Randy T. Lee, Amanda D. Perez, C. Malik Boykin, and Rodolfo Mendoza-Denton, "On the Prevalence of Racial Discrimination in the United States," *PLoS One* 14, no. 1 (January 10, 2019): e0210698, https://doi.org/10.1371/journal.pone.0210698.

21 Mark Lance, David Ragland, Cris Toffolo, Roxanne Marie Kurtz, and Rev. Charles Amjad-Ali, *Nurturing Intellectual Humility through The Truth Telling Project (NIHTTP)* (St Louis, MO: Grant Proposal, 2015).

22 Jarvis R. Givens, *Fugitive Pedagogy: Carter G. Woodson and the Art of Black Teaching* (Harvard University Press, 2021).

23 Patricia S. Parker, *Ella Baker's Catalytic Leadership: A Primer on Community Engagement and Communication for Social Justice* (Oakland, CA: University of California Press, 2020).

24 Laura A. Lowe and Victoria L. Medina, "Service Learning Collaborations: A Formula for Reciprocity," *Families in Society* 91, no. 2 (April 1, 2010): 127–34, https://doi.org/10.1606/1044-3894.3970.

25 Gregory A. Smith and David Sobel, *Place- and Community-Based Education in Schools* (New York, NY: Routledge, 2014).

26 A. A. Akom, "Critical Hip Hop Pedagogy as a Form of Liberatory Praxis," *Equity & Excellence in Education* 42, no. 1 (February 25, 2009): 52–66, https://doi.org/10.1080/10665680802612519.

27 Christopher Emdin, *For White Folks Who Teach in the Hood . . . and the Rest of Y'all Too: Reality Pedagogy and Urban Education* (Boston, MA: Beacon Press, 2016).

28 David Ragland, "Radical Truth Telling from the Ferguson Uprising," in *The Wiley Handbook on Violence in Education* (John Wiley & Sons Ltd, 2018), 519–36, https://doi.org/10.1002/9781118966709.ch26.

29 Pamina Firchow, *Reclaiming Everyday Peace: Local Voices in Measurement and Evaluation After War* (Cambridge, UK: Cambridge University Press, 2018).

30 Roger Mac Ginty and Oliver P. Richmond, "The Local Turn in Peace Building: A Critical Agenda for Peace," *Third World Quarterly* 34, no. 5 (2013): 763–83.

31 Michael Eric Dyson, "Dyson Explores How MLK's Death Changed America," *NPR*, April 3, 2008, www.npr.org/templates/story/story.php?storyId=89344679.

32 This version of Martin Luther King that ignores his militancy also allows commentators to falsely position him as diametrically opposed to other Black leaders as is often the case with comparisons made between King and Malcolm X.

33 Marian Wright Edelman, *The Measure of Our Success: Letter to My Children and Yours* (New York, NY: Harper Collins, 1993).

34 Martin Luther King Jr, "Martin Luther King Jr. Saw Three Evils in the World," *The Atlantic*, May 10, 1967, www.theatlantic.com/magazine/archive/2018/02/martin-luther-king-hungry-club-forum/552533/.

35 Peter Ackerman and Jack DuVall. *A Force More Powerful: A Century of Non-Violent Conflict* (London, UK: Palgrave Macmillan, 2001).

36 Walter E. Fluker, "How Howard Thurman Met Gandhi and Brought Nonviolence to the Civil Rights Movement," *The Conversation*, January 31, 2019, http://theconversation.com/how-howard-thurman-met-gandhi-and-brought-nonviolence-to-the-civil-rights-movement-110148.

37 Erica Chenoweth and Maria J. Stephan, *Why Civil Resistance Works: The Strategic Logic of Nonviolent Conflict* (New York, NY: Columbia University Press, 2011).

38 Howard Zinn, *A People's History of the United States: Teaching Edition* (eBookIt.com, 2012).

39 de Mesquita, *Kingian Nonviolence.*

40 Michael N. Nagler, *The Search for a Nonviolent Future: A Promise of Peace for Ourselves, Our Families, and Our World* (Novato, CA: New World Library, 2010).

41 Louis Kriesberg. *Constructive Conflicts: From Escalation to Resolution* (Lanham, MD: Rowman & Littlefield, 2007).

42 Betty A. Reardon and Dale T. Snauwaert, "Reflective Pedagogy, Cosmopolitanism, and Critical Peace Education for Political Efficacy," in *Betty A. Reardon: A Pioneer in Education for Peace and Human Rights*, ed. Betty A. Reardon and Dale T. Snauwaert,

SpringerBriefs on Pioneers in Science and Practice (Cham: Springer International Publishing, 2015), 181–98, https://doi.org/10.1007/978-3-319-08967-6_13.

43 Johan Galtung, "A Structural Theory of Aggression," *Journal of Peace Research* 1, no. 2 (June 1, 1964): 95–119, https://doi.org/10.1177/002234336400100203.

44 Jagannath Swaroop Mathur, *Contemporary Society: A Gandhian Appraisal* (New Delhi, India: Gyan Publishing House, 2010), 50.

45 Martin Luther King Jr., *Where do We Go from Here: Chaos or Community?* Vol. 2 (Boston, MA: Beacon Press, 2010).

46 Patricia Hill Collins and Sirma Bilge, *Intersectionality* (Cambridge, UK: Polity Press, 2016).

47 Kimberlé W. Crenshaw, *On intersectionality: Essential writings* (New York, NY: The New Press, 2017).

48 Michelle Alexander, *The New Jim Crow: Mass Incarceration in the Age of Colorblindness* (New York, NY: The New Press, 2020).

49 Kelly M. Hoffman, Sophie Trawalter, Jordan R. Axt, and M. Norman Oliver, "Racial Bias in Pain Assessment and Treatment Recommendations, and False Beliefs about Biological Differences between Blacks and Whites," *Proceedings of the National Academy of Sciences* 113, no. 16 (April 19, 2016): 4296–301, https://doi.org/10.1073/pnas.1516047113.

50 Maeve Wallace, Joia Crear-Perry, Lisa Richardson, Meshawn Tarver, and Katherine Theall, "Separate and Unequal: Structural Racism and Infant Mortality in the US," *Health & Place* 45 (May 2017): 140–44, https://doi.org/10.1016/j.healthplace.2017.03.012.

51 John Paul Lederach, *The Moral Imagination: The Art and Soul of Building Peace* (Oxford, UK: Oxford University Press, 2005).

52 Shawn Ginwright, *Hope and Healing in Urban Education: How Urban Activists and Teachers Are Reclaiming Matters of the Heart* (New York, NY: Routledge, 2015).

1 Nonviolence Is a Way of Life for Courageous People

We don't hold up . . . some kind of gold standard (from the curriculum) that people strive for in terms of the risks one needs to be willing to take, what we ask instead is that they experiment with this and try it out. It is a deeply personal matter and one . . . that is explored in community. Nonviolence as a way of life for courageous people . . . These shifts, most often, these shifts in people's views and behavior come about through incremental change.

Ms. Victoria, Director of CTCN

As I search for the door to the CTCN office, located in the basement of a non-descript university hall in West Hartford, I can hear the faint voices of people talking inside. The grey cinderblock walls of CTCN's office are adorned with colorful drawings of the six principles of nonviolence, a large painting of Dr. Martin Luther King, Jr., and photos of trips the youth have taken. This all adds life to what would otherwise be a drab room with little natural light. I am here today because I've been asked to assist Pastor James Lane as he works with a small group of youth nonviolence facilitators[1] who are getting ready to face one of their biggest leadership challenges yet: They are going to facilitate a two-week-long summer nonviolence training called the "ThinKING Summer Leadership Academy" with 25 youth from across the city.

Pastor James Lane is a long-time advocate and leader of faith and a senior nonviolence trainer in the North End of Hartford, where he has lived and worked for more than 30 years. On more than one occasion, Pastor Lane has told me that he is tired of burying young people in the city. He has had to look into the eyes of parents, sisters, brothers and best friends to offer his condolences and to hold a community in grief as some weep and others are numb, having lost another young person before their 18th birthday. Pastor Lane himself has had family members subjected to police brutality. He and his wife have put their children through college, and he understands the many risks youth face in the city and how easily their dreams can be interrupted or destroyed.

Lane's church is in the north end of Hartford, one of the city's highest crime spots, surrounded by boarded-up buildings. The church has a mural featuring the second principle of Kingian nonviolence: I beloved community is the

DOI: 10.4324/9781003243915-2

framework for the future. CTCN led the project, and the mural was designed by local college students in conversation with community members. Many people came by to work on the wall when it was a work in progress, and several predicted that it would be tagged with graffiti before long. Now, seven years later, it still hasn't been touched.

Lane seems to know everyone in the city, as he has worked with a number of nonprofit organizations, coalitions and task forces on issues ranging from gun violence, substance abuse and food insecurity to reentry for people leaving prison. Among Pastor's many roles, none is more important to him than his work mentoring young people to contest these systems, and today he is completely focused on supporting the four youth here for their next big challenge.

I can tell right away that two of the teenage boys, Paris and Tremayne, who I have come to know over the course of several years and who almost always play it cool, are a bit nervous. Both are juniors in high school. Paris is dynamic around young people and adults, quick to make them laugh; Tremayne is philosophical and creative and tends to listen first before offering his perspective. Their voices have an uncharacteristic lilt, brought on by anxiety and their hands shake as they pick up their note cards and run through the content for the upcoming workshop.

When I first join their planning session, Pastor Lane is already starting to engage with the young people His style ranges from satirical to Socratic. He often asks the youth how the lofty ideas they are studying translate into the lives of other residents in the North End of Hartford, or other parts of the city deeply impacted by violence and systemic racism.

"You know you have to make this relevant", he stops to remind them at numerous points. The youth nod in agreement.

Paris starts them off by reflecting on King's writing and talking about several of Dr. King's different definitions of love.

"Philly, think of Philadelphia, right. What comes to mind?" he asks.

He pauses briefly to give people a chance to think but continues on before anyone has time to answer, "Yes brotherly love, you know, like friends, you love them even though they get on your nerves and it's a give and take type situation".

Before long, the students pivot to highlight some of the connections between love and courageous action. Immediately a spirited conversation erupts, with several young people offering insights on the topic at the same time. A number of themes rise to the surface from the discussion – "agape is not sentimental love"; "It is different from romantic or brotherly love"; "agape does not mean one is passive"; "agape is a kind of love that calls us to see the beloved community (principle 2), to envision a positive future and work for it".

Tremayne gets the mic last, pausing and smiling for a moment before he gets serious again.

> Think about the bus boycotts, in all those marches they needed to find common values, it was love that kept them together in the midst's of all

that [violence] . . . you have to have each other, to be able to call on a lifeline in nonviolence!

While Tremayne, Paris and the other youth educators have their explanations and examples of key concepts ready to go for the workshop, they know Pastor Lane is right, that young people hearing about Kingian nonviolence for the first time will want to know if it can be applied to their daily lives. They will need to talk not only about the civil rights movement in the 1950s and 1960s but also about conflicts at the interpersonal, family and school level because these are where some of the most pressing conflicts for youth occur today.

I understand why the boys might be nervous: this would not be an easy task for even the most seasoned teacher or violence prevention expert. To start with, they will be teaching in a school in the middle of summer – hardly an ideal setting for most young people who have already spent all year in school. The workshop participants are part of a larger program that focuses on job training, and they receive a stipend and job placement if they complete the program. If the material does not feel immediately relevant to their lives, then it will seem strangely out of step with the rest of the program, which focuses on workplace skills. Then there is the content itself, which involves difficult conversations about challenges in the community – including violence – with a group of youth who come from different parts of the city and don't know or trust each other. They will also look at issues of injustice not only from the safe distance of history, in Dr. King's time, but also today, in Connecticut, where they live.

And when they open that door to examine issues that affect their lives, there is a great deal to talk about. Connecticut is one of the most racially and economically divided states in the US. Nearly half of the men and women incarcerated in Connecticut come from only three cities: Hartford, Bridgeport and New Haven.[2] Youth in Hartford are impacted by multiple, overlapping forms of structural violence, and most live in poverty.[3] This is part of a wider national trend, as disproportionate numbers of Black youth live in poverty and have the greatest risk of becoming victims of both violent crimes and police brutality.[4] Homicide remains the leading cause of death among Black youth between the ages of 15 and 34 in the US.[5]

The workshop will most likely provoke important questions about how such deep divisions have persisted and, in some cases, worsened. All of that makes for a tough sell with middle and high school youth at 9:00 am on a Tuesday in August. Yet these youth facilitators (YFs) are up for the task. They live in the community, attend public schools and have dealt with significant challenges in their personal lives. Among other hardships, they have lived away from their parents, witnessed violence firsthand, and seen far too many people in their neighborhoods incarcerated. Yet they have also intensely studied nonviolence, embedding themselves in a community of practice at the Center where they have learned with people from many walks of life over the past two years.

Through this work, they have interacted with – and presented to and along-side – activists, street-level violence interrupters, professors, community members just released from prison, police, politicians and more. For several years, they have been conducting their own experiments with nonviolence in their schools, at home and with friends.

Paris and Tremayne's preparation up to this moment has been extensive. They met with Pastor Lane, Victoria and Wilson Torres as well as other adult nonviolence facilitators monthly for what they call "refresher" sessions during most of the school year. In these refreshers, youth discuss the principles of nonviolence in the context of their lives and practice teaching parts of the curriculum for others in the community. Although they have presented many times before, they are now approaching a new milestone; they will be leading sessions at ThinKING entirely on their own. While Pastor Lane and Victoria will be present in the room, they have made it clear that they will not step "onto the floor" at all to co-train with them. That means the youth will lead the sessions entirely, which start at 9 am and end at 4 pm, from start to finish over all two weeks. They will lecture, facilitate discussions, plan activities and manage the lessons for 30 other young people, without intervention from Pastor Lane, Victoria or any of the other adults.

$\star\star$

Like other CTCN YFs, Paris and Tremayne have a number of opportunities to lead their peers through a deeper exploration of the topic of courage and the Kingian first principle: nonviolence is a way of life for courageous people. They will explore with participants how Dr. King's views on nonviolence and courage evolved over time. The topic of courage is not merely abstract or a historical artefact of the civil rights era and will not be discussed as such. Paris and Tremayne spend most of their time during the workshops offering examples from their own lives or from those of other facilitators in the community. They highlight contemporary situations that have required courage.

During this summer leadership academy, it wasn't long before Paris, Tremayne and the other YFs were fielding scenarios and questions about the first principle. The young participants shared situations from their own lives, including fighting between parents or not having their parents at home as much as they would like because they work so much to make ends meet. They also frequently discussed issues with siblings that lead to physical altercations and what to do when, as one participant put it, they "seriously get on your nerves". Students were also eager to discuss the problem of navigating fights at school as well as times when they felt disrespected by teachers, both topics that come up frequently in youth nonviolence workshops. As one trainer puts it, these workshop conversations are some of the places where "shit gets real". This contrasts with students' experiences in their Hartford classrooms, where they feel the content is too often disconnected from their lives.

Victoria Christgau, the executive director of CTCN, has helped lead or observed most of the youth trainings over the past decade, working with thousands of youth and adults. She agrees that workshops cannot be divorced from the challenges these young people face, noting a common dynamic that arises when both youth and adult facilitators lead discussions of the first principle.

When students in Hartford and New Haven learn about nonviolence, she explains, they often are intensely concerned about the idea of being perceived as passive during a fight. Victoria describes participants demanding, "What do you want me to do? Nothing. . . ? When they are coming at me? If they come at me, I need to come at them, Right!?" These are not abstract issues or conversations. Students want to know, literally, what to do when discussing fights that have escalated at school or situations where they have been threatened or disrespected in the past, and at first glance, nonviolence feels like an attempt to encourage passivity in the face of real risk.

Tremayne and Paris have thought deeply about this issue and they face many of the same dilemmas in their own lives. They start off the session on courage by offering examples of times when kids had been talking trash about them personally or someone else in their school and trying to start beef. In these spaces in youth-led workshops, Paris and Tremayne start "freestyling", which they later tell me is their favorite part of being on the floor. For Tremayne, the most powerful moments are "when we're freestyling in the lesson, that's what we call it, when we're not sticking [only] to the curriculum. We're just talking, like basically our prior knowledge, and trying to talk to them [directly]".[6]

As they talk about fights in school, Tremayne quotes LaFayette, the founder of the Kingian curriculum, and writes on a flip chart that "every conflict has a history". One of the other YFs, Enrico, breaks his silence and exclaims "exactly!" in agreement. He follows up with a series of questions about this fight at school and asks the participants to dig into that history: "How do the two people you are talking about know each other? How long has this beef been going on? What other things in their life might be pushing them in this direction?"

One of the workshop participants offers an example of a conflict between two students who had a prior history. A fight was supposed to happen after school, she said, and chronicled how issues had been brewing for months and getting worse. She emphasized that at some point this fight is going to happen, and there is "not much you can do about it". Here, the YFs introduce the idea that conflict escalates and de-escalates – this is referred to in the curriculum as "levels of conflict" – and when a conflict is escalating, before it gets really hot, there may be opportunities to engage with the people involved or with their friends. Both facilitators emphasize this: you can intervene at various points in a conflict, all of which take courage, but if you intervene earlier, then you may have more options for refusal, and it can be less risky.

Paris follows this line of reasoning, asking, are there any people who are tight with both parties? Also, what do you think is going on in their life outside of school? The youth participant offering the scenario is quick to explain that the kid who is pushing the fight "probably has a lot of negative stuff going on in his life" and there are people involved who are friends with both of them. Led by the YFs, the workshop participants then begin brainstorming possible responses. Maybe they could identify people who they might be able to reach out in the days leading up to the fight, including peers as well as a few trusted adults who might be able to handle this skillfully. They agree that while a lot could be done in this situation to possibly guarantee a better outcome, that still doesn't mean *any* of it is easy to do.[7]

Enrico jumps back in to reflect insightfully that "courageous" action in nonviolence is often about finding creative ways to respond to difficult situations, yet that kind of creative action might not appear as courageous at the moment because we've been trained to think that immediate confrontation is most courageous.

He says, "a lot of times I think – it's funny, 'cause people think that if you walk away [from a fight] then you're scared or something. But most of the time, that's not the case".

Key Concepts

Enrico and the other YFs challenge popular conceptions of courage. It is worth noting at the start that it is not self-evident to many people that nonviolence requires courage. In fact, this suggestion goes against common perceptions of nonviolence as either passive – turning the other cheek – or avoiding conflict altogether.[8,9,10] Participants in this type of workshop in Hartford and New Haven often question if nonviolence can be courageous and, if so, how and under what conditions?[11] This is an important starting place for community-based educators who want to reconceptualize the nature of courageous action and discuss the core relationship between courage and nonviolence. It makes sense to start discussions about nonviolence by looking more deeply at how we understand courage itself, and how courageous action can help meaningfully challenge violence.

Over the past 15 years, I have had the opportunity to teach workshops and deliver lectures on the themes of courageous leadership and nonviolent social change in over 20 states. In those workshops on courageous leadership, I often begin with a simple activity of imagining "courage":

Step 1. What comes to mind when you think of courage? Think of an image. What did you see? Describe it in detail. What's missing from this image in your mind? How does the image or images in your mind compare to how bravery is depicted in the media, in your community?

Most people's first associations are images of extreme physical bravery – someone willing to run into a fire and risk their lives to save someone else or scale one of the highest mountains in the world. Unsurprisingly, popular media's representations of heroes and famous historical examples shape many of our images of courage. These stories often glorify people (mostly White men) who take risks in combat. One does not have to look far to see tributes to such heroic stories represented around them. For centuries, everywhere from sleepy small towns to bustling capital cities around the world have prominently displayed large public statues that celebrate the courage of war's victors.

The US is no exception when it comes to extolling the prominent heroism of physical bravery.

In our society, courage is also too often misconstrued as a primarily male quality and one that demands using violence. Americans are deeply influenced by stories that emphasize that "real men" don't show weakness (understood as vulnerability, admitting fault and so on) or emotion (other than anger). Masculine power is often presented as an ability to dominate others.[12,13] From this perspective, courage and vulnerability are often seen as a binary opposition. These ways of thinking about the intersection of courage and masculinity have well-documented negative effects. As a wealth of research has shown, these culturally constructed notions of courage reinforce anti-social behavior, which can contribute in turn to social isolation, violence and a wide range of negative health outcomes.[14,15,16] Furthermore, courage so narrowly conceived is actually disempowering, as it misses a whole range of alternatives and solutions to violence.

> **Step 2:** Who is a courageous person that you have personally known? What made them courageous? In what ways were their actions courageous? When was a time in which you saw them behave courageously?

These prompts often shift the conversation. Participants in my workshops most often talk about family members, mentors and friends. They offer personal accounts of the hardships these people endured while supporting them. These are not the stories of famous people covered in the media or stories of hypermasculine, courageous combat. However, they are powerful, like the story of a grandmother who spent the money she would have used on her own blood pressure medicine to buy food for her grandchildren. Others cite family members who risked everything to leave the Jim Crow South during the great migration in hopes of a better life in the north. Youth often share stories of courage that involve a teacher or guardian who challenged another adult's negative perceptions of them. They describe such individuals as courageous because of their willingness to step in and support these young people, even at the risk of getting into a conflict by taking a side. Importantly, participants reflect back that courage is a quality that manifests itself in many dimensions of life and is practiced by ordinary people they know.

Yet even with this expanded view, I have discovered in my observations and work with community-based educators that many people are hesitant to think of themselves as "courageous", and this is significant for nonviolence education, which tries to cultivate and support the courage to take a stand for justice. There are good reasons for this hesitancy. Popular discourse about courageous leaders often leaves little room to explore the relevance of coura-geous action in our lives. Many young people assume that the most important quality to effect social change is fame or having a prominent role – perhaps as a spokesperson, celebrity, athlete, military general or publicly recognized leader. Similarly, when discussing courage in our society, there is little explanation of the social conditions that support the development of courageous qualities in people. Instead, courageous leaders are often thought of as somehow having the "it factor" of courage. They may be born that way, have a natural proclivity toward taking risks, a higher threshold for pain or are innately adept at making wise choices when faced with seemingly insurmountable odds.

These "stock stories" of courage apply to famous peacemakers as well, including Dr. Martin Luther King, Jr. His "I Have a Dream" speech is replayed to exalt his nonviolent leadership, but with little context; it's as if King appeared fully formed for the first time on the steps of the Lincoln Memorial, mysteri-ously equipped with the courage to challenge White supremacy. For educators, it is critically important to recognize that this oversimplified popular discourse on courage omits the social context in which leaders develop their outstanding qualities over long periods of time and often with great difficulty. It leaves our students with little agency when thinking about major challenges in their lives and communities and tells us a little about the struggles, doubts and fears peo-ple experience along the way to finding courage. In short, this unrealistically polished narrative fails to convey how peacemakers like King actually *became* courageous and *learned* the habit of courage.

LaFayette makes this point by playing with the word "fearless".

"Fearless does not mean having no fear, it means having less fear", he likes to say.

Victoria's point at the opening of this chapter – that CTCN encourages experimentation and ascribes to no single "gold standard" method – is especially important when teaching nonviolence in Hartford and New Haven. This approach is necessary to effectively connect with young people and take seriously the fears that many of them live with on a daily basis due to both lived and vicarious traumas. Being able to front as though you are fearless and invulnerable is often seen as necessary in violence-affected communities, just as it is in the larger society. As Enrico pointed out in the youth-led workshop, showing fear – even simply walking away – can be considered a sign of weak-ness. Young people think it will make them targets for further bullying and other forms of violence. Sometimes kids goad each other into fighting by asking, "What are you afraid of?" a taunt that partly masks their *own* fear. Not fighting back, in other words, gets interpreted as fear. But through nonviolence education, youth can reconceptualize the choice not to engage in a fight and not to respond to verbal provocation with violence as acts of courage. Further-more, they can see the stress that they are feeling, and the pressure to resort to violence, as symptomatic of social systems that devalue Black and Brown people and force them to navigate segregated, underfunded schools with peers who are often experiencing trauma and marginalization. This reinterpretation of nonviolence as courageous and the contextualization of interpersonal conflicts within social inequality is one of the goals of nonviolence education and the nonviolence movement. Nonviolence means fighting back but raises new possibilities about the ways one can do so, and as Dr. LaFayette points out in workshops, "that can be much harder than fisticuffs".[17]

Several ideas and theories about nonviolence underlie the work of CTCN's community nonviolence educators. They work on the theory that nonviolent approaches demand courage and that these qualities can be taught and cultivated; that being a community nonviolence educator is a form of nonviolent intervention and therefore requires courage; that people can become more courageous through active and experiential learning in their everyday lives, and when they are embedded in communities of support and ongoing reflection; that nonviolent action can be contagious and that the involvement of people of various backgrounds in networks engaged in nonviolence sustains and broadens nonviolent social change in our most oppressed urban communities.

Courage has been written about since antiquity and is hardly a new theme, but fresh theories and literature about courage abound today. Courage has become a hot topic across many fields, with books and articles written about the significance of courage in business, education, health care, military studies and a host of other areas. Many authors, from Dr. Brené Brown to Stephen R. Covey, have written bestselling titles on the subject. Yet as much as courage is promoted as an important ideal in many disciplines, the contributions of community educators and social justice activists to the topic are too often missed. Leadership scholar Fredrick Jablin points out that despite a frequent reference to courage in the literature on leadership, little has been written that explores the best practices for cultivating it.[18] Only a few studies have seriously taken up questions about what enables and reinforces courageous action within the context of communities and social movements.[19]

Even so, several concepts and theories of courage apply to community nonviolence education and figure into the workshops and discussions highlighted in this book. As numerous scholars point out, courage can have both an offensive and a defensive orientation. William Ian Miller writes that we should

> think of offensive courage as the courage of the charge, the attack; defensive courage as the courage of standing one's ground under the face of the attack or of maintaining one's fortitude while being bombarded in the trenches day after day waiting for the attack.[20]

Miller's use of the term "attack", while generally associated with violence, is highly relevant when thinking about nonviolent ways to respond to systemic racism. Nonviolence often involves navigating the difficult tension between proactively envisioning and building a more just society alongside the need to respond to daily indignities, assaults, physical violence and lack of opportunities that devastate people's lives. In school, students deal with a host of challenges that raise hard questions about how to respond to the threat of direct physical violence, such as bullying, racial and other forms of discrimination and active shooter drills. Thinking of courage as involving both offensive and defensive actions and approaches expands the range of options. When students engage in defensive forms of resistance to violence as well as offensive actions to influence social change, they tend to forge relationships with others that are guided by a sense of connection in the midst of upheaval and a drive to create new possibilities for the future. This increase in social cohesion and sense of solidarity is at the heart of how nonviolent social movements are sustained over time and build power to influence change.

Community educators also deepen the exploration of courage by discussing the similarities and differences between physical and moral courage. Physical courage involves the risk of injury or death. Certain professions, such as the military or sports, reward physical courage, and it can be a critical component of gaining social legitimacy and respect (as is often the case for youth during rites of passage). Courage, however, is sometimes wrongly associated with hypermasculine standards of domination, self-reliance, external recognition, triumph over physical limits and invulnerability to fear.[21] On the other hand, moral courage may *involve* physical courage, but it entails additional risks and may originate from different motivating factors. Henry Sidgwick, like many other authors, underscores social risk as a key component of moral courage – especially when people face "the pains and dangers of social disapproval in the performance or what they believe to be their [moral] duty".[22]

Since discussions of moral courage entered western literature during the 20th century, it has broadly come to mean "the capacity to overcome fear or shame and humiliation in order to admit one's mistakes, to confess a wrong, to reject evil conformity, to denounce injustice, and also to defy immoral or imprudent orders".[23] The "whistle-blower" comes to mind as an example of this kind of courage; someone risks their job, status and social relations to report abuse. Significantly, for our purposes, this can be a "lonely kind" of courage, as one breaks with popularly held social views or disturbs the silent conformity to the dominant norm.[24]

In teaching about nonviolence, it is important that many nonviolent social justice activists report similar experiences that highlight the pain, fear, loneliness and disappointment that can come from taking such action to challenge the status quo.[25] Recognizing and highlighting these dynamics is key when it comes to educators offering a realistic assessment of what it means to use nonviolence. King was certainly no stranger to the kind of loneliness that comes from taking a moral stand. He was both openly attacked by opponents and ignored or isolated by potential allies, such as White moderates and liberals, who implored him to slow down and abandon nonviolent direct action as a method of struggle. King expressed his concerns candidly in his writing:

> I must confess that over the past few years I have been gravely disappointed with the white moderate. I have almost reached the regrettable conclusion that the Negro's great stumbling block in his stride toward freedom is not

the White Citizen's Councilor or the Ku Klux Klanner, but the white moderate, who is more devoted to 'order' than to justice; who prefers a negative peace which is the absence of tension to a positive peace which is the presence of justice.[26,27]

King is too often caricatured in ways that remove the depth of his philosophy and political methods and bury his commitment to justice under superficial glosses about "turning the other cheek". If we are to be honest with our students in exploring moral courage as a component of nonviolence, then we need then to allow for a realistic exploration of both the potential for positive change, as King's life exemplifies, and the risks and challenges of such an approach, which King's life also exemplifies. Middle and high school students have a heightened sensitivity to the perceptions of others. Having the moral courage to speak out and act against violence, sexism, racial subjugation and other forms of oppression can indeed be a lonely and isolating experience, as others demonstrate indifference or even contempt and hatred for those willing to take action. Students may be highly attuned to these concerns, which raises important questions about how they can take action in these contexts and sustain a commitment to nonviolence over time.

Audre Lorde, the world-renowned Black lesbian feminist author and scholar, famously explained that there simply was no place to hide from injustice for her as a Black woman in America: "My silences had not protected me. Your silence will not protect you".[28] Instead of hiding, Lorde emphasizes the courage to take action,

> for every real word spoken, for every attempt I had ever made to speak those truths for which I am still seeking, I had made contact with other women while we examined the words to fit a world in which we all believed, bridging our differences.[29]

Here, Lorde powerfully highlights courage as a social and collective act and practice. She speaks to how courageous acts, while involving risk, also create pathways for solidarity and connection.

Lorde's insights highlight one of the major limitations regarding how moral courage is often understood in both academic literature and popular culture. In these spaces, moral courage tends to be defined as distinctly individualistic and described largely as a solitary pursuit; for example, the "army of one" or the lone warrior in the Rambo style. These individualistic depictions obscure the power of solidarity and the courage found in communities of people taking a stand together.[30] This is a central point that community educators at CTCN teach about and also try to embody in their work.

The reconceptualization of courage as a social and communal practice rather than an isolated and individualistic one is highly relevant for our exploration of violence in the US, as many of the Black and Brown educators and community members working with CTCN already face elevated risks in the form of direct physical violence and structural violence in their neighborhoods. People in Hartford, for example, must navigate one of the highest violent crime rates and some of the most extreme economic inequality in America. In these contexts, educators can introduce youth to a broader view of courage and explore why people have engaged in civil resistance and other forms of nonviolent action with others to change these systems – even when the risks are extremely high and include the possibility of being attacked or sent to jail.

Community educators emphasize a third concept of courage that it can be learned, especially within the context of movements. The nature of, and ideas about, our courage change over time and through participation in communities and movements. The community in Montgomery, Alabama, for example, inspired Dr. King as much as any of the books he'd read. In Montgomery, he took the next step in his journey to I more courageous by learning with people in the community – people who were already willing to take extreme risks to engage in nonviolent struggle.

Rosa Parks, who was already deeply committed to challenging segregation in her work as a secretary at the NAACP, had taken the next step by putting her body on the line when she refused to give up her seat on the public bus. Like Dr. King, she is often misleadingly remembered during Black History month as a lone protestor, her own background and the larger movement in which she courageously protested all but forgotten. Other women stayed up all night mimeographing copies of flyers to circulate in the community and organized phone banks to encourage people to boycott the buses. Many Black people in the city walked to work instead of taking the bus. Over 90% of the Black community participated in the boycotts in Montgomery, and the action lasted over a year.[31] These efforts made it absolutely clear to King that nonviolence was an active collective process that required dedication and courage if it was to have a chance to succeed. King learned courage from the movement itself.

King's views on nonviolence had already evolved, but in Montgomery, he came to see it as a powerful way to influence change and something that could actually work in practice. This was not a decision, carefully planned in advance by a *savant* of nonviolence, nor was it a preplanned, experiential activity meant for him to practice nonviolence. Rather, the mass movement and the protests were an emergent opportunity that took him by surprise. While his previous study and his connections with other intellectuals had allowed him to contemplate the importance of nonviolence, King writes,

> I had not the slightest idea that I would later become involved in a crisis in which nonviolent resistance would be applicable. I neither started the protest nor suggested it. I simply responded to the call of the people for a spokesman.[32]

At this time, King's intellectual commitment to nonviolence, forged earlier, became grounded in a deeper reality. This evolution happened in a community of people actively struggling and facing great risks and supporting each other in their efforts to change things:

> When the protest began, my mind, consciously or unconsciously, was driven back to the Sermon on the Mount, with its sublime teachings on love, and the Gandhian method of nonviolent resistance. As the days unfolded, I came to see the power of nonviolence more and more. Living through the actual experience of the protest, nonviolence became more than a method to which I gave intellectual assent; it **became a commitment to a way of life.** Many of the things that I had not cleared up intellectually concerning nonviolence were now solved in the sphere of practical action.[33]

Applying the Concepts, and Lessons Learned

Kingian nonviolence educators reframe courage by emphasizing directly and often that *courage can be taught*. People of all backgrounds can learn about and engage in nonviolent action to challenge and uproot systemic racism. Additionally, courage is sustained in communities of practice, so *people don't have to go it alone*. Paris, Tremayne, Enrico and other community-based educators communicate these powerful messages not only by teaching about King but also by modeling nonviolent courage. Making themselves vulnerable, they share stories from their own lives and details about their experiments with nonviolence. Mentors watch and offer support to the YF taking the floor but ultimately defer to their emerging leadership. The YFs introduce how they have developed their courage as part of a wider community of other educators who are exploring how to use these principles to influence change, frequently referring to other youth that attend refresher trainings with them and the many adults who have supported them in becoming community educators. This is very different than teaching about King as a figure on a pedestal, as the emphasis is on the living legacy of which they are part and a method of struggle that is still being developed.

I asked Paris, Tremayne and Enrico to reflect on key moments from the August nonviolence workshop, as it was their first experience leading the curriculum unassisted. They recalled how at first participants were guarded, and that the atmosphere was awkward and intimidating when students were not responding to questions or taking it seriously. Paris points out:

> When they started to like get more familiar, like with us. It was actually after they asked us the personal questions, that's when got like more comfortable with us. That's when more people started like, raising their hands and stuff like that. I feel the reason they start interacting more after like, they found

out the personal information is because they felt like, not . . . I speak for them, but I guess that they felt like, since you're just around the same ages as them, that maybe they should warm up, too. And that, it was, it's not just something that, just being talked [at] by another adult. This is something that everyone is learning [together].[34]

When they step into the classroom, Paris, Tremayne and other community youth educators are demonstrating the courage to teach and learn with their peers and adults who they care about. Teaching is scary for most of us – many people fear public speaking to begin with and would have apprehension about leading a workshop like this. These facilitators are also offering an alternative vision of education, as most of the young people in their workshop are students of color and attending schools where the student body is overwhelmingly Black and Latino, and the teachers are overwhelmingly White and commute from outside the city. So, workshop participants do not regularly see people of color from their communities serving as educators in their public schools.

This point is not lost on other youth participants. When I interview them after the workshop and ask what they thought about having other facilitators of color, students noted that it must be difficult work and that they appreciated having the chance to see their peers lead. Several interviewees emphasized they felt more comfortable to take risks themselves by actively participating in the workshop and applying lessons outside the classroom, seeing someone who had a similar background teaching, and that they recommended it to their friends

Photo 1.1 ThinKING Youth Leaders, preparing for presentations at MLK Birthday Commemorations in numerous CT locations. Wilson Gray YMCA, Hartford, CT 2014 © CTCN

Photo 1.2 ThinKING Youth Leader, Gerina Fullwood, speaking at Legislative Office Building, Hartford, CT 2012 © CTCN

for the following summer. Jennifer, one of the participants who identified as
Hispanic, echoed what several other attendees pointed out, that they felt at
ease and comfortable in the classroom even with such challenging topics. She
explained:

> It feels like they won't judge you like . . . if you do something more like
> slip up – white people they just look at you like, you're just not human like
> [sometimes]-you did something really wrong when you didn't . . . or like,
> some teachers say, 'Well, people of your background,' and I'm like, what

Photo 1.3 ThinKING Youth Leaders, Mahogany Foster and Gerina Fullwood, creating training manuals UConn School of Social Work, West Hartford, CT 2014 © CTCN

do you mean? . . . This is the most comfortable because they understand where we're coming from.

Youth facilitators like Paris and Tremayne model how power can be embodied by stepping into leadership roles as community educators and as a result tacitly giving other participants courage to discuss the oppression they face, their hope for the future and the resources and tools they use to survive and influence change. They employ what LaFayette famously calls "a force more powerful" than violence.[35] Courageous action from this perspective is not primarily about spectacular moments of courage displayed in protest (though that is important) but rather experimentation with *nonviolence as a way of life*. Core principles and skills are applied to how we reimagine not only institutions but also aspects of our own lives. Importantly, our idea of courage does not need to reinforce the use of violent force to influence change, and in a country that so often glorifies violence, this is a radical and countercultural notion. There are other sources of power to draw on, and different meanings of "courage". Specifically, nonviolence seeks to awaken moral conscience by actively challenging violence and inspiring other people to take action against the abuse of power.

Both this vulnerability and persistence are key features of nonviolent courage as community educators step up to embody the change they wish to see in the world. In Connecticut, the community educators are quick to point out that this is not an *invincible* courage, but a reconceptualization of the concept that is communal and vulnerable – the courageous need other people to succeed – and together we can learn to be courageous.[36] Victoria Christgau and the team at CTCN call this a "shared model of leadership".

In Hartford and New Haven, both community-based educators and participants still anchor many of these conversations in historical examples, often with videos and films, of how people took nonviolent action during King's time and consider how these examples might apply today. CTCN regularly uses as a teaching tool *The Children's March*, a film that shows young people's courage in nonviolent movements.[37] King was torn about the involvement of youth and putting them in harm's way. The film features rich conversations about the risks of nonviolent action, the responsibilities of leadership inside a movement and the ways that young people themselves advocated to participate and get involved, despite these concerns. Educators also use the video *A Force More Powerful*, which highlights the prerequisite behind-the-scenes work for direct action in the civil rights movement. Focusing on the role of trainings and workshops, *A Force More Powerful* highlights how sit-ins in Nashville were planned, strategized and coordinated. These narratives of courage differ dramatically from the individual heroism so familiar to us in western culture. At one point in the film, students are in jail because of their protesting, and one asks, "What are my parents going to say about this?" The courage that comes from self-sacrifice is a different kind of moral courage than courage organized around personal gain alone, and this becomes a rich point of discussion in CTCN workshops: educators take seriously these young people's questions, such as what would you tell your parents if you were in jail for your activism during the civil rights movement?[38]

Many students come to CTCN workshops with an idea that Dr. King was born with his formidable leadership qualities all but preordained at birth. However, I'm not convinced that King was born exceptionally courageous; instead, he *became* courageous through an active process of change, and CTCN's nonviolence education shows that process, and King's evolution over time. This journey was unpredictable, difficult, complicated and overwhelming at times, and one that was still very much underway at the time of his assassination. Dr. King's transformation in his understanding of nonviolence was filled with doubt and experimentation.[39] Community nonviolence facilitators in Connecticut often emphasize this key point when they teach about King. While this may not sound particularly controversial, it is an interpretation dramatically at odds with students' views when they enter the workshops, as they have until this moment had the tendency to put King on a pedestal.

Dr. King came to believe that nonviolence was not a passive approach but instead a strongly active one that could leverage significant power for change, the kind of power needed to transform systemic oppression. Nonviolence, in his evolving view, was "one of the most potent weapons available to oppressed people in their quest for social justice",[40] as it could not only address interpersonal dynamics but also radically disrupt existing social structures and allow people to generate power in marginalized communities.

It is not unusual for participants to come out of Kingian nonviolence workshops with increased confidence and a desire to influence change. Educational researchers Sarah Diamond and Jacob Werblow evaluated the ThinKING Summer Leadership Academy with one of the youth cohorts in Hartford and compared before and after survey responses. They found that

> students were 92% more likely to view violence as something more than a direct physical act of aggression, 325% more likely to view themselves as being able to handle situations using nonviolence, and 233% more likely to state that inaction can also be a form of violence.

That increased confidence to engage in nonviolent action, and a heightened awareness of the complexity of violence, is key to building capacity to disrupt and transform structural violence.

Tips for Community Educators

Why does it take courage to be a nonviolence educator? I have observed seven key challenges that Kingian educators in Connecticut often face and overcome:

- *Fear of public speaking:* people are scared of making mistakes in front of others and of public speaking generally, so create opportunities to teach pieces of your curriculum and receive feedback on that teaching with a smaller and supportive group first.
- *Be ready for what comes up:* violence is a serious topic and people carry both insight and trauma around these issues that are deeply personal. Everyone has different experiences and is positioned differently in the community, and so their experiences and ways of making sense of nonviolence are important sources of knowledge that need to be engaged. Questions and resistance are very much to be expected, and many times the people who struggle most with the relevance and applicability of nonviolence go on to become the most committed educators.
- *Stay committed to the long haul:* people feel a great sense of responsibility and urgency to disrupt cycles of violence, but community educators in violence-affected cities often do not see people who look like them in key positions of educational leadership and have been marginalized in formal education settings. To push models of leadership without providing a structure for long-term support can be destructive.
- *Use experiential educational methods to engage diverse learners:* theater, art, role plays and other approaches create multiple ways for learners to engage with this material.

- *Follow the Kingian methodology:* this methodology includes a carefully crafted, set curriculum whose content offers a broad exposure to non-violence and with pre-planned activities that educators can learn. This set curriculum is the scaffolding that allows people to more easily and confidently step into the role of the educator, and then improvise and pursue spontaneous opportunities within that framework. Try to strike a balance between structure and spontaneity.
- *Connect participants to a lineage of struggle:* structural violence is difficult and slow to change. Connections to ancestors and histories of struggle can help sustain and contextualize long-term struggle.
- *Forge connections to the community:* Teach in spaces that people have positive connections to, for example, the library, the YMCA, or a park and to places that stimulate opportunities for people to share their insights. If you ask people to recall their most consequential learning experience, many of those experiences took place outside of the classroom, and with someone who was not a credentialed educator, so try to emulate those spaces and experiences.

Notes

1 I have known these young people for two years, since they first started with CTCN ThinKING program. In fact, most of these young people first encountered the program as part of the Blue Hills program they are about to lead the workshops for. Over that time, we have met many times in Hartford and elsewhere and I have had a chance to watch them grow. They have visited my neighborhood in Brooklyn, NY, exploring the local museum for a show featuring Black artist and later when I moved to DC, I hosted them at George Mason University where I teach conflict analysis and resolution. I arranged for them to meet with our students, many of whom come from conflict zones around the world. There they explained their approach to teaching nonviolence, why they think this type of education can make a difference and the challenges they encounter in their work and lives.

2 Sarah Diamond and Jacob Werblow, *Continuing the Dream: The Effect of Kingian Nonviolence on Youth Affected by Incarceration* (Program Evaluation for the Institute for Municipal and Regional Policy (IMRP), 2013), www.ccsu.edu/imrp.

3 Ibid.

4 Mike A. Males and Elizabeth A. Brown, "Teenagers' High Arrest Rates: Features of Young Age or Youth Poverty?" *Journal of Adolescent Research* 29, no. 1 (January 1, 2014): 3–24, https://doi.org/10.1177/0743558413493004.

5 Patrick Sharkey and Michael Friedson, "The Impact of the Homicide Decline on Life Expectancy of African American Males," *Demography* 56, no. 2 (2019): 645–63.

6 This is not just a knee jerk reaction these young people know that there are risks to looking soft in response to a fight at school – to not standing up for yourself, to being seriously hurt if you don't respond effectively. There are also risks to going to adults in the school where one can be seen as a rat and a snitch or where the adults may not be skilled in handling these situations.

7 In our debrief, I ask the youth facilitators if they have been able to use these strategies and if they had worked in the past. Several responded that they had been able to diffuse some fights in school. Eduardo, however, offers an important caveat, explaining, while it feels good it is also hard, "Because other people still insult you and call you soft if you don't use violence". What he reminds us is that courage in these situations is required

not just during an intervention but long after as there is a reputational risk amongst peers that weighs heavy in those situations for teenagers even when those nonviolent approaches are successful. This is a theme that comes up often in refreshers as nonviolence practitioners and educators support each other in incorporating these ideas into their life in a society that often views nonviolent approach not as courageous but as cowardly.

8 Arun Gandhi, "Nonviolence as a Comprehensive Philosophy," *Peace and Conflict* 10, no. 1 (2004): 87–90.
9 Karuna Mantena, "Another Realism: The Politics of Gandhian Nonviolence," *American Political Science Review* (2012): 455–70.
10 Kurt Schock, "Nonviolent Action and Its Misconceptions: Insights for Social Scientists," *PS: Political Science & Politics* 36, no. 4 (October 2003): 705–12, https://doi.org/10.1017/S1049096503003482.
11 I have made this observation having attended Kingian nonviolence workshops across the US, as well as abroad in Nigeria.
12 Kjerstin Andersson, "Constructing Young Masculinity: A Case Study of Heroic Discourse on Violence," *Discourse & Society* 19, no. 2 (2008): 139–61.
13 R. W. Connell, "On Hegemonic Masculinity and Violence: Response to Jefferson and Hall," *Theoretical Criminology* 6, no. 1 (February 2002): 89–99, https://doi.org/10.1177/136248060200600104.
14 Michael S. Kimmel and Matthew Mahler, "Adolescent Masculinity, Homophobia, and Violence: Random School Shootings, 1982–2001," *American Behavioral Scientist* 46, no. 10 (June 2003): 1439–58, https://doi.org/10.1177/0002764203046010010.
15 James R. Mahalik, Micól Levi-Minzi, and Gordon Walker, "Masculinity and Health Behaviors in Australian Men," *Psychology of Men & Masculinity* 8, no. 4 (2007): 240.
16 Dawn M. Salgado, April L. Knowlton, and Brianna L. Johnson, "Men's Health-Risk and Protective Behaviors: The Effects of Masculinity and Masculine Norms," *Psychology of Men & Masculinities* 20, no. 2 (2019): 266.
17 Peter Ackerman and Jack DuVall, *A Force More Powerful: A Century of Non-Violent Conflict* (London, UK: Palgrave Macmillan, 2001).
18 Fredric M. Jablin, "Courage and Courageous Communication Among Leaders and Followers in Groups, Organizations, and Communities," *Management Communication Quarterly* 20, no. 1 (2006): 94–110.
19 A noteworthy exception here is the work of Kristina Thalhammer and her co-authors in her edited book on *Courageous resistance: the power of ordinary people (PRESS, 2007).* In their book, Thalhammer puts forward a model of understanding nonviolent social change that emphasizes the important role that peer encouragement, communities of practice and support and social relationships have played in emboldening courageous action. Thalhammer and her co-authors make an important contribution highlighting some of the ways that courage is reinforced in social movement spaces. Their work, however, does not explore the role of education in building capacity for courageous action, a challenge I take up here in detail in this book.
20 William Ian Miller, *The Mystery of Courage* (Cambridge, MA: Harvard University Press, 2002), 106.
21 Jessica Meyer, *Men of War: Masculinity and the First World War in Britain* (London, UK: Palgrave Macmillan, 2016).
22 Sidwick in Miller, *The Mystery of Courage.*
23 Miller, *The Mystery of Courage*, 254.
24 Jablin, "Courage and Courageous Communication Among Leaders and Followers in Groups, Organizations, and Communities."
25 George Lakey, "Making Meaning of Pain and Fear," in *The Paradox of Repression and Nonviolent Movements* (Syracuse, NY: Syracuse University Press, 2018), 270.
26 Martin Luther King Jr, "Letter from Birmingham Jail," *UC Davis Law Review* 26 (1992): 835.

27   Interestingly, there have been hundreds of studies that have addressed prosocial behavior (e.g., PsycINFO lists 428 entries from 2007 with the term prosocial behavior in the title), but very little research has referred to prosocial behavior with high (social) costs for the actor (i.e., the person who helps). People often don't think of prosocial behavior and risk, while the literature on moral courage emphasizes this.

28   Audre Lorde, "The Transformation of Silence into Language and Action," *Identity Politics in the Women's Movement* (1977): 81–84.

29   Ibid.

30   In her book, *Courageous Resistance: The power of Ordinary People*, Thalhammer and her co-authors rightly observe that successful nonviolent social movements all over the world teach us an important lesson that people are often more willing to engage in risky actions when they do so with others. This is especially true when it comes to challenging injustice Kristina Thalhammer et al., *Courageous Resistance: The Power of Ordinary People* (Springer, 2007). In fact, even in contexts where collective action is highly discouraged or punishable by death, people still reach out to others and come together to envision strategies for nonviolent social change. See Kristina Thalhammer, et al., *Courageous Resistance.*

31   Ramona Lahleet Hyman, *Montgomery Bus Boycott of 1955: The Literariness of a Political Movement* (The University of Alabama, 2006).

32   Martin Luther King Jr., *The Radical King.* Vol. 11 (Boston, MA: Beacon Press, 2015), 48.

33   Martin Luther King Jr, "Pilgrimage to Nonviolence," The Martin Luther King, Jr., Research and Education Institute, April 13, 1960, https://kinginstitute.stanford.edu/king-papers/documents/pilgrimage-nonviolence.

34   Throughout, I've "cleaned up" the quotes as they move from the aural to the written form (the "ums" and the "likes").

35   Peter Ackerman and Jack DuVall, *A Force More Powerful: A Century of Non-Violent Conflict* (New York, NY: Palgrave Macmillan, 2001).

36   In Fear and Courage: A Psychological Perspective, Stanley Rachman researched the role of education and training on the attitudes and performance of bomb-disposal operators, assault troops and paratroopers. After initially searching for a specific type of psychological profile that would make some people perform better at these high risk tasks he and his coresearchers came up empty handed instead concluding that quality training and support was the most important component of effective performance of high risk tasks. See Stanley J. Rachman, "Fear and Courage: A Psychological Perspective," *Social Research* (2004): 149–76.

37   Robert Houston, *Mighty Times: The Children's March* (Documentary, Short, Drama. HBO Family, Southern Poverty Law Center, Tell the Truth Pictures), www.imdb.com/title/tt0443587/.

38   This question can serve as a writing prompt for students to write a letter to their parents from the point of view of the protestors.

39   As Alex Cromwell summarizes, transformative education occurs when, "people are confronted with something at odds with their frame of reference, they experience a 'disorienting dilemma' (Mezirow 1978; Taylor 1994), also known as 'disequilibrium' or 'dissonance' (Che, Spearman and Manizade 2009; Kiely 2005). People can easily integrate low-intensity dissonance into their mental framework, but when they experience high-intensity dissonance, it requires a change in their frame of reference, leading to transformative learning (Kiely 2005). High-intensity dissonance usually involves a strong emotional reaction caused by this new interaction (Brewer and Cunningham 2009). When a student encounters something so completely at odds with their previous experiences, it is almost impossible to maintain the same assumptions they held previously. Kiely (2005) argues that this type of dissonance results in transformative learning". Alexander Cromwell, "Building a Culture of Peace: The Long-Term Effects of Encounter-Based Peace Education with Pakistani Youth" (Ph.D., George Mason

University, 2019). See Cromwell, "Building a Culture of Peace," https://search.pro quest.com/docview/2247117875/abstract/F029CB67956E4659PQ/1.

40 King, Martin L., et al. *The papers of Martin Luther King, Jr.* (Berkeley: University of California Press, 1992).

2 The Beloved Community Is the Framework for the Future

> In a real sense all life is inter-related. All men [humankind] are caught in an inescapable network of mutuality, tied in a single garment of destiny. Whatever affects one directly, affects all indirectly. I can never be what I ought to be until you are what you ought to be, and you can never be what you ought to be until I am what I ought to be.
> This is the inter-related structure of reality.
>
> – *Dr. Martin Luther King, Jr.*

Community nonviolence educator Wilson Torres first found out about CTCN's work as a part of his community service, mandated by Hartford Superior Court. He did not initially volunteer to work with the Center or to be a nonviolence educator but rather was required to do so as the plea deal the court offered him in lieu of potential jail time. When Wilson first arrived at CTCN he was going through an extremely difficult time. He was 24, and just a few months before he met the team at CTCN Wilson's younger brother Hector, who he called (Manny), was shot and killed on the streets of Hartford. Manny was only 19 years old. Someone Manny considered a friend had paid a homeless man $500 to kill him after an alleged fight.[1,2]

Wilson was close to his brother and they spoke regularly on the phone, sometimes several times a day. He was in shock when heard about Manny's death, and the thought of not having his brother in his life almost immediately manifested into a rage. Within hours after the murder, the Hartford police had found a person with the gun they believed was used to shoot his brother, and Wilson was determined to go to the Hartford Superior Court on the day that the suspect, 36-year-old Gilberto Vargas, was scheduled to appear before the judge. When the bailiffs brought out Vargas, Wilson broke into a full sprint toward the man with the intention of attacking him. He recalled:

> I just – That's the only thing I wanted to do. I didn't want to hurt nobody else, I just want to grab his neck and twist it like in the movies, you know? [laughs]So, that's what I wanna do. I mean, it's – Him – There's no reason that he should live anyway, you know. I mean, you're wasting your life,

DOI: 10.4324/9781003243915-3

you're about 40-years-old, you're a bum – I mean, I'm not saying that he's not worth anything, but, at that time, that's what I thought, you know?

Wilson is built like a football running back, and in a few short steps, he had gained such momentum that when two judicial marshals and a state trooper stepped in to stop him, one was knocked to the ground and injured. Wilson was subdued and eventually charged with a felony:

> So, when I went to court, seen the judge, the judge said, "Hey, oh look, we just added another charge on you of felony and injuring the police officer." I'm like What? Who? I didn't touch any cop?" He said, "Yeah, this marshal broke his ankle trying to bring you down." I'm like, "That's not my problem, man."[3]

Wilson later took the plea deal that included no jail time so long as he stayed out of trouble and finished his community service and other obligations.[4,5] He was comparatively lucky not to see jail time, as many other Black and Latino people arrested accept plea deals that result in incarceration.[6] Black defendants are 19% more likely than White defendants to be offered plea deals that include prison or jail time.[7]

Wilson first began his community service work with Pastor James Lane at the North End Church of Christ. Prior to his work with CTCN, Pastor Lane has served as a long-time community leader in Hartford's North End, where he has lived and worked for more than 30 years. The North End is one of the communities most deeply impacted by gun violence and poverty in the city, and Pastor Lane's church has been a spiritual home and refuge to many of its residents for well over 20 years. The Pastor and his congregation have hosted a wide array of programs that include men's mentoring projects, positive youth development work and visits to support people in prison and after they return home. Pastor Lane is deeply involved in violence prevention programs in the city and is also a substance abuse counselor and one of the senior nonviolence trainers for CTCN. He knew Wilson well, as the latter had spent the first half of his childhood in the North End. As a young boy, Wilson had looked up to Pastor Lane and participated in programs at the church. He trusted him.[8] When Lane found out what had happened to Wilson, he suggested that they visit the Center for Nonviolence to see if he might be able to do his community service work there.

When Wilson first arrived at the CTCN offices in the fall of 2011, he was in a lot of pain from his loss, although it was hard to know that because he was so quiet.[9] In the first few weeks of his volunteer work for the Center, Wilson joined director Victoria Christgau at an elementary school on the predominately Latino South End neighborhood, where he had moved when he was 8 years old. Initially, Wilson assisted Christgau with many of the supporting tasks required for a successful children's program, as he was not yet familiar with the nonviolence curriculum or trained as a community educator.

Wilson and Victoria made quite the team, with obvious differences in both appearance and persona. Victoria is an outgoing, middle-aged White woman who lives an hour away from Hartford in the rural northeast corner of the state. Wilson a Puerto Rican man in his mid-twenties is soft spoken and often keeps to himself in group settings. When I asked Wilson if he would have known anyone like Victoria before they worked together, he replied without hesitation, "Never!"

This relationship was new ground for Victoria as well because even though she had done educational work with people of all ages in Hartford over the past ten years, most of the Center's nonviolence education work with young people had been focused on high-school-aged youth in the North End of Hartford, which was predominately Black. Already, community nonviolence trainers from the North End such as Pastor Lane, Warren Hardy and Cherell Banks were leading nonviolence programs. While CTCN had forged numerous connections with people on Hartford's South End and received this invitation to work in the school, they did not yet have any trainers from the neighborhood. So, when Wilson began his community service work at CTCN, Victoria was grateful for the opportunity to collaborate with him.

Wilson immediately connected with the kids and engaged with each of the students. When I asked Wilson how he did it, he explained

> You know, playing with them outside. Volleyball, soccer, basketball, tag, drawing, you know, I mean, I have fun, I love these kids, man. You know, I've seen – I've seen them [now] from . . . kindergarten, going all the way up to second grade.
>
> So, I've seen them grow for three years and you see the difference . . . a big difference here.

Victoria noticed right away that Wilson's "whole presence was . . . modelling peaceful behavior" in how he interacted with intentionality and care with both kids and adults. It also helped that he knew the kids' neighborhood intimately and speaks fluent Spanish. Wilson was moved by what was happening in the classroom, and he stayed involved well beyond his time of court-mandated participation (and he is still involved in the work a decade later). He was deeply interested in the curriculum about Dr. King and nonviolence and found that he liked working with the director as well.

"And I kinda liked her presence, you know? . . . I was loyal. I didn't- I didn't miss not one class . . . it was three days a week . . . and I was loyal, man, every day".

As Wilson experienced the curriculum for the first time, the theme of a beloved community came up most often and really stuck with him. "Ms. Victoria" emphasized to each of the kids that they had a role to play in building the beloved community right there in their classrooms and neighborhoods. They discussed conflicts and how they could support each other in those moments. They also talked about how often "hurt people hurt other people" and that this cycle can begin even before they are born. The beloved community was an ideal, but Victoria focused on how we build it through daily acts of non-violence in the here and now. If the children in the classroom were upset they could talk about it, if there was a conflict, they made an intentional effort to talk about those issues and find a solution that all parties were satisfied with. Victoria worked with Wilson as she had in other spaces across the city to construct a temporary oasis-a protected place within the city to learn and be together.

On more than one occasion, Wilson told me, he left the classroom and kept thinking about these discussions throughout the week, especially about the possibilities for building a beloved community. His mind raced with lingering questions and thoughts: "Was it possible? In Hartford? What would it take?" He was surprised by how frequently these questions recurred – "when I'm driving my truck, when I am home, you know, talking with my family" – and the deeper he went with his work as an educator the more he grappled with the implications of the beloved community: "I don't know man, a world without guns, and police and prisons?"

Over the course of the summer, as I drove around Hartford with Wilson, he made time to introduce me to his family, take me to his favorite restaurant and share a number of his favorite places. The conversations often shifted without warning, however, as he'd point out one of the many places, from empty parking lots to a front porch to a specific sidewalk, where people who he had known well had gotten arrested or shot and killed. These included the spot where his brother was murdered. I often found myself caught off guard, veering so quickly from relatively mundane moments and places to such deep calamities, and we rarely drove more than a block or two before he pointed to another spot. The privilege I have experienced across my lifetime as a White able-bodied man, living in or with access to safe neighborhoods, meant that even when I had experienced violence it was contained, episodic and something that I could evade or escape. In Hartford, it was relentless, and Wilson understood the difference; on more than one occasion he said to me, "I needed to bring you here, you have to feel it and see it, man".

One day, Wilson Torres gently applied the brakes, slowed down and pointed out the window.

> That's the funeral home over there called De Leon . . . that's where the majority of the Hispanics go and get seen for the last time. Whether you're old or young, it doesn't matter [you could be shot]. Whether it's two or three people at a time.

He wanted me to know that several people could be shot and killed in a short time, sometimes as retaliation for an initial shooting, and on other occasions as unrelated incidents. In either case, there could be so many people lined up that the funeral parlor would need to improvise to serve multiple families simultaneously.

However, I didn't get from Wilson a sense of violence as some chaotic, inexplicable or mysterious phenomenon. He often talked about all the good people that he'd grown up with who got swept up in "hustling" and the "drug game", and he saw clearly how a lack of opportunities in the city had stressed communities, eroded trust between people and put good people in situations where they had limited opportunities. In his brother's case, Wilson saw just how far those pressures could push somebody and warp their relationships:

> Look, man, here in Hartford, friends kill friends. You know, they could – they-they could be hanging out with this person one day and the next day, he's killing [you].

That is exactly what happened to Wilson's brother Manny, and Wilson felt passionately that "you can make just one mistake or not even make a mistake" and it can be all over here. Wilson had his brother's case on his mind constantly – people you cared about and trusted could turn on you, a dramatic opposite to King's vision of the beloved community. And yet despite this huge gap between ideas explored in the workshops and Wilson's experiences in his own life, Wilson kept coming back to the work even after his community service was over. For Wilson, the work of Kingian Nonviolence was not just a glimmer of hope, it was a pathway and a set of beliefs and techniques that could help him not only turn around his own path but perhaps, like laying down train tracks, provide a new path for the community.

Over time it became clear that being with the kids afforded him some comfort, especially seeing how they responded so well to these ideas of supporting and caring for each other, of having hard conversations and of being proactive about conflict and being open to forgiveness and reconciliation. But the kids also did not know fully how unequal the world was yet, so Wilson's questions and doubts persisted. He could feel the children's hope for their futures, but he also knew what lay just beyond their view, and the many risks they would face. These kids would need ongoing and lasting support and, even with that support, the poverty, segregation, racial inequality and persistent violence would make this a long and dangerous journey.

One day at the school, Wilson asked Victoria if she had some time to talk while they were out on the playground. This surprised her, because up until this point, Wilson had mostly talked to her only about logistical issues that came up in their work. She could tell from the look on his face that this was different. Wilson had just realized that "the man who had killed his brother, that man's family lived in the community and their kids could easily be in this elementary school".

Understandably, this gave him deep pause and raised so many questions. He loved working with these kids, and he could see the potential in each of them, but he had to wonder if their parents – and those two parents in particular – should benefit from or be part of this work. They had taken so much from him and his family. This wasn't a question that Wilson was going to answer for himself immediately, and he wasn't even seeking a response or answer from Victoria, but he did want to share how pained he was and how close this work hit home. He was working to build the beloved community, but within the community of the here and now was also the violence that had taken his brother from him. These things co-existed and were not easily reconciled.

It has been eight years since Wilson first got involved with Kingian nonviolence. He is now the father of two school-aged children and still works with the Center. He drives weekly to assist Pastor Lane with refresher sessions in which they guide small groups of high school youth on the application of nonviolence in their lives and prepare them to lead workshops in the community. He has taken the trainings himself and even served on the Center's board of directors.

On one of our drives, Wilson shared his overall impressions about the importance of cultivating the beloved community in the face of violence and his personal tragedy and loss, the importance of having a vision and creating spaces for people to experience that vision firsthand, especially in Hartford and New Haven.

"Just, I mean, [I emphasize the power of] being around positive people, you know, and being able to help these . . . teenagers understand that!"

Photo 2.1 Wilson Torres assisting elementary school child with Beloved Community poster
© CTCN

Key Concepts

As early as 1956, Dr. King envisioned the "beloved community" as the end goal of nonviolent boycotts and other forms of direct action. At a victory rally after the announcement of a favorable U.S. Supreme Court decision on the desegregation of Montgomery's buses, King said:

> The end is reconciliation; the end is redemption; the end is the creation of the Beloved Community. It is this type of spirit and this type of love that can transform opponents into friends. It is this type of understanding goodwill that will transform the deep gloom of the old age into the exuberant gladness of the new age. It is this love which will bring about miracles in the hearts of men.[10]

The scope of change needed for this transformation – now as then – is nothing short of daunting. The pursuit of civil rights for Black people, according to King, would have to be part of a larger and deeper psychological and spiritual journey for the nation. None of Dr. King's work is more well known than his "I Have a Dream" speech which, while not directly referencing the beloved community, highlights how this vision would demand that people of various backgrounds find the moral imagination to envision a society that was not grounded in violence, racial subjugation and economic exploitation. Reconciliation would require not simply idealistic and utopic dreams of positive futures, as King famously articulated in his speech. It would also require pragmatic and realistic "truth-telling", that is, an honest look at the racist, militarist and materialistic orientation that became basic elements of the American experiment. Only then could "the children of former slaves share table fellowship with the grandchildren of former slave owners".[11] Too often, King is commemorated today for his idealistic dream only and not for the pragmatic and incisive ways that he paired the dream of a beloved community to the arduous work and national transformation required to achieve it.

Educators interested in moving from exploring the beloved community as an abstract concept to an approach to learning the models those qualities of the community face a core creative challenge: to find the best ways to support community members in engaging in continuous learning, action and critical reflection on issues of social justice while embodying ethics of mutual aid and compassion. The concept asks us to envision the world we want to live in, but we must do so in the world that we *actually* live in. We must try to embody love, forgiveness and equity in the ways we organize ourselves and our efforts to influence change in the future. To build the beloved community then necessitates not only a commitment to nonviolence values and principles but coming together with people from diverse backgrounds and finding ways to learn together while reflecting on both that which separates us and the strengths and shared values that can facilitate a more just world. This is an exercise, at its core, of building greater solidarity and power as communities as we try to make sense of the complex and intersecting forms of injustice that shape our world. This is not a task that can effectively be taken on alone nor is it a short-term process that can be solved in a two- or three-year grant cycle or with nonviolence training focused on tactics alone.

Given this conceptualization of the beloved community as a learning community, we must ask ourselves: how, then, can we construct supportive spaces for learning that allow us to envision and model the world we desire? How can we respond to conflicts and even violence in ways that help restore and repair relationships? Wilson Torres' challenge in Hartford – to envision a beloved community as he moved through and lived in a community strewn with memories and ongoing realities of violence, injustice and racism – is similar to the struggle that Dr. King faced. King wrote,

> I had grown up abhorring not only segregation but also the oppressive and barbarous acts that grew out of it. I had passed spots where Negroes had been savagely lynched, and had watched the Ku Klux Klan on its rides at night. I had seen police brutality with my own eyes, and watched Negroes receive the most tragic injustice in the courts. All of these things had done something to my growing personality. I had come perilously close to resenting all white people.[12,13]

To evoke the utopic ideal of the beloved community also inevitably agitates the painful awareness that we are very far from the realization of our profound interconnectedness – we are still deeply unequal and divided. A key part of the educational work, then, is taking seriously and engaging with the resistance, fear and concerns that many marginalized people will face when they try to share their vision for better possibilities in a world that so often thwarts them. So too the beloved community in King's conception meant challenging the ambivalence toward oppressed people that many white people have as well as the active and tacit support of violence and inequality.

King was inspired when he saw ordinary people standing up and using nonviolence to model the beloved community even in the face of aggression. He came to believe as a central concept that oppressed people had an important – and even core – leadership role in envisioning and bringing about this future world. King, like many others, was aware that the story of the survival and far-reaching contributions of Black people in America testified to the cultivation of love and the possibility for justice and participatory democracy in a society that too often spoilt those efforts. It is a story of survival, support and hope in the midst of systemic racism, trauma, sexual violence and social exclusion, a subtle power and everyday resistance to the systemic racism that still animates community members in Hartford and New Haven today and helps drive these educational efforts. As King shows us, the crippling forces of racism and violence are not the whole story. If the beloved community would be built, it would be built with the widespread participation and leadership of Black and other marginalized people. Nonviolence community educators work from the understanding that people already have creativity, resilience and key insight into what holds together and sustains a community committed to justice for all and that locally driven education can be a productive way of expressing that desire and collective power.

Pedagogically, the goal then is to foster creative spaces that support and nourish those already existing community practices that foster empathy, solidarity and learning and to allow people to build on them. In our nation's urban schools, far too many classroom teachers are burned out, overwhelmed and myopically focused on covering the content in their subject matter. But the last two decades of increased standardization, standardized testing and school accountability have also left some students feeling detached, isolated and disengaged from the learning process especially when the knowledge being taught is not grounded in the history and realities of their community. This, in turn, leaves a void in which community-led education can play a key role as a driver of these conversations and practices creating spaces and processes for people to explore how they are already and can in the future contribute to building the beloved community grounded in racial and social justice.

The dream does not give license to ignore or forget how the world is now; rather, Kingian nonviolence asks that we hold two worlds in mind at once: an ideal vision and a flawed reality. Redemption, a critical aspect of the beloved community for King, was not only interpersonal but also collective. In other words, it wasn't just about apologies or reparations but the reform and transformation of social institutions and the redemption of American democracy to creates a system that was far more participatory and equalitarian and where systemic harm and humiliation are abolished.[14]

Perhaps most audaciously, Dr. King's concept of the beloved community recognizes that for people who experience oppression and violence, the cultivation of hope with others is a radical act in and of itself. He knew this from his own life, as he struggled to develop and maintain a transformative view in the midst of constant threats and attacks on his family's well-being. The research backs up what King experienced firsthand: societies built on high levels of violence and domination often strip people of hope and reinforce a social world where the status quo is presented as fixed and unchangeable for people at the bottom. Furthermore, a now large body of international research demonstrates that chronic violence and trauma diminish people's sense of agency (their confidence in their ability to influence change) and their hope for the future.[15,16]

Like Wilson, low-income urban youth of color who are exposed to chronic, uncontrollable stressors, struggle with perceptions that the future is too bleak or too uncertain to plan or dream for.[17] I have interviewed young people in Connecticut and elsewhere that believe they may not live to see their 21st birthday. Previous research has shown a correlation between hopelessness and being a victim of or a witness to violence.[18] While youth are particularly vulnerable to the effects of violence, community members of all ages in violence-affected cities experience the negative impacts of overlapping trauma.[19,20,21] Under these circumstances, some citizens feel little reason to strive for peace or work for greater social justice,[22] perceiving the institutions that are supposed to guarantee their safety and rights as unreliable or even openly hostile toward them.

In Wilson's case, for example, even as formal criminal justice procedures were underway surrounding his brother's murder, he took justice into his own hands (literally); he put himself and others at risk while doing so. Wilson had no confidence in the criminal justice system and couldn't imagine a way forward that would successfully disrupt the deep and long-standing cycles that he had seen tear apart his family and community. The same challenges in terms of maintaining a sense of agency and hope hold true in other places of violence worldwide. In Israel and Palestine, 50% of people say they have no hope for a peaceful settlement in the future.[23] This is a common response to multi-generational trauma and a serious challenge for educators who want to explore how an imagined beloved community might inform nonviolent social change. It is indeed a radical act to allow and admit hope in a world of intergenerational violence and injustice, one where the institutions that are supposed to facilitate justice fall so far short.

Applying the Concepts, and Lessons Learned

For Wilson and other community educators working and living in violence-affected neighborhoods, the idea of the beloved community often raises serious questions about the possibilities for change:

- Is it self-indulgent to create spaces to imagine a better future when so many people in our community are suffering right now?
- What if visions for the future do not adequately take into account the profound obstacles we face, setting us up for disappointment and failure?
- On the other hand, if we only focus on problems and how to solve them will we miss vital opportunities to think outside the frameworks of domination?

The concept of the beloved community requires us to ask today:

- What would a world where Black and Brown people's lives matter look like?
- Is justice possible? If so, what would it look like? How can we experiment right now to bring about that world?
- Are racial reconciliation and redemption possible? If so, then what would it look like? How can we experiment right now to bring about that world?

These questions demand creative responses. Learners must negotiate new ways to understand nonviolence in dynamic tension with their ongoing experiences of violence.[24] Alexis Pauline Gumbs, a community educator and scholar, writes in *Octavia's Brood* that "all social organizing is science fiction".[25] In reflecting on the innovative work of Black feminist author Octavia Butler,

Gumbs and her co-authors remind fellow educators and activists that social change demands that we explore a not-yet-realized future. Working toward social justice is a collective and collaborative fiction about what we hope our society can become. These authors challenge us to ask, "What is the world we want to live in?" rather than starting with the question, "What is a realistic win?"[26]

This has valuable implications for educators interested in engaging with nonviolence and, racial justice especially, when teaching with the beloved community in mind. We must cultivate creative spaces and conditions that allow for the (utopic) possible even in the face of the (oppressive) real; *we must create spaces to cultivate hope and envision the future.* This doesn't require that we forget the world as it is now, Gumbs notes, but rather that we also dedicate ourselves to exploring what it might be. Larry Rasmussen calls these collective spaces focused on the future "anticipatory communities" and defines them as:

> places where it is possible to reimagine worlds and reorder possibilities, places where new or renewed practices give focus to an ecological and postindustrial way of life. Such communities have the qualities of a haven, a set-apart and safe place yet a place open to creative risk. Here basic moral formation happens by conscious choice and not by default.[27]

Arts-based pedagogies can help to create these havens and zones of peace. CTCN relies heavily on arts-based pedagogy to support people as they develop both a personal and a collective vision for the beloved community. Community-based educators at CTCN are often working with people deeply affected by systemic racism and physical violence, and in this context, the arts can help participants take familiar aspects of their everyday lives and explore, express and transform them into new possibilities.[28] CTCN is not alone in this arts-based approach to transformation in education as Black artists, educators and activists have often led the way in the US, helping people see through the hypocrisy of America's rhetoric of freedom and justice while also expanding our ideas of beauty and justice.[29]

Wilson Torres noticed when he worked with CTCN's director Victoria Christgau that art could help people open up to the future. Victoria would also break into songs to engage learners or use birdcalls to get people's attention, which was uncomfortable for Wilson ("I was like, what the hell is going on?"). She also brought in artists with expertise in drumming, puppet-making, spoken word, Black art history and other areas. All of these creative arts are potentially valuable when it comes to working in violence-affected communities because they enact the kind of transformation – from a familiar world to something different, something better that is created out of the material at hand – that the beloved community requires.

Christgau developed a program at the Center called "Building the Beloved Community: One Block at a Time", after she struggled to have conversations about the beloved community with a group of youth. She had noticed that discussions of the beloved community often left young people distracted and disengaged, they felt too abstract and so Christgau began to experiment with new ways of engaging with the content.

She had recently visited a thrift store, where she often found supplies for her work, and discovered a large box of usually-expensive wooden blocks at a bargain price. At the same time, the Center had received a grant and was studying the work of Romare Bearden (1911–1988), a Black artist who used collage to depict the complexity and vibrancy of specific blocks in Harlem.[30] One day on Victoria's drive to the Center, an idea came to her: What if the youth painted wooden blocks with each block representing a building in Hartford? The goal then was to *imagine what the Beloved Community would look like if they were to build it one city block at a time.* She brought in photos of buildings from across the city – some large, ornate and occupied; others abandoned. She sought as many different types of spaces and parts of the city as she could, laying out the pictures on the table. Usually, each photo prompted a discussion of the building's location and surrounding area. Christgau recalls, "People would look at a photo and then just start talking about that place, even the adults and people they knew or stories about that place or area".

On one occasion, she incorporated the activity into a larger 24-week program in which youth were learning different artistic mediums, including painting and collage.[31] They used the block-by-block activity as a culmination of their efforts, with adult nonviolence trainers and other supporters of the work from across the city coming together to view students' art and discuss what the beloved community would, could and should look like.[32] Victoria recalls:

> They started drawing on these blocks and started decorating them, the talk went really, really deep. And then they would talk about their violence in their homes, or violence in their families or, uh, what did Dr. King really mean when or how did Dr. King even know how to handle [a specific situation] and it just became [us] teaching them nonviolence while their hands were busy doing something productive.

Cherell Banks, an adult CTCN nonviolence trainer who has led many youth programs, built on this creative momentum to lead discussions with students about the book *Play by the Rules* during breaks from their art sessions.[33] The book focuses on learning more about the laws that govern the state, and CTCN puts an emphasis on how to become advocates and activists to change laws that unjustly impact their communities. CTCN participants' critical engagement with the knowledge in *Play by the Rules* created opportunities to explore how social structures, such as laws, could also be repurposed or changed, even as participants explored ways of altering and creating new physical structures in their art. At the same time, some of the youth participated in weekly refreshers where they revisited the nonviolence curriculum with Pastor Lane and Wilson where they had a chance to share their experiences, talk more deeply about the principles of nonviolence and connect their study of the civil rights movement to their vision for change in the city.

Pastor Lane, who has observed these activities through the years, reflects that "the kids get to be kids again" when creating art. Victoria noticed that students were more fully absorbed in these artistic activities, often going a long time without talking or goofing around.

> Their whole demeanor changed – even the adults were like that. In these arts activities, I would sometimes try to bring an activity to an end and get the attention of the other adult facilitators and they would be totally absorbed in the activity themselves.

One of the participants, Ricardo, reflected that "Working on this painting gave me inspiration. . . . It helped me to focus more. When I'm doing this work, I can feel something deep is going on inside me".[34]

Another youth, Nachaly, noticed that working with watercolors attuned her to subtle thoughts and emotions that she had been unaware of previously. She said, "When it started to flow, it felt like the whisper of my soul".[35]

Her fellow student Mona, agreed, expressing, "I loved how you would begin a painting with nothing and if you work with the ingredients given to you, the art piece actually becomes something beautiful and unexpected".[36]

Christgau, who has led arts-based learning activities with groups across the state for over 20 years, sees this deeper engagement as inherent to the process of making art, which integrates both emotional and abstract elements into the learning process.[37] However, she elaborates that it is vital *to foster a caring and "nourishing" environment to hear your creative voice*, especially when engaging with nonviolence which asks people to be vulnerable, hopeful and experimental – actually, to be vulnerable *by* being hopeful. "I wanted it to be nourishing, No kidding. And I brought cookies and milk and they just devoured the Oreos and had glasses of milk and kept drawing. It was really beautiful".

Community educators at CTCN have adapted the block-by-block exercise to engage people from across the city in an exploration of the beloved community. On MLK day in 2015, CTCN partnered with one of Hartford's museums to host a beloved community block-by-block activity. Through this program, they *created something beautiful and unexpected for the larger community*. Approximately 1,000 people attended the event, which featured tables stacked with thousands of blocks. Participants decorated them and had discussions about the city, envisioning it as a beloved community. To introduce people to Dr. King's ideas about the beloved community, youth and adult nonviolence trainers stood up and read passages from King's writings that addressed the concept and explored themes such as love, reconciliation interconnectedness and an end to injustice, which prompted conversations about these themes at tables. Nonviolence trainers also did several "walk abouts", where people were asked to leave their tables and pause their art-making projects to move around the room and imagine themselves at different moments in the life cycle – as small children, parents or elders – and to move through the space from that point of view. They hoped the activity would encourage people to appreciate that they are connected to and with each other, at various points in their lives and that the beloved community needs to work for everyone.

"The blocks were a surprise", shared Jada, one of the youths who had recently started to attend CTCN's programs.

> We started to look at places we see every day in our neighborhoods through new eyes. It made us see where we live in a completely different light – each time we added more color or trees it made the community more fun. . . . We even added the Kingian Six Principles as signs throughout the community. This project really made me appreciate my community more. It was like where we all live really became the Beloved Community Dr. King talks about. I'll never see my community the way I used to. Now I can actually see what it might become.[38]

Ariel, an experienced YF, observed from the activity, "Art is something you have to practice and practice, just like nonviolence".[39,40]

MIT Professor Peter Senge explains that "the fundamental difference between creating and problem solving is simple. In problem solving we seek to make something we do not like go away. In creating, we seek to make what we truly care about exist".

The community nonviolence educators that I observed and interviewed rarely saw problem-solving and creative vision as separate projects. Indeed, their efforts teach us the value of creating a pedagogical space that primarily nurtures people's hope and vision in a world fraught with problems. The beloved community does not just occur in some theoretical future, but in relationships and social processes that are modeled in the learning environments we construct. Importantly, we can see aspects, albeit incomplete, of the beloved community in the here and now. Working toward our vision for justice demands connecting the means and ends in this way. Most Americans remember the dream element of King's "I Have a Dream" speech but setting aside spaces that draw on an array of pedagogical approaches to discuss how to achieve it right now are vital.

These spaces can be critically important for healing as well. By modeling aspects of the beloved community, we intervene in the present by reshaping internal beliefs, immediate relationships and even institutions while we simultaneously lay the groundwork for future change. The underlying assumption here is that the most reliable guarantor of the future we wish to have is how effectively we develop processes to live in peace today.

This movement, or dual vision – between the ideal future and its implementation (however circumscribed) in the here and now – is an important component of the beloved community. CTCN directly explores how to connect their visioning sessions and exercises to current policy debates as well as local and state-level advocacy. Yet educators must balance set plans for the

Photo 2.2 ThinKING Youth and Adult Trainers, board and volunteers celebrating the completion of Principle Six mural on the 224 Ecospace building, Hartford, 2016 © CTCN

curriculum with emergent opportunities that arise while working in the community. The building "blocks" for change in the block-by-block exercise are not only the city buildings and familiar institutions such as a church or school or even the laws, policies and democratic structures but the learning process and community through which this collective imagination, power and resistance to the status quo take shape.

Tips for Educators and Peacebuilders

*   *Don't underestimate the relationship* between imagination and personal transformation. Envisioning and expressing a positive vision for the future often requires self-reflection and challenging deeply held beliefs and deeply entrenched emotions.
*   *Create a nurturing environment for students and community members to envision a better future* for themselves, their families and their community. Consider having the class collaborate on a mural or collage that illustrates what the beloved community would look like for their school or community.

- *Help students explore visions of the future beloved community from a variety of viewpoints.* For example, a child studying the ecosystem might assume the perspective of a grasshopper to think about chemical fertilizers and insecticides used prevalently in private residences throughout the community. Or a teenager might take the perspective of an elderly person on a fixed income or a political leader representing the state in Washington, DC. Given their positionality, how can they work to help advance the beloved community?
- *Embrace the future.* The concept of the beloved community requires mustering hope, embracing ambiguity and taking risks to imagine what is not yet known. But it takes courage even to have hope and dreams in a world of systemic racism and violence. Given the exciting but potentially unsettling nature of the work, be attentive to the pedagogical demands of supporting people in taking these risks together. Resistance is a natural response for many to thinking in this way.
- *Experience the future.* Arts-based pedagogies powerfully create experiences where learners can feel they are in that future world. Art takes vision, and it challenges people, literally, to give shape and form to that vision. Through sculpture, painting, collage and dozens of other media, learners can see and touch those visions for the future. Through theater, they can also explore the beloved community in an embodied way. These creative mediums enact the very transformation – from the world at hand to the world that we seek – of the beloved community.
- *Experiment with your vision now.* Emphasize the creation of support systems for people as they experiment with community-building and visions for the future. This daily work can be slow in comparison to a vision of the "ideal state" and will likely be filled with surprises and disappointments along the way. Create everyday peace indicators to track progress in the small ways peace is built every day.
- *Try putting youth in the lead.* King was inspired by the competencies and leadership that he observed in ordinary people who courageously enacted a nonviolent ideal in a violent world. Likewise, youth and their strengths should be at the forefront. Young people will spend the most time living in this future world that we are envisioning and hoping to create, so we need to create opportunities for youth voices and leadership.
- *Consider ways to connect your experiments* at the micro-level to macro-level efforts for change: national and international social movements are working toward a world without war and with more equitable and sustainable societies. Seek out connections between larger movements and smaller-scale programs. King, for example, connected the beloved community to the American dream, and likewise, we can explore how efforts to engage in local nonviolence education connect to work taking place to create change in state-wide and national institutions such as the criminal justice system.

- *Start a community peace center.* One way to create spaces to incubate the beloved community is to create a nonviolence center or youth club where participants can learn about nonviolence and explicitly model the beloved community. CTCN has been developing this model in a number of schools, both in New Haven and Hartford, with increasing success. These spaces can refer to a building or a culture of relationships informed by nonviolence and Dr. King's thinking about nonviolence and the beloved community. In this space, youth can make explicit the key values they wish to practice and their commitments about building a supportive and loving environment. They can practice nonviolence conflict interventions. Over time, as the center gains momentum, youth and adults can partner to evaluate cultural practices and competencies in the larger community and make recommendations for institutional changes. Through nonviolence competency trainings with students, staff and families on nonviolence, participants can help build capacity for wider change and help develop a shared language and vocabulary.

Notes

1 "Marshals Tackle Shooting Victim's Brother," *New Haven Register*, July 28, 2017, www.nhregister.com/news/article/Marshals-tackle-shooting-victim-s-brother 11632603.php.
2 David Owens, "Man Sentenced To 20 Years in Murder for Hire Scheme," *Hartford Courant*, April 17, 2014, www.courant.com/community/hartford/hc-xpm-2014-04-17-hc-hartford-murder-guilty-plea-0418-20140417-story.html.
3 Wilson's ordeal – that he had was being charged for trying to attack his brother's killer in court – didn't draw much widespread interest in the local media. Only a single short piece was written about Manny's murder in a city with one of the highest murder rates in the country where these kinds of conflict are all too common.
4 Innocence Project, "Report: Guilty Pleas on the Rise, Criminal Trials on the Decline," August 7, 2018, https://innocenceproject.org/guilty-pleas-on-the-rise-criminal-trials-on-the-decline/.
5 Emily Yoffe, "Innocence Is Irrelevant," *The Atlantic*, August 5, 2017, www.theatlantic.com/magazine/archive/2017/09/innocence-is-irrelevant/534171/.
6 Carlos Berdejó, "Criminalizing Race: Racial Disparities in Plea-Bargaining," *BCL Review* 59 (2018): 1187.
7 Gene Demby, "Study Reveals Worse Outcomes for Black and Latino Defendants," *NPR*, July 17, 2014, www.npr.org/sections/codeswitch/2014/07/17/332075947/study-reveals-worse-outcomes-for-black-and-latino-defendants.
8 Pastor James Lane was one of the first people that Victoria Christgau met when she first arrived in Hartford looking to see if there was any interest in nonviolence education and he helped introduce her to numerous people around the city that were involved in violence prevention and community empowerment work.
9 Pastor James Lane came to the work following the immediate loss of someone close to him, similar to Tanisha in the opening chapter. This work is not just about civil rights and peacemaking as abstract notions but is also deeply personal.
10 Martin Luther King, *The Papers of Martin Luther King, Jr., Volume III: Birth of a New Age, December 1955-December 1956.* Vol. 3 (Oakland, CA: University of California Press, 1992).

11 Charles Marsh, *The Beloved Community: How Faith Shapes Social Justice from the Civil Rights Movement to Today* (New York, NY: Basic Books, 2008), 2.

12 Martin Luther King Jr., *My Pilgrimage to Nonviolence* (The Martin Luther King, Jr., Research and Education Institute, September 1, 1958), https://kinginstitute.stanford. edu/king-papers/documents/my-pilgrimage-nonviolence.

13 Wilson offers a similar reflection recounting how most of the people he had known in positions of power growing up were white and how he had been looked down upon for where he grew up and went to school.

14 Robert Michael Franklin, "In Pursuit of a Just Society: Martin Luther King, Jr., and John Rawls," *The Journal of Religious Ethics* 18, no. 2 (1990): 57–77.

15 Andrés Moya and Michael R. Carter, "Violence and the Formation of Hopelessness: Evidence from Internally Displaced Persons in Colombia," *World Development* 113 (January 1, 2019): 100–15, https://doi.org/10.1016/j.worlddev.2018.08.015.

16 Ijeoma Opara, David T. Lardier, Isha Metzger, Andriana Herrera, Leshelle Franklin, Pauline Garcia-Reid, and Robert J. Reid, "'Bullets Have No Names': A Qualitative Exploration of Community Trauma Among Black and Latinx Youth," *Journal of Child and Family Studies* 29, no. 8 (August 1, 2020): 2117–29, https://doi.org/10.1007/s10826-020-01764-8.

17 Dana Landis, Noni K. Gaylord-Harden, Sara L. Malinowski, Kathryn E. Grant, Russell A. Carleton, and Rebecca E. Ford, "Urban Adolescent Stress and Hopelessness," *Journal of Adolescence* 30, no. 6 (December 2007): 1051–70, https://doi.org/10.1016/j.adolescence.2007.02.001.

18 Amanda N. Burnside and Noni K. Gaylord-Harden, "Hopelessness and Delinquent Behavior as Predictors of Community Violence Exposure in Ethnic Minority Male Adolescent Offenders," *Journal of Abnormal Child Psychology* 47, no. 5 (May 1, 2019): 801–10, https://doi.org/10.1007/s10802-018-0484-9.

19 Melissa E. Smith, Tanya L. Sharpe, Joseph Richardson, Rohini Pahwa, Dominique Smith, and Jordan DeVylder, "The Impact of Exposure to Gun Violence Fatality on Mental Health Outcomes in Four Urban U.S. Settings," *Social Science & Medicine* 246 (February 1, 2020): 112587, https://doi.org/10.1016/j.socscimed.2019.112587.

20 Mohsen Bazargan, Sharon Cobb, and Shervin Assari, "Discrimination and Medical Mistrust in a Racially and Ethnically Diverse Sample of California Adults," *The Annals of Family Medicine* 19, no. 1 (January 2021): 4–15, https://doi.org/10.1370/afm.2632.

21 Maureen R. Benjamins and Megan Middleton, "Perceived Discrimination in Medical Settings and Perceived Quality of Care: A Population-Based Study in Chicago," *PLoS One* 14, no. 4 (April 25, 2019): e0215976, https://doi.org/10.1371/journal.pone.0215976.

22 Oded Adomi Leshem, "The Pivotal Role of the Enemy in Inducing Hope for Peace," *Political Studies* 67, no. 3 (August 1, 2019): 693–711, https://doi.org/10.1177/0032321718797920.

23 Oded Adomi Leshem, "What You Wish for Is Not What You Expect: Measuring Hope for Peace during Intractable Conflicts," *International Journal of Intercultural Relations* 60 (September 1, 2017): 60–66, https://doi.org/10.1016/j.ijintrel.2017.06.005.

24 King was aware of the idea of Beloved Community, which was initially used by the philosopher-theologian Josiah Royce, who founded the Fellowship of Reconciliation to which Dr. King was a member.

25 Walidah Imarisha and Adrienne Maree Brown, *Octavia's Brood: Science Fiction Stories from Social Justice Movements* (Stirling, UK: AK Press, 2015), 10.

26 Walidah Imarisha, Alexis Gumbs, Leah Lakshmi Piepzna-Samarasinha, Adrienne Maree Brown, and Mia Mingus, "The Fictions and Futures of Transformative Justice," *The New Inquiry* (blog), April 20, 2017, https://thenewinquiry.com/the-fictions-and-futures-of-transformative-justice/.

27 Larry L. Rasmussen, *Earth-Honoring Faith: Religious Ethics in a New Key* (Oxford, England: Oxford University Press, 2015), 227.

28 Maxine Greene, *Releasing the Imagination: Essays on Education, the Arts, and Social Change* (San Francisco, CA: Jossey-Bass, 1995).

29 Van Anthoney Hall, "Black Aesthetics, Art and Social Justice," *Journal of Intercultural Disciplines* 11 (2013): 51.

30 Schuyler Price, "'The Block' Is Hot and Romare Bearden," *Black Art in AMERICA™*, December 3, 2020, www.blackartinamerica.com/index.php/2020/12/03/the-block-is-hot-and-romare-bearden/.

31 Setting where youth met weekly to create art and learn about Kingian Nonviolence and civic engagement with a special focus on the beloved community.

32 As is the case in many of CTCN programs, they partner with artists in the community to engage community members in exploring the themes of the curriculum. The youth learned how to paint, sculpt and collage. They partnered with the Harford Public Library and explored the Harlem Renaissance art movement, its connection to civil rights struggles in the US and other Black-led artistic movements.

33 Lisa Worth Huber, "Building the Beloved Community One Block at a Time," *CT Center for Nonviolence*, July 5, 2016, https://ctnonviolence.org/news-events/building-beloved-community-one-block-time/.

34 Ibid.

35 Ibid.

36 Ibid.

37 Stefano Mastandrea, Sabrina Fagioli, and Valeria Biasi, "Art and Psychological Well-Being: Linking the Brain to the Aesthetic Emotion," *Frontiers in Psychology* 10 (2019), https://doi.org/10.3389/fpsyg.2019.00739.

38 Huber, "Building the Beloved Community One Block at a Time."

39 Ibid.

40 Hartford Department of Families, Children, Youth and Recreation Assistant Director Trish Torruella, one of the funders of the event, commented on the importance of the intergenerational component and how processes that allow for visioning push up against the world as it is "It's clear there is great power in the generations coming together. Today I observed how these students have developed a sense of pride through these art projects. Too often their circumstances make them feel criticized and dismissed. It is just beautiful to see them experience a community where they are listened to, heard, and appreciated". – Quote from Huber, Lisa Worth. 2016.

3   Attack Forces of Evil, Not Persons Doing Evil

Pastor Lewis and I have the windows down as we drive up a long, serpentine hill in New Haven toward his childhood home. For a moment, time seems to stand still as the city disappears from our rearview mirror, and I am surprised by a pleasantly cool breeze.

"You see I used go up and hang out at the top of this hill and, man, every time I come up here, especially these corners, I remember those go-carts we used to have", Pastor Lewis reminisces. "We used to soup them up and fly down this hill, sometimes we didn't even have a steering wheel just a rope and you would never think we could make it around these corners at that speed but we did!"

Pastor Lewis is in his mid-fifties and has a deep voice that can easily cut through a room full of people. He is six-foot-three and has been practicing martial arts since he was a teenager. Now a Blackbelt, he's also a sensei (instructor) who teaches classes regularly in addition to preaching at his church in the Dixwell neighborhood. But today, when Pastor Lewis laughs, for a moment I can hear the 9-year-old boy in his voice.

"I always had what we called the Limo", he continues,

> it was the longest one and it used to take these corners. You see, Artie, I grew up around nature, the whole-time man, and there used to be fresh springs over there and we used to go up with bottles and get water with Dad.

The Pastor stops the car suddenly and waits for a moment.

> Listen, you hear how quiet it is? All you hear is that river! This was my church – nature. Man, I always been so connected to nature. We had all that right here in the city and I wasn't really connected to the city as a kid, I was connected more to nature.

"Here, Artie, at the top of the hill", he says, gesturing to a row of newly rebuilt townhouses, "They tore it all down and redid it. Low-income housing.

DOI: 10.4324/9781003243915-4

Still, it's nice, they keep it nice up here [now]. And that's our little community center, yeah, they still using it!"

He smiles. "They had a lot of great programs for the kids there when I was coming up".

Pastor Lewis' early years were happy. His father, a veteran and sanitation worker, was around a lot in the evenings, and all the kids in the neighborhood knew the Lewis family in part because, as the Pastor explains, "We had the best dogs, and the other kids in the neighborhood used to come out to check them out when we were walking them". The Pastor was a quiet kid and never liked fighting – he was more likely to keep to himself. His mother worked long hours, traveling out to affluent suburbs to do domestic work for a White family.

While Pastor Lewis' early life was filled with love, things deteriorated when he was getting ready to head to high school. At that time in the early 1980s, New Haven was buckling under the weight of massive disinvestment, increasing poverty and White flight. From 1950 to 1980, New Haven's population dropped over 23%, down to 126,109. After a modest increase to 130,474 in 1990, the city then shrank further, with current population estimates as low as 120,000 – a number comparable to the city's 1905 population.[1]

During this time, worsening poverty and the crack cocaine epidemic besieged Black neighborhoods like Pastor Lewis' in cities across the country and dramatically changed families. His father, like many war veterans, fell deep into the grips of alcohol and drug abuse. Lewis recalls, "Around that time, that's when [drugs] started to really flood those communities. Fathers were getting strung out, leaving the house, children abandoned, mothers raising them. And so you had everything in place. Prison ready for 'em!"

In fact, prisons were being built at a record pace to incarcerate increasing numbers of people, especially Black men and, later, Black women most of whom were impacted by poverty and drugs. After holding steady from the 1920s through the 1970s, the population of incarcerated people exploded in the 1980s and has more than quadrupled in the four decades since. Legal Scholar Michelle Alexander writes that during the late 1900s and early 2000s, "[The] rules of acceptable discourse changed, however, segregationists distanced themselves from an explicitly racist agenda. They developed instead the racially sanitized rhetoric of 'cracking down on crime'".[2] With these racialized 'tough on crime' policies, the US prison population grew at an unprecedented rate as the most vulnerable were criminalized at the same time that programs to help families in poverty were cut.

Initially, Pastor Lewis didn't know what had happened to his father. "I didn't know what it was . . . we used to always just have to go out there and get my dad out of the car", he recalls. "You know, my mom would say dad was drunk or something, but then find out later on it was drugs".

The strain of his father's addiction changed Lewis' life at home drastically. "And so we were five in the household. They had me take care of the household, you know?" Come home, go to sleep and go back to work. And I think that's another part of me wanting to sell or getting to, you know, selling drugs and stuff [to try and help the family out] but that turned into its own prison".

With upheaval at home, and the neighborhood growing more chaotic and dangerous under the stress of deepening poverty, Pastor Lewis fell behind in school and started to get involved with selling drugs. By the tenth grade, he was still functionally illiterate and falling further behind in school.

That same year, young Pastor Lewis brought a gun to school, not because he had any intention to use it but because he wanted other kids to respect him, take him seriously and not threaten him. School staff found the gun on him and just a month earlier there had been a shooting at a local high school and a law had been passed to make the possession of firearms in school a more serious offense. Pastor Lewis recalls that the school acted swiftly and the result altered his life: "I was put out [of school] indefinitely".

Without any connection to the school, increasing stress at home and the neighborhood turning sharply for the worse, things quickly spiraled out of control. Pastor Lewis was jailed on drug-related charges. "I still remember my number . . . I was on the eighth galley . . . I knew everybody . . . you know from the neighborhood – I couldn't believe it but I never liked that [seeing so many other Black men I knew]".[3]

After he got out, Pastor battled drug addiction and depression. Many of his friends were still incarcerated; others had been killed while he was away from the community. "You become desensitized [to loss, to violence]", he says. After he was released from prison, Pastor was at a desperate point in his life. He describes this experience of being released from prison as chaotic – it was a vulnerable time for him and he had little support. He wasn't alone in this perception. He saw many of his friends and other people in the city who wanted to stay out of the system, only to get sucked back in as they came back to the city with no money or long-term housing and extreme difficulties finding a job with a criminal record. He says, "People feeling their way through and were doing the best they could. Come on, bro. What else do you expect? Why wouldn't they be desensitized [after being in prison and coming back to a community in disarray]". People need support when they are facing this many problems all at once, and this cemented Pastor Lewis' conviction that young people in these precarious situations need mentors and support (such as Kingian nonviolence).

At this fragile moment, the young pastor met a mentor who changed his life. "Yeah", he reflects, "I met [a guy] . . . in the bathroom, uh, selling drugs and [later] he said, 'Yo, man, come down to the program, man, I'm telling you, we can help you.'"

When Lewis went to the program, his mentor, John Goyle, was the "only white guy sitting there . . . Just a happy, lively guy and – this is my first real encounter coming out from the street, you know, with some white guy".

His mentor looked at the Pastor's name tag and exclaimed, " 'John Lewis.' You know, that's a famous name", referring to the civil rights leader, and close friend of Dr. King, John Robert Lewis. "Do you understand how valuable and how great you are?"

"And this- this white guy saying that to me", Pastor Lewis recalls,

> And I say, "Man, what are you talking about, man? I came down here to get some help." "And I'm helping you," he said. "The value of who you are is going to be the greatest help for you ever in your life, and I'm going to help you find that, and I'm not going to stop until you see it." He saw something in me, whatever that was then. And I'm gonna tell you, this man never stopped!

Pastor Lewis thought John Goyle reminded him of his own father. He had impeccable integrity, spoke the truth and was deeply loyal. "Don't ever let nobody demean you – Just because you're Black, don't ever let them – don't ever let them. Man – He was a beautiful soul". Goyle stood by Lewis [putting him in community organizing and leadership positions] "sitting at a meeting with the university president and the Chamber of Commerce. And the Mayor. This junkie who's coming out the projects or a drug dealer – ex-drug dealer".

These experiences with Goyle helped pave the way for Pastor John Lewis' work with the Center for Nonviolence, as he immediately recognized the importance of Black-led education about nonviolent social change, and the need to add depth to how people engaged with Dr. King and other people who sacrificed to challenge systemic racism. He talks often about the importance of transforming systems, such as criminal justice, but also that these changes alone are not enough.

> Here's the other thing. So with all that said, with us being able to identify the flawed system, now, what you gonna do? Unfair to the hilt but if you understand how to take advantage of that and build your inner strength, absolutely mind-blowing. Because if you don't take advantage of the unfairness, you'll become a victim [of] what it has done [to you].

Pastor Lewis recognizes that his life experiences have been profoundly shaped by historical and social forces, institutions, laws and changes in his neighborhood that made racial injustice, violence, even desperation and despair, a daily reality for him and so many other Black people. As he seeks out ways to address the injustices that have impacted his community, Lewis also engages this deeper analysis in exploring the possibilities for redemption; one can hate the systems but not others or oneself. In his words, "Black Love" is one of the most powerful forces in America and as result Pastor Lewis resonates with King's strategic approach to "Attack problems, not people".

Key Concepts

Kingian nonviolence principles helped Pastor John Lewis think about the "forces of injustice" in more precise and actionable ways. But what are the "forces of injustice" that nonviolence educators in Connecticut refer to? This graphic is one way of seeing how many different institutions reinforce inequality, especially along lines of race.

King articulated the "forces of injustice", to recall, as "the triple evils" of racism, economic exploitation and materialism, and militarism. By "forces", Dr. King meant social structures and systems as well as cultural values and norms.[4] He focused on attacking these and not people or individuals. He made clear that the civil rights movement must not rest until the entire edifice of racial segregation is dismantled. This is an excellent starting place for King's principle. Students can consider: what constituted the edifice of racial segregation in America during King's time? What pillars of support held it in place? How did

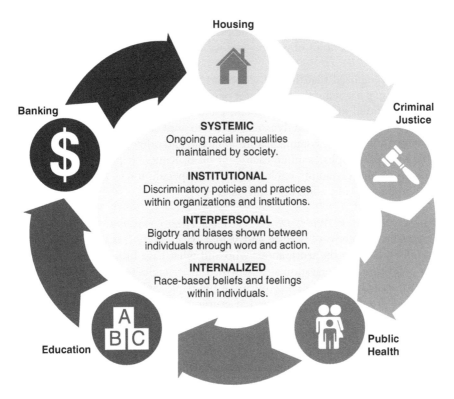

Figure 3.1 Frank Porter Graham Child Development Institute

Source: What Racism Looks Like: An Infographic. Frank Porter Graham Child Development Institute, University of North Carolina at Chapel Hill. Available at: http://fpg.unc.edu/sites/fpg.unc.edu/files/resources/other-resources/What%20Racism%20Looks%20Like.pdf

the civil rights movement weaken or destroy those pillars? The edifice included, for example, the entire Jim Crow system of racial segregation and inequality which included discriminatory laws, racial terror and violence such as lynching, cultural practices that mocked and diminished Black people – including racialized art and advertisements and sexualized images of Black women and girls – and a host of other racist practices.

People have an understandable psychological tendency to feel powerless toward "the system", which is notoriously slow, vague and difficult to change and to direct frustration instead toward the individual. They can enjoy a more immediate catharsis if they call out individuals for their shortcomings. The Kingian curriculum instead uses an aggression/conciliation model to encourage people to change this dynamic by directing their conciliation (compassion) toward individuals and their aggression toward systemic injustice.

To push people toward more systemic thinking, King explained:

> True compassion is more than flinging a coin to a beggar; it is not haphazard and superficial. It comes to see that an edifice which produces beggars needs restructuring. A true revolution of values will soon look uneasily on the glaring contrast of poverty and wealth . . . and say "This is not just".[5]

King recognized that the full scope of these forces were often hard to see, for those experiencing the full weight of oppression but even more so for those who benefitted materially from them. He drew on a range of metaphors and concepts to describe these dynamics to try to awaken white people and other potential allies to the systemic nature of racism and other forms of oppression.[6] The next paragraphs examine each concept of King's "triple evils" of racism, militarism and economic exploitation – the specific forces that nonviolence and nonviolent education must challenge.

In his 1967 book, *Where Do We Go From Here: Community or Chaos*, King begins his chapter on "Racism and White Backlash": "It is time for all of us to tell each other the truth about who and what have brought the Negro to the condition of deprivation against which he struggles today".[7] Dr. King saw the *racism and White supremacy* pillars of the triple evils as the most problematic and grievous. Racism perverted everyone who internalized its logic by creating a false sense of superiority or inferiority in people's sense of self and their place in the world. Although anti-racist work and critical engagement on systemic racism are growing areas of interest for educators – and "systemic racism" almost a buzzword in popular culture – King's views on how deeply racism has shaped and deformed our entire country are often omitted or glossed over in King commemorations and celebrations, which tend to focus on his rhetorical flourishes and at best on a few iconic episodes and events of resistance, especially the Montgomery bus boycotts, and Rosa Park's refusal to give up her seat. Fortunately, educators have a vast array of available resources to discuss systemic racism as they educate about King. For example, King clearly defines the concept of racism and a host of problems that arise from White supremacy:

> Racism is a philosophy based on a contempt for life. It is the arrogant assertion that one race is the center of value and object of devotion, before which other races must kneel in submission. It is the absurd dogma that one race is responsible for all the progress of history and alone can assure the progress of the future. Racism is total estrangement. It separates not only bodies, but minds and spirits. Inevitably it descends to inflicting spiritual and physical homicide upon the out-group.[8]

Dr. King warned that racism affects both individual attitudes and major institutions that often invisibly shape some of the most important aspects of our life – where we live, the quality of our schools and health care, our opportunities and the likelihood of experiencing trauma in our lives. Left unchecked a racist worldview (which doesn't require being a card-carrying KKK member) can all too easily lead to mass violence.

For King, it was not hyperbole to call this a genocidal logic. "Our nation was born in genocide", he wrote, "when it embraced the doctrine that the original American, the Indian, was an inferior race. Even before there were large numbers of Negroes on our shore, the scar of racial hatred had already disfigured colonial society".[9] King noted that "while America has not literally sought to eliminate the Negro in this final sense, it has, through the system of segregation, substituted a subtle reduction of life by means of deprivation".[10]

Pastor John Lewis himself was caught up in one of the most severe, recent iterations of these systems: the mass incarceration of millions of people (mostly Black and Brown) who are not only locked up but also stripped of their voting rights and, in many cases, their future opportunities. That is why the Pastor was surprised, and horrified, to realize that he knew most of the people in jail with him. The population of US prisons has increased by over 400% in the last 40 years,[11] the majority of people in prison are there for nonviolent drug offenses, and this trend has disproportionately affected Black people.

Dr. King understood that the very first step was to *see* these forces, yet doing so meant subverting popular narratives that still hold power today. These narratives that emphasize "Black on Black crime", "single parent households", "urban violence" or other racial codes shift focus away from America's history of racism and obscure the way our institutions and social policies function. It is important for educators to know that King, who was deeply conversant with these arguments, underscored that Black people are not in their current position because they are inferior, lazy or have not struggled enough individually to change or rise above their conditions. Too often commemorations of Dr. King only spotlight his emphasis on personal transformation and inner strength and conveniently elide the ways that King closely paired this sort of change to a steadfast understanding that the "forces of injustice" that required dedicated efforts to change the education, employment and other sectors of society to create greater racial justice.

King centered his work and words on Black people's experiences of racism, but he also confidently explained that its solution – since racism was a system and force, and thus implicated all Americans in different ways – was not to look at Black people in isolation but rather to dissect the "world of white people". This was a controversial claim then, as it still is today, because it seeks to reveal the usually invisible aspects of White privilege and White-serving institutions and prove how racial oppression and White supremacy exist beyond individual malice or goodwill. This system is reinforced by both large institutions and everyday behaviors and choices. A now widely used resource, the Pyramid of White Supremacy, illustrates some of King's insights on this topic.

Like other Black leaders before him,[12] King perceived White America as *psychologically conflicted and internally contradictory* – on the one hand professing the highest ideals of democracy and on the other hand engaging in practices

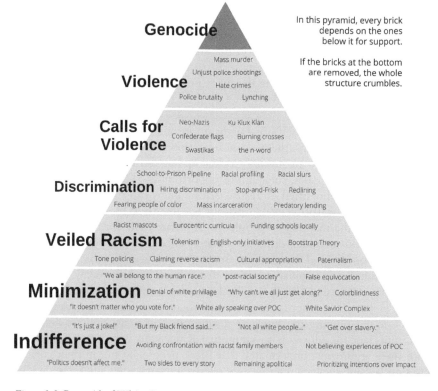

Figure 3.2 Pyramid of White Supremacy

Source: This figure is an adaptation of the "Pyramid of White Supremacy", a visual model developed by Ellen Tuzzolo at Partners for Collaborative Change. It has been included here with Tuzzolo's permission.

that humiliate and deprive Black people and undermine democracy. King challenged White Americans to develop the spiritual fortitude to accept the historical impact of racism, come to grips with the guilt, analyze our own tendencies to ignore, minimize or stand on the sidelines and take accountability for America's racial inequality.

King noted that even after a long and bloody battle for equal rights in the South, he still observed apathy from White people across the country. He wrote, "As the nation, Negro and white, trembled with outrage at police brutality in the South, police misconduct in the North was rationalized, tolerated, and usually denied". Leaders in Northern and Western states "welcomed me to their cities, and showered praise on the heroism of Southern Negroes", King described. "Yet when the issues were joined concerning local conditions, only the language was polite; the rejection was firm and unequivocal".[13]

As part of the solution to *de facto* segregation, attacking the forces meant that White people had to be willing to take risks and forego some of the privileges and comforts afforded them by racial and economic inequality.[14] For some White people, this meant donating to the movement, providing housing for activists, teaching family, co-workers and other members of their community about the issues and why activists demanded action. King asked White people to join marches, voter registration efforts and other forms of direct action. Many people heeded the call, including activists such as Viola Liuzzo, a mother who left her comfortable life near Detroit to participate in the Selma, Alabama march across the Edmund Pettus Bridge after King called on people nationwide to join. Liuzzo was subsequently stalked and killed by local members of the Ku Klux Klan. Similarly, James Reeb, an American Unitarian Universalist minister, came to join the march and was killed the night before.[15]

For Black people, King called for an awakening of confidence and a recognition that justice would not be given voluntarily by those in power or with the help of White individuals of good will alone. This is a vital part of King's approach to nonviolence that is often omitted in overly simplistic comparisons to the Black Power Movement. Even while he called for making good on the higher values articulated by founders of the US, he did not believe that these changes would occur without a fight, or without Black people and other oppressed groups taking direct and often militant action. The radical King, for example, said:

> I come here tonight and plead with you, believe in yourself and believe that you're somebody . . . nobody else can do this for us. No document can do this for us. No Lincolnian emancipation proclamation can do this for us. No Kennedisonian or Johnsonian civil rights bill can do this for us. If the negro is to be free, he must move down into the inner resources of his own soul and sign with a pen and ink of self-assertive manhood his own emancipation proclamation.[16]

King famously declared, "freedom is never given voluntarily by the oppressor; it must be demanded by the oppressed".[17] Attacking the forces of injustice, then, requires a personal transformation through a process of education, not only for Black people but also for White people and other allies as well, though the work for each is distinct. Nonviolence at its best, then, allows for fierce resistance in addition to compassion for everyone entangled in these systems.

Dr. Martin Luther King, Jr. realized that the roots of White supremacy and racism were very deep, and education excavates and makes them visible. For example, slavery was often ignored, glossed over or, even worse, justified in US history books.[18,19] Looking from our vantage point today, Dr. King might not be surprised that the first national lynching museum was established only in 2019, or that the first museum dedicated to African American Culture in Washington, DC, was built as recently as 2016. He might be disappointed but not surprised that America's Black ghettos remain and have even worsened in many places.

Dr. King might have told educators committed to engaging with these uncomfortable truths that they could expect resistance. A large body of scholarship shows that attempts to reflect on issues of race, especially in schools, are often met with persistent minimization, resistance, deflection and other negative responses.[20,21,22] King's term "white backlash" described people who blamed him and the civil rights movement for the violence when racist mobs attacked protestors or bombed activists' and other Black people's homes. Labeling and dismissing activists as "outside troublemakers", the White backlash held that violence happened not because of the deep history of racial violence and inequality in America, but because people like King "stirred up trouble" and "supported riots".[23] King certainly would have recognized the tendency to blame the White backlash today on Black activists, having written in 1967:

> The white backlash of today is rooted in the same problem that has characterized America ever since the black man landed in chains on the shores of this nation. . . . for the good of America, it is necessary to refute the idea that the dominant ideology in our country even today is freedom and equality while racism is just an occasional departure from the norm on the part of a few bigoted extremists.[24]

Racism, King teaches, was a force of injustice that extended beyond a few isolated bigots, something that could only be resolved through an attack on the "force" itself rather than merely fixating on individual evildoers.

When it comes to the second pillar of the triple evils, militarism, King arguably took one if the biggest risks of his life. Dr. King spoke out against the Vietnam War in April of 1967. King saw connections between racial and economic injustice at home and US wars abroad, identifying war as the second pillar of the "triple evils". "I cannot segregate my conscience", he declared in his famous speech, "Beyond Vietnam", at the Riverside church in New York City:

> I knew that America would never invest the necessary funds or energies in rehabilitation of its poor so long as adventures like Vietnam continued to draw men and skills and money like some demonic destructive suction tube. So, I was increasingly compelled to see the war as an enemy of the poor and to attack it as such.[25]

For King, racism emerged out of a colonial project that had wreaked havoc not only on People of Color in America but, ultimately, around the world. As King saw it, the country could make a choice to break with this legacy by truly supporting the cries of people of color everywhere for self-determination and economic equality. "I am convinced that if we are to get on the right side of the world revolution, we as a nation must undergo a radical revolution of values". He said of the Vietnam war:

> By entering a war that is little more than a domestic civil war, America has ended up supporting a new form of colonialism covered up by certain niceties of complexity. Whether we realize it or not our participation in the war in Vietnam is an ominous expression of our lack of sympathy for the oppressed, our paranoid anti-communism, our failure to feel the ache and anguish of the have-nots.[26]

For Dr. King, these conflicts reflected "racism in its more sophisticated form: neocolonialism", whose primary goals were domination and economic exploitation. To use education to attack the forces of evil was to decolonize education and our wider societies and dismantle the military–industrial complex.

King analogized the poverty of America's brutal ghettos to "a system of internal colonialism not unlike the exploitation of the Congo by Belgium".[27] War was the spectacular projection of that kind of violence to people abroad and, as we see with the militarization of the police today, a homecoming of that violence afterward.[28]

> This way of settling differences is not just. This business of burning human beings with napalm, of filling our nation's homes with orphans and widows, of injecting poisonous drugs of hate into the veins of peoples normally humane, of sending men home from dark and bloody battlefields physically handicapped and psychologically deranged, cannot be reconciled with wisdom, justice, and love. A nation that continues year after year to spend more money on military defense than on programs of social uplift is approaching spiritual death.[29]

The problems of American militarism have worsened after five decades of continuous war and military engagement abroad. While the US maintains the highest military spending in the world, it has experienced racial and economic inequality, political division, violence and instability at home.[30] King saw this trend and felt morally that he had to call it out. It is important when learning about this principle of attacking the forces of injustice that Dr. King was widely criticized for not only addressing racism at home but for raising issues of militarism. President Johnson was furious about it, and King's allies worried that expanding his focus beyond civil rights would alienate other people supportive of civil rights, and they were correct. Well-known activists and organizations like the NAACP lamented King's decision to publicly express his views on the War.[31] But Dr. King felt he *had to* address these issues, because in his view, the dynamics of war abroad brutally reinforced racism and economic exploitation at home.

To begin a conversation about the third pillar of the triple evils (economic exploitation), ask your students these questions: What was Dr. King doing when he was assassinated? Why was he in Memphis? Many might be surprised to learn that he was there to join the picket line with sanitation workers striking for a five-cent raise.[32] While Black people, Latinos and Native Americans bear the heaviest burden of economic inequality, the US has grown increasingly unequal overall. The 50 richest Americans in 2020 have the same net worth as the poorest 165 million people combined.[33]

Over the course of his short life, King evolved in his thinking toward growing concern over *economic exploitation and materialism*, which he named the third element in his "triple evils". King saw vividly how poverty and the lack of opportunity for meaningful work stripped people of dignity. This commitment to shifting the economic model in the US came through clearly in his speech entitled, All Labor Has Dignity in 1968, and he fiercely advocated for a massive federal anti-poverty bill and a basic income on numerous occasions.[34] King grappled with a question that has eluded US political thinkers since the founding of the republic: what good are representation and other political rights if people cannot escape cycles of poverty? "America's greatest problem and contradiction", he posited in a statement to the Southern Christian Leadership Conference (SCLC), "is that it harbors 35 million poor at a time when its resources are so vast".[35] King supported the idea of a "Poor People's Campaign", which he announced with key aides from the SCLC in November 1967:[36]

> We ought to come in mule carts, in old trucks, any kind of transportation people can get their hands on. People ought to come to Washington, sit down if necessary in the middle of the street and say, "We are here; we are poor; we don't have any money; you have made us this way; you keep us down this way; and we've come to stay until you do something about it".[37]

From this point on, the problem of poverty, more pronounced for Black people but afflicting White people as well, became the major focus of his work. King saw poverty as a systemic issue that required stronger unions, more equitable sharing of profits and worker influence as well as a universal basic income which has more recently drawn interest by political thinkers on both the right and the left.[38] At his Nobel lecture, King highlighted the need for bold policy to attack these forces, "The time has come for an all-out world war against poverty. The rich nations must use their vast resources of wealth to develop the underdeveloped, school the unschooled, and feed the unfed. Ultimately a great nation is a compassionate nation".[39] According to the 2020 census data, the poverty rate for Black people was at 18.8%, Hispanics at 15.7%, Asian people 7.3% and non-Hispanic whites at 7.3%.[40] Further inequality is dramatically increasing for more than 70% of the global population, and the recent pandemic has only exacerbated these divisions.[41,42]

In the final years of his life, King saw clearly the connections between all "triple evils" and moved decisively toward addressing economic issues, recognizing that guarantees of civil rights are of limited value to people deeply mired in poverty.[43] King faced the daunting problem, however, of demonstrating why poverty should matter to the rest of society that reaped the material benefits of these systems and why people should take immediate action to help support a comprehensive response.

King continually encouraged the movement to "attack" these three forces, and he had several reasons for his second admonition that the movement remain disciplined and *not* attack people. Nonviolence recognizes that those who engage in direct violence and injustice are also caught up in systems that reinforce these values and choices – that White supremacy warps a person's moral and ethical compass. Too often, attacks on people leave the larger system unaffected, create a dangerous illusion of change, and reinforce resentment and resistance. Attacks on individual racists exhaust vital energy needed for the longer and more complex work of transforming social policy in ways that can guarantee a living wage or shift funds away from the military and toward communities of color that bear the heaviest weight of inequality. Furthermore, political violence too often allows the opposition to shift the focus away from the deeper issues of inequality and helps promote more militaristic responses to dissent. In contrast, violence by the state or others on unarmed people in nonviolent actions dramatizes the deeper problems and challenges people's consciences. People on the fence (either passive supporters or passive resistors of change) may feel compelled to reconsider their positions and those that are already active may consider more radical forms of direct action.

However, King was resolute that political violence devalues human life and causes psychological harm. As a result, individual relationships matter as well even in the heat of the battle, and nonviolence helps foster them:

Nonviolence seeks friendship and understanding with the opponent [whenever possible during the struggle to influence change]. Nonviolence does not seek to defeat the opponent. Nonviolence is directed against evil systems, forces, oppressive policies, unjust acts, but not against persons.

Through reasoned compromise, both sides resolve the injustice with a plan of action. Each act of reconciliation is one step closer to the 'Beloved Community'.[44]

Drawing on his both theological and historical knowledge, Dr. King did not believe that powerful institutions could or should solve problems with little engagement from marginalized people. For King, like many other nonviolent theorists, when people withdraw their consent and creatively resist the ruling elites, the power dynamics can begin to shift.

Applying the Concepts, and Lessons Learned

Policing and criminal justice is one of the most important and difficult areas today in which to try and apply the Kingian principle of attacking "forces" of injustice and not individual perpetrators of it. Recently, police shootings of Black people in the US have garnered a great deal of national and international attention, which began following the 2012 murder of 17-year-old Trayvon Martin in Florida, and shortly thereafter, that of 18-year-old Michael Brown in Ferguson, Missouri. On May 25, 2020, after the COVID-19 pandemic had already exposed the consequences of systemic racism, the tragic murder of George Floyd by a police officer in Milwaukee, Wisconsin and Breonna Taylor in Louisville shortly thereafter unleashed public rage and anger once again. Large numbers of Black Lives Matters protestors and sympathizers demanded a move away from incremental change and toward serious overhauls of racially biased systems (most notably, policing). The size, spread, and frequency of these demonstrations took many analysts by surprise, as did the appearance of a new generation of organizers and activists. As many scholars and analysts have noted, police violence against Black people is not an isolated incident. Over-all, Black people were almost three times more likely to be killed than White people in the US according to data from 2013 to 2017.[45] In addition, African Americans constitute a third of the unarmed population killed by the US police between 2013 and 2019, despite making up less than 20% of the total population.[46] Studies reveal that law enforcement is responsible for the death of 1.6% of African American males aged between 20 and 24; this number is 1.2% for American Indian/Alaskan Native, 0.5% for Asian/Pacific Islander, 1.2% for Latino and 0.5% for White males. Those numbers are 0.2% for Black women and American Indian/Alaskan Native women, 0.05% for Asian/Pacific Islander women, 0.16% for Latina women and 0.11% of all deaths for White women.[47]

These high-profile shootings provoked one of the longest sustained periods of nonviolent protest in the US in nearly five decades. Consequently, many Americans have called for greater accountability from the police, includ-ing reforms in how departments investigate police officers who have been involved in shootings and the removal of qualified immunity.[48] Others have advocated a variety of reforms – improved police training, eliminating the use of military-grade weapons and the development of policing models that may foster better relations with communities of color. At the same time, given the deep sense of betrayal and distrust in hyper-policed communities there are growing calls to shift funds away from law enforcement and into nonviolent forms of crisis response staffed by mental health and social work practitioners as well community-led conflict resolution approaches[49,50]

In 2014, Pastor John Lewis made it one of his top priorities to engage police in New Haven as the community outreach coordinator for the CTCN. Activists in New Haven were more insistent on change, and Pastor Lewis had already worked to strengthen relationships with individual officers and local law enforcement leaders and activists, so he and Victoria began to explore the possibility of law enforcement training programs. Then, in 2014, the New Haven police asked CTCN to lead a number of nonviolence trainings for police cadets, with a specific focus on conflict de-escalation, as well as professional development for more seasoned officers.[51]

With trepidation, CTCN's director Victoria assembled a special team of community educators and developed a model that they hoped could connect police officers more directly with the communities they served through nonviolence education and help them more effectively de-escalate conflicts.[52] She and Pastor Lewis were hopeful that by learning how to analyze conflicts (especially long-standing issues of racial inequality) in the community while considering nonviolent interventions these cadets would be able to better serve the communities they work in. In this way, these educators sought to attack the "forces of injustice" rather than solely focusing on individual police officers by taking education and elements of police reform into their own hands and grounding that education in nonviolence. But this is precarious work and the CTCN leadership team had reservations from the outset about how much support they would receive in seeking institutional change while supporting officers to make sense of their professional identities and the responsibilities of ethical policing in a country with a deep history and ongoing legacy of systemic racism, economic inequality and militarized approaches to problem solving. Victoria worried that this simply may not be possible given the limited influence they had on the wider department and the prevailing ethos of militarization.

If you were to walk in the New Haven Police Academy during a Kingian nonviolence training you might first notice that the training team is a mix of community members and police officers. This is unusual, as police trainings in the Academy usually feature trainers who are all law enforcement officials and, often, ex-military. In the later examples, the training team is multiracial and drawn from many different backgrounds. It includes CTCN director Victoria Christgau; Pastor Lewis; Rich Tarlaian, a former police captain in Rhode Island and a Vietnam veteran who met Dr. Bernard LaFayette and worked with him to implement Kingian nonviolence in his Department and New Haven police officers Sam Bradford, Samantha Brown and Patricia Hilliger.[53]

The police officers have gone through extensive preparation for the program, which itself is unique in that it brings together police officers and community members. To become nonviolence trainers, the officers had to join the "training of trainers" offered to community participants, who are primarily from Hartford and New Haven. Those trainings are held regularly by CTCN at various sites in Hartford and New Haven – libraries, colleges, community centers and elsewhere. Police officers are trained alongside racial justice activists, teachers, frontline violence interrupters, people recently released from prison, volunteers from the suburbs, funders and others. They engage each other about the best ways to disrupt cycles of violence and integrate nonviolence into their personal and professional lives. Together they learn models for analyzing types

Photo 3.1 Community Outreach Director, Pastor John Lewis, New Haven Police LT. Pat Hilliger and Senior Trainer, former Rhode Island, Police Captain Richard Tarlaian on break during the Yale University Police Dept. training In New Haven, CT 2018 © CTCN

Photo 3.2 Hartford, youth trainers conduct segment of Certification Training for a mix of New Haven, Community members and New Haven Police department

Photo 3.3 Pastor John Lewis, Hartford Training 2017

and levels of conflict, the principles of nonviolence and the action steps used in key historical civil rights campaigns of the 1950s and 1960s.

The community educators in this case are mostly Black and live in Hartford or New Haven. Violence has impacted many of them directly. At a TOT, students will be taught by senior trainers such as Victoria and Pastor Lane and by others such as Pastor Lewis and Cherell Banks, who live in Hartford and help lead youth trainings and run nonviolence centers in schools. Most likely, these officers and other trainers in training will be taught by the youth of color from the community who model lesson plans and share their experiences at many of CTCN workshops and presentations.

To complete this course, officers will need to learn the Kingian curriculum manual content and gain enough understanding of how they can lead others in learning it for the first time. This means that the three police officers, like others in the class, will do mock teaching lessons in front of this mixed group of nonviolence trainers and community members before they try to teach fellow officers. Along the way, they'll receive constructive feedback from both adult and youth educators from the community.

On numerous occasions, I've been part of the team that offers feedback and coaching for police officers in Connecticut. Like many of the participants in CTCN's community workshops, these officers are not professional educators and may have limited experience with public speaking; it's a very vulnerable moment for all of them. They, too, may have had negative experiences with formal schooling, and so the thought of stepping back into the classroom can be daunting. Even if participants have spoken publicly before, it is nonetheless challenging to lead a participatory educational process where people role play emotionally-heated conflict scenarios or facilitate unpredictable conversations about complex topics with others from such a wide variety of backgrounds. For these police officers, it takes a great deal of courage and humility to stand in front of community members who you are being trained alongside, and then receive feedback in front of everyone about how you can improve your teaching and the way you respond to conflict. This can have a leveling effect, even if it is a temporary one. In some of the rewarding moments I've observed, youth like Tremayne demonstrate how to teach the nonviolence curriculum and basics of facilitation, such as projecting your voice, giving clear instructions for an activity and asking open-ended questions. This temporarily reverses power dynamics normally skewed in the other direction when these Black youth encounter police on the street.

The police officers must step far outside their comfort zones in the training. When they step into that room full of law enforcement back in New Haven, they will be claiming the title of a nonviolence trainer in front of their peers, something that carries its own uncertainty – the risk of looking weak, out of touch, a pawn for the captain or the Mayor's new pet project. There is also a central commitment to loyalty in law enforcement, what some call "the blue curtain", which stresses the importance of not divulging information with people outside of the police force. Any perceived breach of this loyalty can even result in officers being seen as "traitors" to the "culture".

All of this raises a number of potential issues for both nonviolence educators and law enforcement participants: How much can we expect other officers to share about the impacts of violence in workshops? When it comes to non-violence training for police, some may ask; Is that a joke? Police are literally *sanctioned* by the state to use violence and most often that violence is levied toward marginalized communities. Finally, why should cops listen to people from the community? These officers know it will be challenging to walk into the police academy with a group of nonpolice from the community. What do they know about the daily realities of being a police officer, and what do they have to teach? A lot will be riding on these officers' shoulders as they begin to engage with this unfamiliar curriculum and content.

At 9 am on the morning of Police Academy Training in New Haven, about 35 cadets shuffle into the room, walking past the flip chart paper and the group of nonviolence trainers assembled at the front. I've been to many nonviolence training sites in the community, but this is my first time at the Academy. One of the first things I notice when I walk in is a cleaning station for officers' guns, as well as unused paper targets leaned up against the wall. It reminds me that this is an unusual site for a nonviolence training.

Rich Tarlaian, the retired Providence police force captain, makes an opening statement:

> I am privileged to have been introduced to this work [while I was working in law enforcement]. This is not a shoot or "don't shoot" course – this is mostly about the use of force. I only realized this point after I was introduced to my first course. Doc [LaFayette] led that training and I have seen him train people all over the world, including many people who have been deeply involved in violence. Sometimes the people that have used violence are the ones that know exactly how limited it can be, how bankrupt that approach can be. I'm one of those people. I have had a gun in my hands since I was 18 and I became a police officer just weeks after I got back from Vietnam. When I heard Doc [LaFayette] talk in my department I thought he was crazy and after I was captain I have had people tell me they thought I was crazy for bringing this in. They call nonviolence the sword that heals. If I cut you with a knife that is a felony, right? but if the surgeon uses the knife to heal, then we applaud them!

Rich's opening remarks are provocative. For him, the question is not whether an officer will use force but what *kind* of force they will use and for what purpose. This training asks the question, *what is power, and force*? Force can not only be used to dominate, humiliate and render passive, but it can also be used to preserve and sustain life. Rich is also well aware that changes in individual officers attitudes while important often do not lead to consistent or widespread shifts in police violence.

With Rich in the lead, this discussion around language often expands beyond the interpersonal to include dynamics between the police and the community, especially communities of color and poor areas of the city. He asks the officers, "So what do you call those houses where you get frequent and repeated calls?"

The officers stare at him nervously, and blankly.

Rich presses them, "You know the one where the call comes in and you look at your partner and say, oh these guys again?"

Several of the officers become visibly tense and shift in their seats, and no one raises a hand. He continues, "I'll tell you, we used to call them, *animal houses*, and some people said things that were worse than that!"

People let out a nervous laugh.

Rich makes a broader point here: our social perceptions influence our view of people – sometimes before we even meet them – and this becomes normalized in many police departments. Those views are based on race and class, and many times on where people live, their neighborhood and zip code, and as a result, communities are policed differently and working-class black communities are often the most surveilled and policed spaces in the United States. But there is another implication here too, that our stance – in other words, the view we bring to a situation – can influence what we see as possible. For police, this perception of what is possible in a given situation can have life or death consequences. Sometimes preconceived ideas of risk and the gradual dehumanization of people in majority-Black and Brown neighborhoods can unconsciously or consciously justify the use of violent force by police in situations where it is not justified. Conversely, it results in under-policing neighborhoods deemed "good", safe, stable or affluent. In a society with a high degree of inequality, people come to believe that some groups are more worthy of compassion and care than others.

Pastor Lewis' interventions here are important, as he builds on Rich's point with a sense of authority grounded in his personal story and experiences. "Remember I was one of those youth and I am standing in front of you here today". He lived and still lives in a neighborhood that is over policed. He struggled to make it and faced challenges that were not unique to him or his neighborhood but have been formative for many Black people across the country. He emphasizes that it takes work to "see the man" and not just the neighborhood.

Rich offers an example from his work to delve more deeply into the use of force. He talks about an intervention at a home that he and his partner had visited numerous times before in response to disturbances. When the officers get to the front door and knock, the cracked door swings open and they immediately see two brothers fighting. One brother was chasing the other around the house with a knife, and the mother was standing near them, frozen. At that moment, Rich surveyed the scene and noticed that the stove flame was on – someone had been cooking before all the mayhem broke out – so he yells,

"Hey, what are you guys doing, the beans or whatever you got cooking on the stove are about to burn. Help your mom out". The brothers stop for a second or two. He addresses the young man with the knife by his first name and says, "Drop the knife, let's talk". The other officer is able to step between them and the young man puts the knife on the table.

Rich turns to the officers in the classroom and asks,

> What am I trying to do in that situation? I am trying to create space, to buy some time, and if possible slow things down. I want to do that and not degrade or insult someone, to not escalate this. I want to give them a way out. You know? To save face, where they don't have to look like they lost or gave in. In my head in that moment, I'm thinking, something I learned in nonviolence, and I'm asking myself that question: how can I do something *genuine and unexpected.*

Rich understands that a conversation about the use of force and conflict de-escalation needs to be relevant to potentially dangerous situations officers may face, but in so doing, he is highlighting types of force that might otherwise be missed. In this example, he appeals to the young men's sense of responsibility; "Help your mom out". Rich does not see this person as incapable of shifting his behavior, even while he is engaged in antisocial and violent behavior. He highlights the element of emotional control and the importance of being able to think critically. He employs the weapon of surprise and thinks about "force" in terms of providing a way to restore some semblance of human connection. Even a little space, and a chance to disarm the young man, can de-escalate the conflict, not in a way that is universally transformative, necessarily, but that may create new possibilities for the restoration of relationships.

Police officers are schooled to think about a spectrum of force and to always look for risk. The first two levels of force are the "physical presence" of officers in uniform and "clear verbal commands", and after that things get physical – wrist locks, for example. In contrast, the Kingian method envisions a far wider array of communicative options prior to or instead of verbal commands. When I join the community educators in Connecticut in speaking with the officers about the spectrum of force, I often start by asking officers, "Let's say you come home, and you are hungry. You want your partner to cook you a meal, ideally quickly! You use the force continuum as a guide. They are in the kitchen, and you stand there. You're using 'physical presence', but they don't seem to notice. So then you move to 'clear verbal commands' – something like, 'move toward the refrigerator and get out some food, then immediately proceed to the stove to start cooking'.

I ask the officers how they imagine this would go over at home? The officers always laugh. 'Oh, you would be in trouble. You might get the pan upside your head'" and so on. They already understand the limits of this understanding of force and use other methods in their everyday lives.

But through the aforementioned example, Rich explores "force" on a deeper level, and the theme is not as controversial as I might have expected with officers in the sessions I observe. Nonviolence looks at the force inside of us – the ability to maintain compassion even in the face of violence. It is also about the force needed to change complex and historically embedded systems often through protest and other forms of direct action that are vitally important in a democratic society. At a basic level, for officers, that means acknowledging racial and other forms of injustice and trying to promote justice by protecting the rights of people in the society, especially minority communities that are most at risk. This can feel overwhelming or a bit abstract and at points in the discussion some of the officers' eyes drift off. Pastor Lewis is sure to emphasize that police cannot mend broken relationships by themselves or fully upend social injustice, and others will need to take the lead on that work as well. Police are limited in their ability to change underlying conditions in a neighborhood with scarce economic opportunities, where children often experience trauma and their education is insufficient, even with wealthy suburbs just a few miles away, and they still have to contend with the realities that they work in a society with prevalent firearms.

Pastor John Lewis is one of the first community educators to step to the floor. The room is completely quiet, and there is a nervous sense of curiosity. He begins,

> I am a lifelong resident of New Haven and this is a powerful moment for me. This training is about relationships, to see where we are going and about always looking for ways to bridge the gap with the community. So the conversations can be real, they have to be real, so we can talk about what separates us. The Center has helped with this, providing a curriculum for us to learn together [and have that conversation]. Today I ask you have an open mind. This is not a test but a journey. That means today we will create dialogue and I can guarantee one thing: at some point along the way you will be surprised.

After Lewis' remarks, the police training resumes with a new look at the civil rights movement of the 1950s and 1960s. CTCN's police training includes the study of major civil rights movement campaigns in Birmingham, Montgomery and Nashville. It emphasizes how these movements aimed to demolish Jim Crow laws and push America to become a fuller democracy, extending beyond basic political rights to Black people. Officers learn about the strategy, planning, and discipline involved in organizing these major turning points in the movement. They also learn about specific organizers, beyond Dr. King. Victoria has made it a priority to expand the original curriculum for the center in all their programs to encompass many of the women who played key roles in organizing for change, including Ella Baker, Claudette Colvin, Rosa Parks, Diane Nash and many others.

In addition to getting a "behind the scenes" look at participatory democracy and the intensive education and preparation involved in this work, police officers attending the trainings can view footage of the violence inflicted on nonviolent activists in the civil rights movement. For example, officers learn in depth about the frequent attacks suffered by Black people in Birmingham, Alabama. This includes the infamous 16th Street Baptist Church bombing that killed 4 children and left 22 others injured.[54] Bombings were so frequent that many in the Black community dubbed the city "Bombingham". While these were shocking acts of racialized terror, CTCN trainers are careful in this discussion with police not to categorize these as isolated incidents that occurred only during a particularly tense time but as an extension of longstanding practices, such as the lynching of Black people across the US for over 400 years, economic sabotage and a lack of accountability in the criminal justice system for White people who perpetrated violence against Black people.

Here, the conversation shifts to Black people's vulnerability in these systems, then and now, even in the most mundane moments. Victoria asks the cadets (who are mostly White) if anyone is familiar with the story of Emmett Till. Not one of the White cadets raises a hand.[55] She explains that he was simply visiting family in Mississippi when he was accused of being a threat, much as Trayvon Martin had been a few months before this workshop. Till was murdered at the age of 14, drowned in the Tallahatchie river because people claimed he looked at a White woman.[56] His mother demanded an open casket funeral so that the world could see the brutality that her innocent child had endured, and *Jet* magazine published the photos, which galvanized more support from previously indifferent Whites.

Lieutenant Sam Brown explains to the training group, "[*Look*] magazine ran a story [where the murderers] admitted killing him and yet still no one was found guilty".[57] This is an opportunity to focus on the forces of injustice, or what King called the "edifice" of racial segregation – the major pillars, including the legal system, that supported and enabled segregation.

Soon, the conversation takes a more personal turn toward the role of police in this system. A White cadet raises her hand and says, "I have noticed when I'm walking [the beat] that people look at me and they don't know me, and they have a problem with me being there and they don't even know me". Police during the civil rights era, and for centuries before, reinforced racist laws and abetted the lack of accountability in criminal justice for White people who threatened, attacked, and killed Black people – not only in the South but across the US. Watching civil rights movement films, this cadet is struck by the realization that the relationship between police and the Black communities she will be serving is deeply influenced – and soured – by this history, and it's a jarring realization.

When this training occurred in Connecticut, the Ferguson Uprising was still in full swing in Missouri and several police officers had been shot in Dallas a few days earlier. Similar to the civil rights era, police confronted many

Black Lives Matter protests with violent force and military-grade weapons eliciting outrage and concern from around the world. Several cadets talked about this but saw it very differently; their sentiment was that the civil rights movement was nonviolent, but today the police are "actually the ones that were nonviolent and protestors were the violent ones". Yet, this is an over-simplified and inaccurate remembering of history. In fact, when people stood up to injustice through nonviolence in the 1950s and 1960s, much like today, protestors were inaccurately labeled as violent and as outside agitators, and police were asked to violently quell these "uprisings". Further where some officers contend that Black Lives Matters protests put them at risk police killings decreased in many cities with increased protest and other forms of civic engagement.[58]

King remarked on the deep hypocrisy of this position when he wrote,

> You warmly commended the Birmingham police force for keeping "order" and "preventing violence." I doubt that you would have so warmly commended the police force if you had seen its dogs sinking their teeth into unarmed, nonviolent Negroes. I doubt that you would so quickly commend the policemen if you were to observe their ugly and inhumane treatment of Negroes here in the city jail; if you were to watch them push and curse old Negro women and young Negro girls; if you were to see them slap and kick old Negro men and young boys; if you were to observe them, as they did on two occasions, refuse to give us food because we wanted to sing our grace together. I cannot join you in your praise of the Birmingham police department.[59]

Issues of police brutality come to the forefront when officers watch the film *A Force More Powerful*, which highlights the efforts in Nashville, Tennessee, to desegregate lunch counters. The film includes several clips of Bernard LaFayette, then 18-years-old, and rare footage of the extensive nonviolence trainings that took place in preparation for the sit-ins. In one part of the film, Dr. LaFayette talks about how they were told in advance that the police were going to let the "white hoodlums" beat them up without intervening for the first 10 minutes and that nonviolent protestors needed to be prepared to be beaten without protection from the police.

Police trainings might also include *The Children's March*, a film that shows how King struggled behind the scenes with the moral dilemma of whether children should be allowed to march alongside adults and be subjected to such violence and indignity. As police officers review the brutal images of firemen spraying protestors with high-powered water hoses and police attacking people with dogs and batons, the room is quiet. Many of the protestors were children, and so inspired by the civil rights movement that they wrote essays to try and "win" their place in the protest by showing how much they wanted to be part of it. Children who joined the march faced violence not from members of the general public but from firemen, police officers and officials at jails, where they were also hosed with water, subjected to police brutality and held in makeshift cages.[60]

As I look across the room at this police training, many of the cadets are clearly bothered when watching this footage. Some wince at many points in the film, especially during the scenes where protestors are attacked. Others sit with their arms folded.

After the end of the screenings, Lt. Sam Brown leads the debrief. He begins with a question. "How do you feel, how would you feel, knowing that you just unleashed your dog? He makes a reference to the fifth principle of nonviolence: Would that cause internal violence?"

I'm surprised to hear Brown use the term "oppressor" when he follows up to ask if participants thought the police were doing the work of the oppressor. The room is quiet for a few moments and Victoria joins him, asking the group to share reactions to the films. Several White cadets speak up first: "This is ridiculous – this was just a few years ago". Another agrees before someone else adds, "This was not in my lifetime but still is my background". One of the Black officers joins in and speaks to the reality that the activists navigated: "It was brutal but it was courageous". A White colleague agrees, "It was awesome – they changed it for all of us".

Pastor Lewis steps back in, to build on Sam Brown's last point – social changes that come about through nonviolence "tend to last longer". He continues,

> we still have a lot of work to do, though, and we stand by that principle, and that work still continues and people are still doing the work! Why do we talk about this? We are at a time where a lot of this is rearing its head, the civil unrest, and you are at the forefront of responding to what is happening today. This is pertinent and it helps to know that history [because today you see] a lot of subconscious behavior.

Pastor Lewis goes on to talk about the riots born out of despair and frustration following King's assassination and the White flight that followed. How a system like this can make people lose hope and believe that they are not valued by society, even pushing some toward violence.

CTCN's director Victoria Christgau then speaks directly to her experiences as a White woman. "There comes a time when you have to choose which side of justice you want to be on. To see things and talk about them", she says, "Being a white person in the movement required taking risks too, to stand up to racism. [That is why] Viola Liuzzo was killed".

Victoria makes the point that Liuzzo was a housewife who was probably socially ostracized for doing what she did. Liuzzo left the comfort of her suburban home in the Detroit area to support the movement in Alabama. Liuzzo's story has inspired Victoria and she raises her voice when asking one last question, making explicit something that has been implicit the whole time as they study the history: "When are we willing to take a stand? What are we willing to sacrifice for?"

The community educators make several potentially controversial points in the training. The first is that the protests are an outgrowth of deep systemic inequalities and that kind of challenge to the status quo is needed. Further police bear a responsibility to keep people safe especially the most marginalized people in society while also protecting those civic spaces for people to demand change. The second is that the threat of protestors and the focus on possible violence during protests during the 1960s parallels discussion of Black Lives Matters protests today which have been overwhelming nonviolent. It is difficult to tell however if these points are understood by officers as CTCN only shows historical films of police brutality missing recent images of violence against unarmed Black Lives Matters protests across the country. As a result, discussion of the relevance of these human rights abuses today are more abstract and prevailing narratives in police departments that minimize these abuses may remain largely unaltered.[61] Some educators like many community members also question if the police in the US can become less violent? Even if they can, is that good enough? Can they become guardians of democracy and support changing a status quo that marginalizes Black people and other oppressed people?

These questions weigh heavy on some of the community educators' minds, and Victoria and Rich frequently raise questions like these when considering the possibilities for change in these spaces. They know that nonviolence education requires that they support people in confronting various forms of violence, what King called the forces of injustice. What is troubling is they recognize the possibility that nonviolence can also perpetuate violent systems by failing to contribute to enduring and redemptive transformation not only of individuals but also of institutions. While nonviolence education may lead to more peaceful relationships with individual police officers, can it produce significant declines in police violence or even crime and homicide in the city? Community educators are uneasy with the possibility that departments may be engaging in limited educational efforts without a deep commitment and plan to engage in transformative change. It is in this uncertain context that they continue to explore the possibilities for change when working with police.

Typically, police officer de-escalation training focuses on reducing officer use of force in situations where violence is already imminent, often referred to as "shoot or don't shoot" scenarios.[62] For example, a person has his hands in his coat and the officer fears that he may have a gun and needs to make a split-second decision about how to respond. These trainings look at immediate strategies to manage violence in high-risk moments, and not on what came before, or on the prevention of escalation in the first place. However, hypersensitivity to risk can also amplify fear, bias and lead to rushed or reactive decision-making and create many other problems.[63,64]

In contrast to this, CTCN's community educators focus on early intervention, that is, how to prevent conflicts from escalating to a point where violence is likely to be used by one or both parties in a conflict and using communicative and other strategies to shift behavior.

In this training, cadets learn the same conflict modules that are taught in any other Kingian training. The difference is that they will also run through examples that are drawn from their experiences and those of other police officers, and they will look at conflict not only with the community but also with other officers or in their personal lives. They are taught a model with several different types of conflicts and three levels of conflict intensity so that they can track escalation: normal, pervasive and overt levels. As is common in conflict resolution workshops, Kingian trainers explain that conflict is a normal function of social life and it can be either destructive or constructive. Conflict doesn't have to be negative; in fact, it can have either productive or destructive outcomes. Community educators elaborate that conflict, when not productively engaged – when underlying tensions are not addressed, or people's basic human needs denied – can lead to more intense conflict.

In interpersonal dynamics, the "normal" level of conflict is characterized by dialogue, debate, and even heated exchange. A conflict could escalate to the "pervasive" level, where the parties start "othering" by using dehumanizing language, silencing or threatening the other person. At the "overt" level of conflict, direct physical violence happens. Trainers use a shorthand for these levels of escalation: normal is mostly dialogue (even if it is heated); pervasive is mostly monologue and insults; overt is picking up a log (as in, hitting someone over the head with it). People often remember this usefully simple phrase after the training ends.

Victoria, Pastor Lewis and the two officers lead a discussion about how language changes according to the intensity of the conflict. The normal level can be tense; people might feel "triggered" and upset, but to some extent, they are still able to hear each other. The overt level shifts to language that dehumanizes, generalizes or "others" other people. For example: "The problem with people like you" or, worse, the adversary is no longer a person but an animal. Officers share several examples: "You could call people a dog"; "or a pig"; someone adds, being called "a bitch, which is a female dog". Physical violence breaks out at the overt level – domestic violence, bar fights, gang wars and police shootings, to name just a few that the group discussed.

The trainers in this session highlight the importance of being able to see a conflict as it is developing, maintain an analytical disposition and respond rather than react. The trainers' overarching message is simple: there are more options with fewer risks when you intervene at the normal or pervasive levels than at the overt level. Intervention into overt conflict carries with it the most risk and usually affords chances only to manage the conflict rather than resolving or transforming the conflict dynamics. Nonviolent interventions at this stage may involve creating space between the parties, disarming them with the least amount of force possible, distraction and redirection and other immediate strategies. In some cases, as in hostage negotiation, a certain amount of dialogue may be possible. These tactics are important, valuable and sometimes necessary, but if possible it is best to notice lower-level conflict dynamics and respond before they reach the overt level.

At this point, the more experienced officers will frequently reflect that they are being asked to do things that they are not trained to do and that these are not problems that policing can fix. Today we have all the "forces" that King wanted to attack. We have systemic racism, housing insecurity, a lack of affordable health care, poverty and problems caused when people self-medicate to escape despair – and eventually, sometimes at the end stage of problems, the police get involved. They are asked to evict people from their homes or to deal with the scourges of addiction. Even if interactions with the police in these episodes are more human and humane, the larger social systems remain unequal and unjust.

CTCN's program raises these issues explicitly, drawing attention to another important role that officers play, as protectors of democratic space. For example, when police unleash dogs on nonviolent protesters, they are not only causing violence to those individuals but also shutting down spaces of democratic resistance, where people withdraw consent and challenge unjust and racist laws.

Even so, it is a tall order to "attack the forces of injustice" when those forces are complex and will require work on multiple levels simultaneously. Dr. James Lawson, to recall, was the nonviolence trainer recruited by Dr. King to do trainings in Nashville and who influenced some of the most dedicated activists, including Diane Nash, James Bevell, and Bernard LaFayette. I queried Lawson about how we can change systems that are so complex and multifaceted. He responded with a question: "How do you eat an apple? You take a bite. And what happens if you try to eat the whole thing [[at once]]? You choke".

The point was clear: you do need to make strategic choices about the best place to start, but you will not bring down the whole system at once. In his own work, Dr. Lawson and others were trying to dismantle what King referred to as "the whole edifice of segregation". They were working to unmake the laws, institutional practices and attitudes that scaffolded Jim Crow, and they succeeded in abolishing many of these laws and shifting attitudes about race in America. Yet many aspects of systemic racism survived, impervious – they shifted form and endured.

If we look at CTCN's efforts in these trainings, to change police behavior, we can see both the strengths and limits of this approach. The strength is that these programs help law enforcement consider their position within a society that has a deep history and ongoing presence of systemic racism, and to consider what ethical behavior looks like from that position. As Lt. Brown comments,

> This was something I could relate to, it hit home . . . because King was much more than the dream. He learned from philosophers, he wanted

to internationalize and institutionalize this work, and these are the only things that worked in addressing deep social change.

The limits are, as officers themselves note, that one program cannot dismantle the edifice on its own. We have to question if and how ethical policing is possible in a society with:

1. A deep history of White supremacy and racial inequality, where streets, entire neighborhoods and sometimes large sections of a city are still segregated and can therefore be policed differently?
2. The widespread availability of guns and the common potential of a high-risk encounter for police, even in the most mundane situations?
3. Weak mechanisms for accountability when officers engage in abuse?
4. Inadequate training in conflict de-escalation?
5. Officers who often do not live in the neighborhoods they police or come from different racial, cultural and sometimes linguistic backgrounds?
6. A society that criminalizes Black people at every turn?
7. Unmet trauma and mental health needs especially in impoverished communities of color?
8. Inadequate economic opportunities?
9. Schools that are inadequately funded and segregated, which diminishes opportunities for mobility or even dreams?

Finally, Lt. Brown's opening comments at the Academy session raise perhaps the most stunning and transformative questions of all: could you have a police force that institutionalizes *non*violence in the US? That challenges racism in its ranks but also in the larger society? These questions are not answered in the training, but they are at least raised.

Tips for Community Educators

- *Attacking forces, not people: the forces can be defined.* Nonviolence education requires understanding the systems that reinforce and produce inequality. While complex, educators can play a key role in helping to demystify and define those systems (forces of injustice). For example, White supremacy can be defined. As Frances Lee Ansley defines it, the

> political, economic, and cultural system in which White people overwhelmingly control power and material resources, conscious and unconscious ideas of White superiority and entitlement are widespread, and relations of White dominance and non-White subordination are daily reenacted across a broad array of institutions and social settings.[65]

- *Systemic racism occurs because of specific ways that society is organized and historical momentum. Students can learn this and connect it to their experiences in their daily lives.* During initial three-week youth nonviolence trainings, researchers found that "youth were 92% less likely to define violence as only a physical act and 81% more likely to describe violence as something that is both physical and nonphysical".[66] This more robust understanding of what constitutes violence raises questions about student understanding of violence as the result of structural conditions. Evaluation of the program in 2015 directly asked the youth if they could give an example of "systemic or structural violence", either past or present, and 59% provided concrete examples. Some youth gave historical examples, mentioning segregated schools, bathrooms or water fountains or not having the right to vote. Others gave contemporary instances of police brutality or Black people being killed by White police officers, as well as examples such as racial slurs or, more specifically, being called an "oreo" (a person who is Black but is perceived to "act White"), and "television showing us [violence] is okay".[67]

- *Connect the past and the present with a focus on those who have taken action to influence systemic change.* There is a rich history of people taking action to address issues of injustice, and those efforts are very much alive today and often led by youth. These efforts include movements led by youth addressing mass incarceration in the US, climate change, food justice and an array of other areas.
- *Organizing takes time and requires persistence.* Organizing for wider change can seem impossible when only looking at the present moment and the enormity of challenges people face. Attacking forces is more than a protest, a hashtag or an online petition. It takes effort to sustain a protest, build communities of practice and shift attitudes and policies.
- *While strategy and planning are important, so are creativity, spontaneity and allowing for experimentation.* There is a balancing act between emergent strategies and actions and planned, coordinated actions that are consistently implemented.
- *Connect movements.* Any single campaign to address change will necessarily be limited, so efforts to connect with other activists and advocates who are working on related issues are important. This is often called intersectional organizing.
- *Attack forces – and still think about people.* For example, coal miners will still need work, even if fossil fuels are phased out. People proactively engaging in efforts to ensure public safety will still be needed even if police are scaled back. This necessitates building alternative institutions and practices in the here and now, and this can happen in a school or at the neighborhood level as people step into the role of active peacemakers.
- *Expect resistance.* King called some of this resistance "White backlash" when it came to organizing for racial justice. This backlash needs to be contextualized in relation to a long history of backlash – after slavery ended, during Reconstruction, with White flight and (directly relevant to students today) in response to school integration.

• *Use diagrams and visuals.* The diagrams introduced in this chapter illustrate more concretely the otherwise abstract "forces of injustice" and evil, and this kind of visualization should be used in nonviolence education. There are also activities where students can map systems that are reinforcing problems and explore the *pillars of support* that reinforce those systems in order to find ways to shift the power dynamics at play.

Notes

1 Connecticut State Register and Manual, "Population of Connecticut Towns," Prepared by the Office of the Secretary of State, accessed March 8, 2021, https://portal.ct.gov/SOTS/Register-Manual/Section-VII/Population-1900-1960.

2 Michelle Alexander, *The New Jim Crow: Mass Incarceration in the Age of Colorblindness* (New York, NY: The New Press, 2020), 43.

3 It was not surprising that Pastor saw many of the people he knew and loved from his childhood and from across the city in prison. Even as recently as 2015 African Americans were incarcerated at 5.1% times the rate of whites (Nellis, The color of Justice: Racial and Ethnic Disparities in State Prisons Published by The Sentencing Project, Washington DC, 2016, https://www.sentencingproject.org/wp-content/uploads/2016/06/The-Color-of-Justice-Racial-and-Ethnic-Disparity-in-State-Prisons.pdf), and African American youth comprised 35.1% of juvenile arrests (Bureau of Justice Statistics, Prisoners in 2015, Washington DC, 2015, https://bjs.ojp.gov/content/pub/pdf/p15.pdf).

4 Dr. King has been criticized for not speaking up enough for women's rights and the rights of the LGBTQ community. This is an issue that can make for rich discussion and Coretta Scott King dedicated much of her time and energy to addressing these issues as part of what she saw as their shared work building the beloved community. See Michael Long, "Coretta's Big Dream: Coretta Scott King on Gay Rights," *HuffPost*, 32:03 500, sec. Queer Voices, www.huffpost.com/entry/coretta-scott-king_b_2592049 and also The University of North Carolina at Chapel Hill, "Carolina Celebrates a Civil Rights Leader at Annual Lecture | UNC-Chapel Hill," February 18, 2020, www.unc.edu/posts/2020/02/18/carolina-celebrates-a-civil-rights-leader-at-annual-lecture/.

5 Martin Luther King Jr., "Beyond Vietnam: A Time to Break Silence," *Speech, Riverside Church, New York, NY*, April 4, 1967.

6 One way to envision these forces is to think of the pillars of support that hold these structures in place. Here is an image that students can use to think about what pillars hold up a specific form of oppression. For example, segregated schools today. www.nonviolent-conflict.org/wp-content/uploads/2019/02/Pillars-of-Support-PNG-English_Page_2.png.

7 Dr Martin Luther King Jr, *Where Do We Go from Here: Chaos or Community?* (Boston, MA: Beacon Press, 2010).

8 Ibid.

9 Jesse Jackson and Martin Luther King, *Why We Can't Wait* (New York, NY: Signet Classic, 2000), 110.

10 King Jr, *Where Do We Go from Here.*

11 The Sentencing Project, "Criminal Justice Facts," accessed March 29, 2021, www.sentencingproject.org/criminal-justice-facts/.

12 James Baldwin, *The Fire Next Time* (New York, NY: Vintage International, 1993).

13 Jeanne Theoharis, "We Remember How Martin Luther King Jr. Revolutionized the South. But We Can't Forget His Struggles in the North," *Washington Post*, April 4, 2018, www.washingtonpost.com/news/made-by-history/wp/2018/04/04/we-remember-how-martin-luther-king-jr-revolutionized-the-south-but-we-cant-forget-his-struggles-in-the-north/.

14 There are numerous resources that critically examine what it means to be an ally across race lines including:

K. T. Brown and J. M. Ostrove, "What Does it Mean to be an Ally? The Perception of Allies from the Perspective of People of Color," *Journal of Applied Social Psychology* 43, no. 11 (2013): 2211–22; A. J. Barton, "What Does it Mean to Be an Ally?" *Journal of Nursing Education* 59, no. 10 (2020): 543–44.

15 DeNeen L. Brown, "Slaying of Civil Rights Activist James Reeb in 1965 Is Reexamined in the Face of New Evidence," *Washington Post*, accessed March 8, 2021, www.washingtonpost.com/history/2019/06/19/slaying-civil-rights-protester-james-reeb-is-reexamined-face-new-evidence/.

16 "Dr. Martin L. King Jr.: 'I'm Black and I'm Beautiful' [VIDEO]," *NewsOne* (blog), January 20, 2014, https://newsone.com/2843703/dr-martin-l-king-jr-im-black-and-im-beautiful-video/.

17 Martin Luther King Jr., "Letter from Birmingham Jail," *UC Davis Law Review* 26 (1992): 835.

18 Susan C. Pearce and Rachael Lee, "Missing Colonies in American Myths of Slavery: Where Is the 'Deep North' in Sociology Textbooks?" *Sociology of Race and Ethnicity*, January 12, 2021, 2332649220980474, https://doi.org/10.1177/2332649220980474.

19 Latisha Jensen, "A Portland Parent Found Her Daughter's Textbook Racist. Her Teacher Has a Contract That Says He Could Use It Anyway," *Oregon Herald*, March 9, 2021, www.oregonherald.com/oregon/localnews.cfm?id=14464.

20 Arthur Romano and Rochelle Arms Almengor, "It's Deeper Than That! Restorative Justice and the Challenge of Racial Reflexivity in White-led Schools," *Urban Education* (2021): 0042085921998419.

21 Prudence L. Carter, Russell Skiba, Mariella I. Arredondo, and Mica Pollock, "You Can't Fix What You Don't Look At: Acknowledging Race in Addressing Racial Discipline Disparities," *Urban Education* 52, no. 2 (February 1, 2017): 207–35, https://doi.org/10.1177/0042085916660350.

22 Ricky Lee Allen and Daniel D. Liou, "Managing Whiteness: The Call for Educational Leadership to Breach the Contractual Expectations of White Supremacy," *Urban Education* 54, no. 5 (June 2019): 677–705, https://doi.org/10.1177/0042085918783819.

23 Anjali Kamat, "'Go after the Troublemakers': How Trump and Barr Targeted the Black Lives Matters Movement," *Mother Jones* (blog), accessed March 10, 2021, www.motherjones.com/politics/2020/11/go-after-the-troublemakers-how-trump-and-barr-targeted-the-black-lives-matter-movement/.

Safia Samee Ali, "False 'Thug' Narratives Have Long Been Used to Discredit Movements," *NBC News*, September 27, 2020, www.nbcnews.com/news/us-news/not-accident-false-thug-narratives-have-long-been-used-discredit-n1240509.

24 King Jr, *Where Do We Go from Here.*

25 King Jr, "Beyond Vietnam."

26 Martin Luther King Jr, "The Casualties of the War in Vietnam," *Speech, Los Angeles, California*, February 25, 1967, https://investigatinghistory.ashp.cuny.edu/module11D.php.

27 Arthur Romano, "Martin Luther King's Vision of an Interconnected World Is More Relevant than Ever," *Waging Nonviolence* (blog), January 16, 2021, https://wagingnonviolence.org/2021/01/martin-luther-king-world-house/.

28 Krishnamurti, J. *Living in an Insane World: A Selection of Passages for the Study of the Teachings of J. Krishnamurti* (Ojai, Calif: Krishnamurti Foundation of America, 1989). Print.

29 King Jr, "Beyond Vietnam."

30 "Costs of War," Watson Institute, Brown University, https://watson.brown.edu/costsofwar/.

31 "National Association for the Advancement of Colored People (NAACP)," The Martin Luther King, Jr., Research and Education Institute, June 12, 2017, https://kinginstitute.stanford.edu/encyclopedia/national-association-advancement-colored-people-naacp.

32 "Memphis Sanitation Workers' Strike," The Martin Luther King, Jr., Research and Education Institute, June 2, 2017, https://kinginstitute.stanford.edu/encyclopedia/memphis-sanitation-workers-strike.

33 Ben Steverman and Alexandre Tanzi, "The 50 Richest Americans Are Worth as Much as the Poorest 165 Million," *Bloomberg*, October 8, 2020, www.bloomberg.com/news/articles/2020-10-08/top-50-richest-people-in-the-us-are-worth-as-much-as-poorest-165-million.

34 The book *All Labor Has Dignity*, which is a 2010 collection of King's writings by Beacon Press offers deeper insight into King's approach to economic issues.

35 Martin Luther King Jr, "Statement on Black Power to Southern Christian Leadership Conference," October 14, 1966, www.crmvet.org/docs/6610_mlk_power-poverty.pdf.

36 "Poverty," National Civil Rights Museum, MLK 50, accessed April 2, 2021, https://mlk50.civilrightsmuseum.org/poverty.

37 Heather Dockray, "50 Years Later, MLK's Poor People's Campaign Is Back – and More Needed than Ever," *Mashable*, April 4, 2018, https://mashable.com/2018/04/04/poor-people-campaign-mlk-revival/.

38 Jordan Weissmann, "Martin Luther King's Economic Dream: A Guaranteed Income for All Americans," *The Atlantic*, August 28, 2013, www.theatlantic.com/business/archive/2013/08/martin-luther-kings-economic-dream-a-guaranteed-income-for-all-americans/279147/.

39 Martin Luther King, *The Quest for Peace and Justice* (Nobel Peace Prize Lecture, December 11, 1964), www.nobelprize.org/prizes/peace/1964/king/lecture/.

40 John Creamer, *Poverty Rates for Blacks and Hispanics Reached Historic Lows in 2019* (The United States Census Bureau, September 15, 2020), www.census.gov/library/stories/2020/09/poverty-rates-for-blacks-and-hispanics-reached-historic-lows-in-2019.html.

41 UN News, "Rising Inequality Affecting More than Two-Thirds of the Globe, but It's Not Inevitable: New UN Report," January 21, 2020, https://news.un.org/en/story/2020/01/1055681.

42 Valentina Romei, "How the Pandemic Is Worsening Inequality," *FInancial Times*, December 31, 2020, www.ft.com/content/cd075d91-fafa-47c8-a295-85bbd7a36b50.

43 Surprisingly, writes Anderson and Delgado, "some of King's sternest critiques were aimed at the black middle class, which, he charged, had succumbed to the sin of forgetfulness." King said, "Many middle-class Negroes have forgotten their roots and are more concerned about 'conspicuous consumption' than about the cause of justice". He accused middle-class blacks of sitting "in some serene and passionless realm of isolation, untouched and unmoved by the agonies and struggles of their underprivileged brothers". "This kind of selfish detachment", he added, "has caused the masses of Negroes to feel alienated not only from white society but also from the Negro middle class". They feel that the average middle-class Negro has no concern for their plight – From: Victor Anderson and Teresa Delgado, "For the Beauty of the World: VISION and Moral Order in Martin Luther King Jr.'s World House," in *Reclaiming the Great World House*, ed. Vicki L. Crawford and Lewis V. Baldwin, The Global Vision of Martin Luther King Jr. (University of Georgia Press, 2019), 28, www.jstor.org/stable/j.ctvfxv9j2.6.

44 "The Triple Evils," The King Center, accessed March 8, 2021, https://thekingcenter.org/about-tkc/the-king-philosophy/.

45 Gabriel L. Schwartz and Jaquelyn L. Jahn, "Mapping Fatal Police Violence Across U.S. Metropolitan Areas: Overall Rates and Racial/Ethnic Inequities, 2013–2017," *PLoS One* 15, no. 6 (June 24, 2020): e0229686, https://doi.org/10.1371/journal.pone.0229686.

46 Deidre McPhillips, "Data Show Deaths from Police Violence Disproportionately Affect People of Color," *US News & World Report*, June 3, 2020, //www.usnews.com/news/articles/2020-06-03/data-show-deaths-from-police-violence-disproportionately-affect-people-of-color.

47 Frank Edwards, Hedwig Lee, and Michael Esposito, "Risk of Being Killed by Police Use of Force in the United States by Age, Race – Ethnicity, and Sex," *Proceedings of the National Academy of Sciences* 116, no. 34 (August 20, 2019): 16793–98, https://doi.org/10.1073/pnas.1821204116.

48 Akela Lacy, "Massachusetts' Progressive Lawmakers Push Congress to Abolish Qualified Immunity," *The Intercept*, March 1, 2021, https://theintercept.com/2021/03/01/qualified-immunity-ayanna-pressley-ed-markey/.

49 Laura Santhanam, "Two-Thirds of Black Americans Don't Trust the Police to Treat Them Equally. Most White Americans Do.," *PBS NewsHour*, June 5, 2020, sec. Politics, www.pbs.org/newshour/politics/two-thirds-of-black-americans-dont-trust-the-police-to-treat-them-equally-most-white-americans-do.

50 Matt Gutman et al., "Police Officers, Communities of Color Reflect on the Struggle to Build Trust," *ABC News*, accessed March 8, 2021, https://abcnews.go.com/US/police-officers-communities-color-reflect-struggle-build-trust/story?id=73076677.

51 "Yale Medical Students Hold 'die-in' to Protest Race, Gender Discrimination," *New Haven Register*, December 10, 2014, sec. Colleges, www.nhregister.com/colleges/article/Yale-medical-students-hold-die-in-to-11379088.php.

52 This work was based on Kingian Police training work that had taken place previously in FL and elsewhere. There is an academic article on Florida and elsewhere. See David E. Barlow, Melissa Hickman Barlow, Joani Scandone, and Walter A. McNeil, "Restorative Justice, Peacemaking, and Social Justice: The Application of Kingian Nonviolence Philosophy in Community Policing," *Criminal Justice Studies* 17, no. 1 (March 1, 2004): 19–31, https://doi.org/10.1080/08884310420001679343.

53 Arthur Romano, "Police Should Put Away the Military Gear and Build Connections with Young People," *The Conversation*, August 12, 2015, http://thcconversation.com/police-should-put-away-the-military-gear-and-build-connections-with-young-people-44947.

54 "Six Dead After Church Bombing," *Washington Post*, September 16, 1963, www.washingtonpost.com/wp-srv/national/longterm/churches/archives1.htm.

55 Similarly, in preparing to watch these films about the movement they ask the officers if anyone had seen the film *Selma* (2014, Dir. Ava DuVernay) which had recently been out in theaters. Not one had.

56 History com Editors, "Emmett Till," *History*, accessed March 8, 2021, www.history.com/topics/black-history/emmett-till-1.

57 To read the confession in January 1956 read www.pbs.org/wgbh/americanexperience/features/till-killers-confession/.

58 Tonya Mosley and Allison Hagan, "Police Killings Decreased in Cities That Saw Black Lives Matter Protests, Study Finds," *WBUR*, March 12, 2021, www.wbur.org/hereandnow/2021/03/12/police-killings-decrease-study.

59 King Jr., "Letter from Birmingham Jail," 835.

60 This is still a problem in the US. Small children, especially children of color in the US are often arrested in school. Bill Hutchinson, "More than 30,000 Children under Age 10 Have Been Arrested in the US since 2013: FBI," *ABC News*, October 1, 2019, https://abcnews.go.com/US/30000-children-age-10-arrested-us-2013-fbi/story?id=65798787.
    The US is also one of the few advanced industrial countries that imprisons children for life. Malcom Jenkins, "Why Is America the Only Country Still Sentencing Children to Life without Parole?" *NBC News*, December 6, 2017, www.nbcnews.com/think/opinion/america-only-country-world-still-sentencing-our-kids-die-prison-ncna826471.

61 Erica Chenoweth and Jeremy Pressman, "Analysis | This Summer's Black Lives Matter Protesters Were Overwhelmingly Peaceful, Our Research Finds," *Washington Post*, October 16, 2020, www.washingtonpost.com/politics/2020/10/16/this-summers-black-lives-matter-protesters-were-overwhelming-peaceful-our-research-finds/.

62 For resources exploring the limits of current ideas about use of force, see http://useof-forceproject.org/#project.

63 Eamonn Arble, Ana M. Daugherty, and Bengt Arnetz, "Differential Effects of Phys-iological Arousal Following Acute Stress on Police Officer Performance in a Simu-lated Critical Incident," *Frontiers in Psychology* 10 (2019), https://doi.org/10.3389/fpsyg.2019.00759.

64 Kelly A. Hine et al., "Exploring Police Use of Force Decision-Making Processes and Impairments Using a Naturalistic Decision-Making Approach," *Criminal Justice and Behavior* 45, no. 11 (November 1, 2018): 1782–801, https://doi.org/10.1177/0093854 818789726.

65 Frances Lee Ansley, "Stirring the Ashes: Race Class and the Future of Civil Rights Scholarship," *Cornell Law Review* 74, no. 6 (1989, 1988): 993–1077.

66 Sarah Diamond and Jacob Werblow, *Continuing the Dream: The Effect of Kingian Non-violence on Youth Affected by Incarceration* (Program Evaluation for the Institute for MunicipalandRegionalPolicy(IMRP),2013),www.ccsu.edu/imrp/projects/files/CTCN-Evaluation-Report.pdf.

67 Sarah Diamond, *Results from ThinKING Leadership Academy* (New Haven: Diamond Research Consulting, 2015).

4 Accept Suffering Without Retaliation for the Sake of the Cause to Achieve the Goal

If you were to check Facebook at two or three in the morning, many nights you'd find Warren Hardy live-streaming from the streets of Hartford. His mood in the videos ranges from calm to desperate. On one night, he begins with a circle of candles on the sidewalk on a quiet street where there have been a number of shootings in Hartford's North End. Hardy, a local nonviolence educator, activist and violence interrupter, lights each candle, and the flames fight to stay alive against the wind. He pleads with people watching his video.

"Family, we have to do this together", Hardy implores.

> Some nights I am lighting these candles because we lost somebody, but tonight I'm lighting them like I do every night because we need to care, to sacrifice before some else gets gunned down. Remember family, there is no love without sacrifice.

He often describes the situation in the city as life or death and reminds viewers, some of them hundreds or even thousands of miles away, "we need all of you".

Warren Hardy was born and raised in Hartford; every day he navigates the exhausting demands of working to disrupt violence in the city and support people who are dealing with its aftermath. He has worked for years with Peacebuilders, an organization on the frontlines of violence prevention in the city and as a nonviolence educator, where he often engages with people on the streets of Hartford who are on the verge of being involved in a shooting – often young people from the poorest parts of the city who are armed, including some who have already pulled out their guns and are actively threatening to shoot someone on the street. It is extremely difficult work. In the summer months, people are killed every week by gun violence, and others who survive are left with lifelong disabilities.[1] For example, in the summer of 2019, nine people in Harford were shot, and two were killed in the span of eight days.[2] Hardy knows firsthand how deeply this trauma impacts people's lives.

"Before I even picked up a gun", he recalls,

> I remember seeing my aunt get beaten until she was unrecognizable, and I ended up stabbing the person who beat her up. At age 12, I witnessed my

DOI: 10.4324/9781003243915-5

first shooting right in my backyard. I was standing there in awe, and just watching a person get shot.

Warren was part of Hartford's notorious 20 Love gang at an early age and was sentenced to 12 years in prison when he was just 21 years old.

"It was like, 'welcome to the club,'" says Hardy. "A lot of parents had adopted the survival syndrome, or 'Keep it moving' syndrome. I think it got accepted as, 'This is the way life is, this is where we live at, what are you gonna do? Deal with it.'"[3]

As soon as Warren got out of prison, he knew he wanted to work to try to break the cycle of violence in the city. Shortly after joining Peacebuilders, he encountered CTCN's nonviolence workshops. Regarding adjusting to the latter, Warren describes,

> you know, that takes some serious getting in tune to, you know what I'm saying, your insides, and kinda building up that love for humanity, to where you don't have that "I don't give a Fuck" type of attitude. Because that's easy to develop. I mean, so many people have it, and they just display it in different forms throughout their everyday life.

Warren suggests that "I don't give a fuck problem" is not only a response to the daily indignities of violence but also to the reality that suffering in communities like his are so often pathologized, dismissed or completely overlooked in the wider society. He sees Hartford, like other cities impacted by the relentless effects of poverty, racial inequality, gun violence and crime as at a crisis point that needs "an all-hands-on deck approach". That approach in his view requires sacrifice not only from people impacted by the violence and racism most directly but also from people in positions of power or in the comfortable suburbs surrounding the city.

This is not easy work. Warren puts his body on the line and stretches himself thin, as he is underpaid and often gets far too little sleep. He explains,

> I lead by an example. There's no love without sacrifice. Because I found myself constantly sacrificing whether it was my body, whether it was money, whether it was time. Whatever the case may be, I found myself sacrificing for what it was that I love.
>
> I'm trying to lead by an example, meaning . . . I come from a lifestyle of you hit me, I hit you back, so I come from that. So now that I am trained [in nonviolence] I want to be a person that, you know, leads by an example. I'm all conscious of that – one of the things that I regret so much is that I wasn't conscious of the negative things that I was doing, and how many people were paying attention to me.

After years of working as a street-level violence interrupter[4] on Hartford's most dangerous streets late at night, the nonviolence workshops provided

Warren a space to process his insights from those experiences. The workshops emphasized the transformative power of suffering for a cause, a hallmark of his own work, and provided a supportive space to think through what it might take to transform these cycles. Warren explains his approach:

> So, I'm conscious of these [nonviolence] principles. . . [I've] been trained in and it kind of helps me to . . . stay afloat. Stay afloat. And one of the things that made this training even more valuable to me was the fact that during my time as a Peacebuilder, at least at that time, Peacebuilders was a program that's designed to work with individuals who have been shot or they're the perpetrator. They're the ones shooting or those that have the sensibility to commit one of these crimes. So, in the process of doing Peacebuilder work we're stopping a person from getting shot today, they'd still get shot tomorrow. We're stopping a person from getting beat up or beating somebody up today, and then it will happen . . . the next day [so I appreciate the long-term vision of sustaining sacrifice in nonviolence]. The bottom line is that, Black people, didn't have the same opportunities as white people, you know. Things just weren't available. So, so you [have to] fight to get equal rights. You don't accept a system that's going on, you know what I'm saying, you keep fighting.

Key Concepts

When Warren Hardy and other community educators lead discussions about nonviolence, no principle is more controversial than the third: to *accept* suffering without retaliation for the sake of the cause to achieve the goal. It is one of the most difficult tenets – that unearned suffering can be both redemptive and transformative – for both the nonviolence practitioner and society at large. A serious exploration of King's legacy and the power and pitfalls of nonviolence must grapple with this idea that nonviolence often requires choosing actions that may create risk, pain and suffering for the nonviolent practitioner. In the context of CTCN's outreach, this tenet is especially controversial, since many in their workshops are Black and Latino people who have faced and continue to face suffering as a result of systemic racism and economic exploitation.

Further complicating the theme of suffering is a long history in the US *of dominant institutions* telling people of color, especially Black people, to passively accept suffering for some later reward. White people who benefited from racial inequality often conveyed this message. Missionaries and slave owners would sometimes excise from their Bibles passages likely to incite rebellion – as much as 90% of the old testament and 50% of the new testament.[5]

That tendency to enshrine a passive approach to one's own oppression in religion or custom was not solely a vestige of slavery – it has endured in the centuries since and resurges whenever Black-led movements for social justice engage in direct action. In several of the Kingian workshops that I have attended, this theme emerges when students read Dr. King's "Letter from a Birmingham Jail". Many are unaware the piece was a direct response to a letter written by White clergy while Dr. King sat in a Birmingham jail. The clergy, considered moderate by the White establishment at the time, wrote from the comfort of their homes, admonishing King and other activists in the movement to slow down and halt nonviolent demonstrations in favor of more passive and *proper* approaches.

> We the undersigned clergymen are among those who, in January, issued "An Appeal for Law and Order and Common Sense," in dealing with racial problems in Alabama. We expressed understanding that honest convictions in racial matters could properly be pursued in the courts, but urged that decisions of those courts should in the meantime be peacefully obeyed.
>
> We are now confronted by a series of demonstrations by some of our Negro citizens, directed and led in part by outsiders. We recognize the natural impatience of people who feel that their hopes are slow in being realized. But we are convinced that these demonstrations are unwise and untimely.[6]

The words of the eight clergymen in Alabama in 1963 echo today in similar pleas for more incremental or gradual approaches that do not involve active approaches to suffering or confrontational nonviolent protest. The preference for gradualism or mild protests is still evident, as prominent leaders from NFL Commissioner Roger Goodell to a wide range of political pundits have criticized an array of nonviolent protests focused on racial justice. In recent years, protests ranging from Colin Kaepernick taking a knee to marches against police shootings of unarmed Black people to protestors who blocked highways have been met with condemnation from a wide array of leaders. The persistence of activists, however, has had an impact on popular opinion, as more people have come to see issues related to racial justice as in need of attention and these forms of protest as acceptable.[7] For opponents of change, including those who consider themselves moderates in favor of less antagonistic approaches, there may be *no* acceptable time for nonviolent direct action. Part of the suffering of nonviolent protest, then, is the sheer resistance that it provokes – the stigma of being labeled an outsider, agitator, radical, extremist and even in many cases "violent" for engaging in nonviolent civil resistance.[8]

King conceded the challenge that he was asking people who have already suffered so much to take additional risks and suffer yet more. He even made time in his "I Have a Dream" speech to pay homage to those who had helped make the movement possible, the "veterans of creative suffering":

> I am not unmindful that some of you have come here out of great trials and tribulations. Some of you have come fresh from narrow cells. Some of

you have come from areas where your quest for freedom left you battered by the storms of persecution and staggered by the winds of police brutality. You have been the veterans of creative suffering. Continue to work with the faith that unearned suffering is redemptive.[9]

Dr. King, however, was initially skeptical of the power of love to influence political and social change. He reflected on this when he was a college student grappling with Nietzsche's *Will to Power*, later writing, "during this period I had about despaired of the power of love in solving social problems".[10] In fact, this was one of the aspects of nonviolence that he found most challenging – that loving one's enemy and sacrificing and suffering for justice could eventually change their view. Dr. King accepted early on that suffering could bring about positive internal transformation under the right circumstances and have constructive effects on friends, family, co-workers and other interpersonal relationships, but he remained unconvinced that it could effectuate bigger political changes. That skepticism weakened when he reconsidered Gandhi's approach, by which the endurance of suffering was a way to build the power needed to fight against injustices. Embracing that vulnerability brought people together, often from different walks of life, and could be used strategically. Their participation in this wider resistance to unjust laws and institutional practices that dehumanize people in turn dramatizes the violence of those institutions and their racism, which are often otherwise hidden from view for all but those who experience them firsthand.

King grappled to reconcile his understanding that we need to embrace suffering for the well-being of others, grounded largely in his Christian ideals, with the realities of how those with political and economic power had used the concept to keep people down. Where slave-owning Whites had used specific verses to promote the acceptance of suffering, King rejected the idea of passively accepting one's fate and of religion as a tool to anesthetize that suffering. Instead, he saw suffering as a tool against injustice:

> We are gravely mistaken to think that Christianity protects us from the pain and agony of mortal existence. Christianity has always insisted that the cross we bear precedes the crown we wear. To be a Christian, one must take up his cross, with all of its difficulties and agonizing and tragedy-packed content, and carry it until that very cross leaves its marks upon us and redeems us to that more excellent way which comes only through suffering.[11]

Religion studies scholar, Ron Large writes that "a major portion of King's involvement in the struggle for civil rights was the effort to alter the elements of character, to develop a *moral character* that is capable of rejecting violence".[12] That internal pivot is at the heart of nonviolence.[13] It is the indomitable understanding of self-worth and the commitment that it inspires to uproot, challenge and destroy the forces that humiliate and marginalize

Black people and threaten that dignity, both individually and collectively. At the same time, King recognized that the most effective way to challenge and transform violence is through nonviolent resistance to injustice and constructive efforts to build the beloved community, both of which realistically require suffering.

King was the most well-known spokesperson and guide, but he knew that it was the *collective power of so many people taking these risks together that had made the sacrifice effective.* The transformation of systemic racism requires reconfiguring deeply entrenched power dynamics, and this demands that people make sacrifices in many different capacities and from various life experiences and backgrounds. King knew this, acknowledging as he did in (his Nobel Peace Prize acceptance speech) that:

> Most of these people will never make the headlines and their names will not appear in Who's Who. Yet when years have rolled past and when the blazing light of truth is focused on this marvelous age in which we live – men and women will know and children will be taught that we have a finer land, a better people, a more noble civilization – because these humble children of God were willing to suffer for righteousness' sake.[14]

This vulnerability and willingness to suffer when taking strategic, nonviolent action can put one's adversary in a difficult position, as the use of violence often demonstrates weakness, exhausts resources and tends to win new converts to the side of nonviolent activists. This is what social movement scholars Lester Kurtz and Lee Smithey aptly call "The Paradox of Repression".[15] It held true during King's time when White mobs and police attacked civil rights activists and forced a wider national conversation about racism and segregation. These violent attacks raised awareness about racial inequality, and the shocking images pushed some White people and others who had been on the fence to reconsider their position. King articulated the paradox, and the powerful meaning of suffering, in his most consequential calls for nonviolent militancy in the movement:

> Do to us what you will, and we will still love you. Bomb our homes and threaten our children, and as difficult as it is, we will still love you. But be assured that we'll wear you down by our capacity to suffer, and one day we will win our freedom. We will not only win freedom for ourselves, we will so appeal to your heart and conscience that we will win you in the process, and our victory will be a double victory.[16]

For the past six years, people have taken to the streets to mobilize against police violence in order to demand change and have taken serious risks having been met with violence by police, Alt-Right groups and people who oppose their efforts.[17] While this has drawn further attention to police violence, the paradox of repression, however, is a theory and not a guarantee. It does not ensure that those taking risks are always able to persuade people that injustice needs to be changed.

"Human progress is neither automatic nor inevitable . . ." King said. "Every step toward the goal of justice requires sacrifice, suffering, and struggle; the tireless exertions and passionate concern of dedicated individuals".[18]

Major campaigns against systemic racism from King's time to the present day have tended not only to galvanize concerns about injustice for Black people but also sparked backlash towards those efforts with exaggerated claims of property destruction, outside agitators and infiltration by "Marxists and anarchists".[19,20] For this reason, it is important to have the long view, like King suggested – where unearned suffering is used to *combat the shift in focus away from systemic racism.*[21]

King's view of the transformative power of suffering was not grounded in a naive sense of the world that people with wealth and power or with deep-rooted hatred would readily change. Nor did he think that institutions would easily be transformed. On the other hand, when King called for the use of nonviolence or the radical and militant use of love, he was not thinking solely of short- and medium-term political goals. He saw nonviolence and chosen suffering as necessary in a world where we are profoundly interconnected, tied together in "a mutual garment of destiny" that demanded serious action. Injustice needed to be challenged and oppressed groups must demand and force change but not through violent force which furthers resentment, distracts from the underlying issues and too often fuels a cycle of retaliation.

The "mutual garment of destiny" was not just a metaphor to King. His recognition of profound interconnectivity was grounded partly in an understanding that security comes from the quality of our relationships, the systems we have to support people when things get hard or disaster strikes and an ethic of care where we cannot simply discount the humanity of people who oppose us. Strategic suffering then serves the purpose of trying to awaken people, even those who are not interested in your cause to the moral and pragmatic necessity of changing the status quo. This is part of what the violence interrupter Warren Hardy is attempting to do when broadcasting from the streets in Hartford at night. He is working to challenge the indifference and build a bridge across the disconnect between people in Hartford and the surrounding suburbs. That divide is not just a matter of personal disinterest and a lack of empathy but is also reinforced by the often hidden dynamics of restrictive housing policies, where the suburbs fight to keep out the poor and retain localized school districts (by town) prevent desegregated schools and access to better economic opportunities across school lines. When Dr. King said that "injustice anywhere is a threat to justice everywhere" or that we are tied together in a "mutual garment of destiny", these were not just moralistic platitudes about the importance of demonstrating kindness toward each other. They were statements about the nature of our world, and that human security is grounded ultimately in a sense of solidarity, of mutual aid and care. Ultimately, suffering and militant love are needed to forge those bonds and provide a framework for repairing them when the connections are violated.

Applying the Concepts, and Lessons Learned

During an evening refresher class for art educators from across the state, YF Tremayne teaches principle 3. He focuses on the importance of ongoing reflection when one commits to practice nonviolence. He begins his lesson,

> No matter where you go in life, where you come from, or what you do when you have a goal that's ahead of you, a goal that's in your reach, it's not going to be easy, to be 1 2 3 or ABC, it's not going to be all easy like you probably see in the movie where it always has a happy ending. You got to make a happy ending . . . you have to get to, what really matters is the journey . . . throughout a part of the journey is where the suffering comes in a lot of the time. We ask ourselves is suffering bad? In order for Diamond to be produced, carbon got to be really compressed under really high pressure, you gonna turn to diamond or you going to turn to coal? You accept the suffering . . . to get your goal however Pastor Lane is . . . always telling me, you got to look at the goal and *compare it to the value of the suffering.* [Is it worth it?]

Tremayne makes several points that come up frequently in community workshops. The first is that *nonviolence is a creative act,* and as a result, in some situations, you are choosing actions that may create suffering in order to influence change. This emphasis on the creative, active and strategic components are critically important, he explains, as he reflects on his work with other youth in the city who face violence and poverty:

> When you're trying to accept suffering, . . . you can't just look at suffering from one path, you've got to go a different . . . path, because . . . just getting whipped on [isn't necessarily going to make a difference] . . . it's like you've got to look at different ways to take that suffering. You can't just look from one perspective of suffering.

Tremayne's central point when teaching nonviolence is that a refusal to retaliate with violence does not equal inaction or a passive acceptance of suffering or degradation. To explore this active approach to nonviolence in relation to Dr. King's philosophy, community educators focus both on historical examples of civil resistance, where people heroically put their bodies on the line to resist unjust laws, challenge racism and advance justice and work through possible responses to everyday challenges that participants face in the community. But some of the examples they offer are less iconic; Warren Hardy is quick to point out that sometimes sacrifice is "going to get food for the cookout or driving to a workshop after I worked all night".

When they teach the civil rights movement, for example, Tremayne, Warren, Victoria, Pastor Lane and the others usually focus on four major campaigns: Montgomery, Birmingham, Selma and the Freedom Rides which are outlined in the training manual. In these sessions, they pay concerted attention to the organizational details of each campaign. They are acutely aware that to simply show dramatic flashpoints of protest, those peak experiences, without showing the behind-the-scenes work fundamentally misrepresents nonviolence struggles and the meaning of suffering for the cause. Warren, Victoria and Pastor Lane are all quick to teach and underscore that "nonviolence demands sacrifice to achieve the goal" of greater social justice and that sacrifice can take many forms. It would make for a shallow and fundamentally misleading view to emphasize struggle without teaching the specifics of how people committed themselves over the long term and made sacrifices, including the small but consequential, hidden prerequisite steps to the dramatic action. When this happens Dr. King and other highly visible activists are rendered saintly, and larger movement victories almost magical outcomes that seem to have happened out of nowhere. Instead, in CTCN workshops, participants learn the stories of key but previously unknown and anonymous players.

Dr. Bernard LaFayette played a critical and often overlooked role in the Nashville lunch counter sit-ins, Selma and the Freedom Rides, so Connecticut educators often weave in his firsthand accounts.[22] Where community members may have heard, for example, of Dr. LaFayette's close friend Congressman John Lewis' experience, they may never have heard LaFayette's perspective or learned about the story of Amelia Boynton and the pivotal role she played in Selma. A teacher and Black woman who registered voters in Selma, Boynton risked her life for decades without significant national recognition, playing a key part in challenging Jim Crow in Alabama. It was Boynton who took LaFayette into her home when he arrived in Selma at just 23 years of age as a field organizer for the SCLC. She laid the groundwork for later success there and took extreme risks as she ventured out in an area where racial terror was a norm, especially for Black people traveling country roads and traversing the city to organize people to vote.[23]

All of these campaigns had specific goals – to desegregate downtown businesses, interstate busing or to register voters. Each of these major chapters of struggle had many people working in less visible roles than Dr. King. Bayard Rustin, a brilliant strategist, deeply committed nonviolence practitioner and a gay Black man, helped orchestrate the March on Washington and was repeatedly targeted for his sexual identity. Ella Baker organized working-class Black communities across the country. The bus boycotts in Montgomery had over a 90% participation rate[24] and lasted over a year,[25] and hundreds of people, mostly women, helped to mimeograph and post flyers informing the community about the boycotts. They organized rides for people to and from work and school (Montgomery has had a thriving Black-owned taxi service ever since), made food for meetings and played many other roles.

Conversations in the workshops in Hartford and New Haven are not solely focused on major campaigns for social justice in the past or present. In workshops, Tremayne and the other youth educators field tough questions about suffering in the context of everyday relationships and resisting oppression and complicity in everyday life. Some of the youth are most engaged when they are exploring challenges they face at home, with their friends or in school. One of the common dynamics is that youth often feel stuck as if they have few choices in life. In fact, many of these young people are dealing with serious and complex stressors in their lives in Hartford and New Haven that are not easy to change. In addition, as young people, they often do not feel heard. This is where Tremayne points that suffering is not an end in itself becomes critically important. It is a means to influence change and a way to channel personal frustration, aggression and righteous indignation into *creative action* especially when you feel stuck. Tremayne and other facilitators underscore that the question is how you make sense of suffering and use it. Victoria likes to make this point explicitly clear both in workshops and in all trainings for new community facilitators:

> The other thing we always talk about is this doesn't mean we are suffering for the sake of suffering sake. It's not, because Beloved Community is the goal and if you are staying in a marriage let's say that is damaging body spirit and mind, then you're not helping to create the Beloved Community. It is the antithesis of Beloved Community and I distinguish that right from the jump . . . if I don't [then naturally] people start to [and should] ask me about that.

During workshops, Victoria often explores a difficult, yet all-too-commonly experienced example with participants: domestic abuse. She explains that in cases of domestic abuse, people who have been victimized may think that if they continue to love the person and not fight back or get angry, then the person may change their behavior – they are suffering without retaliation. In practice, this rarely if ever changes the abuser's behavior. In the workshop, Victoria turns to participants and asks, "At this point, what else can be done?"

Community members jump right in to brainstorm an array of ideas for responding to violence in the home: "They could leave the house to seek safe shelter"; "Friends and family could step in or help plan an intervention". Others suggest "calling a social worker".

After discussing the risks, strengths and limitations of each approach, Victoria asks, "Do these other options require sacrifice or suffering?"

Participants are quick to point out that each proposed approach requires some form of sacrifice or suffering. Good, Victoria continues, then it is a question of which form of sacrifice has the best chance of working.[26]

But Victoria, Tremayne, Pastor Lane and other community educators like to draw another distinction. Domestic violence is about power. Perpetrators threaten those they victimize, to feel in control, to use their position to make those they abuse dependent on them. In contrast, suffering without retaliation for the sake of the cause is about *disrupting* those power dynamics in the short term and sacrificing to transform the systems that reinforce this abuse of power in the long term.

The benefit, according to Dr. King and nonviolent educators in Connecticut, is that nonviolence allows you to fight and do so with compassion, love for yourself and without a desire to violently attack your adversaries. This does not mean that nonviolence dictates a sentimental love for people who inflict harm on your life, but rather the recognition that they, too, are influenced by these deforming and unjust systems. The challenge is to acknowledge a sense of interdependence while working to dismantle the systems that reinforce this suffering. You don't have to use the master's tools, in the form of violence, or give in or back down. From this more muscular view of suffering, sacrifice can fortify one's sense of being more fully human in the face of violence. Put simply, nonviolence practitioners convey a commitment that "I will accept suffering not for suffering's sake, but in order to remain or change myself into a more compassionate person and erode the sources of power that hold white supremacy, patriarchy and other forms of violence in place".

King contrasts this with the embrace of hate and retaliatory violence, which he contends twists the human spirit because it amplifies fear, anxiety, despair and a potentially fatalistic sense of one's place in the world. In practice, that sense of rage and *realism* rarely inspires transformative change or moves us closer to the beloved community. As Warren Hardy says:

> I love my community. I love helping people. So, with that being said, you don't need a whole lot of money to do this. You just need to genuinely believe that we can build a relationship that's going to, you know what I'm saying, eventually spread it. It only takes a block. You can start out with a block and if that block is able to show the benefits of us working together opposed to us acting like it's every man for himself then that's what we need to try . . . to create together.

Warren talks about the kinds of sacrifices and risks that more privileged people must make as well. For Warren, the "I don't give a fuck" attitude doesn't just refer to people in his neighborhood who have lost hope because of violence. Especially when he is leading workshops for participants who are largely White and privileged, Warren emphasizes that the "I don't give a fuck" attitude is present in the suburbs too. He explains, "the people who actually could . . . make a difference but choose not to . . . do something different, in an attempt to, you know, not [Focus on themselves and say] "Yeah, I'm only gonna take care of my family". Warren sees this behavior as contributing to the perpetuation of violence in Hartford, especially when it is driven by indifference to those who bear the heaviest weight of inequality.

But then Warren turns to King's quotation, "What affects one directly affects us all indirectly":[27]

> Injustice, you know what I'm saying, anywhere is a threat to justice everywhere. So, those things can be very vivid and . . . you can illustrate them,

Photo 4.1 Warren Hardy, Community Activist, Founder H.Y.P.E (Helping Young People Evolve) and Vice Chair of the CTCN's board since, 2010. Hosting his Community Cook Outs in Hartford, 2018 © CTCN

Photo 4.2 Pastor James Lane, Kathleen Sartor and Warren Hardy, first Harford, Kingian Certification Training at University of Hartford, 2009 © CTCN

like, at the drop of a dime. It doesn't take – you don't need, like, a whole lot of pulling things together to paint that picture [that] this injustice to me is gonna be injustice everywhere.

You don't have to go far out to try to show a person that, you know, if I'm having a bad day I can affect you and you, you know what I'm say, don't got nothing to do with it. I use Sandy Hook . . . as an example all the time.[28]

Warren continues that Sandy Hook dispelled any idea that "bad things only happen to bad people", or that people can "think that we're safe, because of the area, geographical area that we live in".[29] He explains:

Like, in Sandy Hook . . . I never thought anything like that would ever happen in that safe little neighborhood. It just goes to show that, you know, it's not selective, . . . So when that happens, . . . I wasn't shocked. I did want to go and show my support, just as an individual that deals with gun violence on a regular basis. And I'm still connected with them. Every year we go to Washington and we lobby for safer gun laws, and we do a vigil and, you know, we try to have a conversation. But one of the things

Photo 4.3 Pastor James Lane and Warren Hardy, prepping for Kingian certification training Hartford, CT 2009 © CTCN

I try to discreetly get across to them is that, yes, we need safer gun laws, but we also need a way of life.

Warren is reaching out to and connecting with people in Newtown and courageously pointing out that gun violence had been happening down the street from them for decades, but it didn't prompt action; then gun violence happened to them, and they asked others to sacrifice to make changes. Pastor Lewis has a vivid and astute image for these moments when a community that has been shielded from the weight of violence in America, and benefited from inequality, becomes the victim of violence: "Sometimes people [White folks] need to understand that to get to you, to mourn with you, I have to climb over dead bodies in my own community to get there, so it may take an extra minute".

Victoria points out that there is a critical role for White people to play in inspiring and modeling for each other ways to accept suffering for the sake of the cause. But this role goes beyond simply caring about issues of racial justice or even regularly attending protests or marches. The third principle serves as an opportunity to have a broader conversation about the strategic goals behind accepting suffering and points toward a deeper recognition that people of color have already suffered a great deal and need allies willing to challenge complicity and take risks for change politically and in their everyday lives. The multi-racial learning community in Connecticut then becomes a place to embody these practices.

In the *Paradox of Repression*, Rachel MacNair argues that there are a number of factors that make more privileged people willing to directly participate in repression or refuse to take action against suffering when they know that it's occurring. Group solidarity is one factor, as people perceive external threats that increase group solidarity and decrease their willingness to challenge the group. Another major factor is fear, which includes fear for physical safety as well as intangible fears of diminished privilege or social standing.

Victoria explains that there are complex dynamics at work for White people who engage in nonviolent workshops or attempt to break that chain of complicity. She has observed in her own life and with White participants in the workshops that

> when there is *suffering*, when you become blatantly aware of the inequity and the imbalance in our country . . . it's such a heavy sense of suffering, in fact, that it could lead you to inertia or complacency if you don't have a fire, or you don't have a belief in a higher power to help you. If you don't have something [else] to hold on to, some anchor, that gives you the strength to keep going into the flames, you will feel the suffering without any of the glory.
>
> You'll feel the suffering without any of the joy that comes with motion forward. The biggest joy I have received at all is the trust that my Black colleagues have placed in me. That's utter joy because then I feel like this work is not in vain. That the suffering is worth it. I've crossed a bridge – there's incredible suffering with a desire to do something, and going through the struggle of learning what it is to do. You get this desire, 'I've got to do something' . . . [that happened for me] in 2003 when I got my first training. That gave me a sure sense of what to do.

Victoria sees that awareness of one's own privilege and the scale of Black America's suffering provokes complicated emotions of guilt, yet awareness of these issues does not automatically result in action.[30]

"Well, one way I describe it", she explained to me, "is that I've come to see that White America and Black America seem to be two totally different worlds. Two different worlds in terms of urban America and suburban white America . . . I liken [systemic racism] to Chinese water torture. You keep dropping that little bit of water but if it happens over multiple times you're tortured, you're tormented. It's a terrible analogy. Microaggression basically, is no longer micro. It's a way of being in this world in our country that makes for such acute pain over a lifetime".

She explains how, through her work of nonviolence and personal experiences as a White person, she sees a troubling and chronic degree of disconnect in her White peers.

> I marvel at the weight that a Black American has to carry. I marvel at it and the "suffering" that I experience is the constant [microaggression of] sweeping statements like, "Well, who doesn't want to eat organic food?" or, "Who wouldn't want to go swimming? Oh, that lake is so beautiful . . . We go there all the time. The sailboats. Oh my gosh." . . . Just this constant [obliviousness] . . . I can be with a whole crowd of people. They won't even mention Black Lives Matter right now, today. [For example] I was with a farewell group . . . this dear friend . . . moving into a town it's just so white. She never once said, "Yes, I'm really a little troubled. It's all-white". That wouldn't even have crossed her mind. I feel that [extreme disconnect], often when I'm with other white people.

Victoria frequently discusses suffering and White privilege with Pastor Lane, who talks about

> an awareness that comes with wisdom, that can separate you, in a way, from others, because now you have insight that others may not have. I feel [that] living with this insight is intense, productive suffering and . . . I . . . mostly feel more whole, in some ways, when I'm in the Black community because I can just breathe differently because I know they know.

This is why King encouraged people to study Whiteness, because there is a cost to this silence and disconnect, and as Victoria points out, the disconnect endures today.[31]

Violence interrupter Warren Hardy knows firsthand that suffering is no magic wand. To Hardy, the principle of suffering means sacrificing to challenge violence in the community and supporting youth who are at risk of losing it all, either as perpetrators of that violence or as victims of it.

In practice, educators teaching about Dr. King's understanding of nonviolence must face the hard truth that there is no guarantee that nonviolent resistance will empower its practitioners, and inviting suffering can also have negative psychological effects in nonviolent movement spaces. I have also observed participants experience self-doubt as they experiment with nonviolence in their relationships with family members, peers, teachers, legislators and others – with mixed results.

These risks and doubts are part of the reason why Warren, and other community educators saw it as essential not only to focus on large-scale protests but also to actively experiment with "mini beloved communities" in some of Hartford's most hard-hit areas. These constructive everyday activities highlight something that is too easily missed when talking about nonviolence social change; that great joy comes from sacrifice as well. Warren broadened his focus from direct crisis intervention to proactive community building, in particular organizing cookouts in some of the most hard-hit streets in the city. His goal was to highlight the resources, compassion and love already present in the neighborhood. The fact that Black and Brown communities are still here is a testament to this sustained love in the face of violence. Warren feels adamant about this. Communities like Hartford have vital resources that, if "we create greater unity in our community", can lead to "peace in our streets". One of the first neighborhood cookout events I attended lasted several hours longer than Warren and the other organizers had planned. Initially, people came out slowly, and once they started to enjoy themselves, they texted friends, family and neighbors. Kids rode their bikes home to grab the other siblings and friends, and by the end, the gathering included people of all ages. In addition to the food people enjoyed music, kids played games and made suggestions of the DJ, and neighbors who hadn't seen each other caught up.

From these first cookouts, Warren's work has grown.

"We do community cleanups with kids [now] on a regular basis", he says. "We do barbecues, basketball tournaments, and sometimes volunteer to feed the homeless. We volunteer to read to the elderly".

He would like to work with CTCN to build smaller centers in the community through which people work on issues at the micro-neighborhood level. The "center" might not be a fixed building or place at all – it might mean working out of a car, or someone's home – but it would be about meeting needs in the smallest capillaries of the community and then, perhaps, building a network of civic engagement throughout the city. Warren says he "owes it to myself to leave here knowing that I've . . . tried to make a difference and then . . . to those that I've seen pave the way for me":

> A lot of people have this . . . mindset that, you know, "It's no use, in doing anything, like there's no hope." Like, "Why even bother to do that." But I'm thinking based off of where we were and where we are [now], if they had – if those people had thought like you – imagine where we would be.

Warren Hardy is on fire in workshops when he teaches King's themes of suffering, sacrifice, the militant use of love and interconnectedness. While his knowledge comes from a careful reading of King, he also viscerally understands the principles from his own experiences navigating life and death in Hartford. Harsh realities harden people, and they hardened Warren. Racism and inequality also desensitize privileged people living just a few miles away that could help make a difference but do not see it as part of their responsibility. It is not just a challenge for young people, who have seen so much violence, to open up and take a risk for each other and to build the beloved community – each of the adult community educators and peacebuilders experiences these challenges regularly. But that is only part of the story as love sustains people and it is that sense of connection that allows people to grow together, to build collective power together and to open up to each other. There is a joy event when facing these imposing odds.

Tips for Educators and Peacebuilders

Don't avoid difficult conversations or dynamics – make meaning out of suffering. King makes challenging claims about suffering that raise difficult issues and provoke important questions. To take King seriously, we have to wrestle with his call for a heavy sacrifice, and not minimize the risks or hide the everyday, too often invisible work of that sacrifice. At the same time, and especially when working with youth, it is an ethical burden to suggest that Black communities and communities of color, which have already shouldered a disproportionate weight of inequality and violence, should be martyrs in the fight for justice.

On top of this, many public school teachers and educators who have dedicated their careers to working in these communities also are suffering – from burnout, anxiety and high rates of teacher attrition.[32,33] In an effort to engage, train and mobilize this group of people, in recent years, CTCN has begun leading nonviolence professional development workshops in schools in Hartford. One, Hartford, High School now has a Nonviolence Lab, which is staffed by one of CTCN's lead facilitators four days a week.

Both teachers and students spend time in the Lab, which is used as a resource to manage conflict in the school and maintain an ongoing practice and study of nonviolence. As Victoria describes it, "We are consistently reinvigorated by the commitment of some, and the resistance from others, to develop a culture of nonviolence in daily interactions throughout the school".

In this way, CTCN is helping provide teachers and the youth with additional skills needed to identify and deescalate conflict and to channel their day-to-day stress, anxiety and other forms of suffering to become a creative act that supports change.

Nonviolence workshops provide a vital space for a wide range of community members, whether its peacebuilders like Warren Hardy working out on the streets or educators embedded in local schools attempting to make meaning out of suffering. That suffering is real and pervasive for far too many young people in Hartford and New Haven who must contend with the daily indignities and stressors of systemic racism on their families and friends. Students in CTCN workshops consistently report that they do not have adequate opportunities in school to critically think about and respond to the challenges of violence and poverty in their lives, even when they are learning about the civil rights movement and Dr. King.

Validate your suffering and the suffering of others. Many public school teachers and community educators suffer from stress, being overworked, underpaid and under respected among other factors., But if we step back and analyze the systems that they work in – underfunded and segregated public schools, communities that have been fractured by decades of job loss, mass incarceration and a lack of adequate health care – then we see that these institutions and environments too often systemically promote suffering among the individuals who reside within them. Here, suffering should be expected. It is predictable. So, the first step is to simply validate that the toxic stress and burnout that so many people living and working in these communities feel. As one facilitator said,

> Do you feel stress? Anxiety? Somedays wish that you would just quit? Yes, I feel that too! The system is designed to make us feel that way, and once we recognize it we can begin to see possibilities to change it. So is the system broken? Yes. Do we want to live in a better system? Yes and so in the meantime what are we willing to risk to change it?

Critically look at what issues are worth suffering for. The youth educators and community participants that attend the workshops comment on how powerful it is to see community members who look like them teaching about suffering and what is worth sacrificing for. As one of the youth participants put it, "in this state we learn about these three people MLK, Rosa Parks and Malcolm X but we don't really learn about what is behind this [work]". This student is not alone as both adult and youth have also critiqued how on some occasions King is relegated to the past or, even worse, used as a disciplinary tool to convey the "right" way to behave when protesting or speaking about injustice that imagines resistance without any emotion or disruption. This version of King omits nonviolent principles highlighted in this book and can gloss over the democratic, economic and social vision that animated his nonviolent concepts. By exploring suffering explicitly potential peacebuilders are drawn into conversations about their personal worlds and what is at stake.

As Viktor Frankl's work and a half-century of research since have demonstrated, people who experience oppression often have a vital need to make meaning of violence and injustice while in the midst of it. It is critical both in terms of resilience (having the ability to persevere through suffering) and in terms of removing the causes of that injustice – as King was fond of saying, to "tear down the entire edifice" of racial segregation and inequality. Where Frankl discovered in his community the need to make meaning from within the concentration camp, Black people in the US have had to make sense of a society where their labor is exploited, their bodies are targets of state-sanctioned violence, and they are alienated from education.

Strategic suffering is transformative. Voluntary suffering for the sake of the cause or to achieve the goal is different from involuntary suffering when a person suffers because of injustices that they cannot identify or feel helpless to change. Sacrifice is a weapon that can be used creatively to engage with oppression. Strategic suffering is a creative force because courageous nonviolent action can generate a greater sense of agency, righteous indignation, anger and the conviction to fight against rather than acquiesce to injustice. And strategic suffering has to be understood in a world with injustice, where some level of sacrifice and suffering is inevitable. If you try to avoid pain you will suffer (especially if you are in a vulnerable group); if you fight back using nonviolent approaches, then this too will entail suffering and sacrifice. Victoria emphasizes this lesson in her example of domestic violence and asks CTCN participants to consider which kind of sacrifice works best to achieve goals.

Suffering is a transformative force, but it is not the goal. Early in his life, Dr. King grappled with the enormous question of how he could best fight back and take action against racism and injustice such that movement participants could embrace their full humanity and avoid moral injury.[34] He reflected:

> As my sufferings mounted, I soon realized that there were two ways in which I could respond to my situation – either to react with bitterness or seek to transform the suffering into a creative force. I decided to follow the latter course.[35]

That transformation is the theme of the next chapter. CTCN educators contend that to sustain the work of challenging injustice and dismantling the "edifice" of racism, we also need to develop practices that bolster people's spirits in the midst of this struggle and allow for positive emotion and joy. Otherwise, the suffering can veer dangerously close to masochism, as if suffering itself is the goal.

Notes

1 Renegade Dreams by Laurence Ralph is an excellent book that focuses on the lifelong impacts for people injured but not killed by gun violence and how they work to survive and change their cities.

2 Nicholas Rondinone, "In Eight Days, There Were Nine People Shot, Two Fatally, in Hartford. But Officials Say There Are Fewer Shootings than Last Year," *Hartford Courant*, www.courant.com/breaking-news/hc-br-hartford-shootings-two-dead-follow-20190702-m2ookk2yvrggtkffwartuv3tfy-story.html.

3 Rebecca Lurye, "Never the Same: In Hartford, Gun Violence Rarely Far from Children's Eyes," *Hartford Courant*, sec. Community, Hartford, www.courant.com/community/hartford/hc-news-hartford-gun-violence-childhood-trauma-20180927-story.html.

4 "*Violence interrupters* are connected to the streets of the toughest neighborhoods with the unique ability to identify and intervene in individual, group and gang-related conflicts before they intensify." There are violence interrupters working in cities across the US, www.youthalive.org/wp-content/uploads/2015/07/Violence-Interrupter-Job-Description-2018.pdf.

5 Michel Martin, "Slave Bible from the 1800s Omitted Key Passages That Could Incite Rebellion," *NPR*, December 9, 2018, www.npr.org/2018/12/09/674995075/slave-bible-from-the-1800s-omitted-key-passages-that-could-incite-rebellion.

6 "Statement by Alabama Clergymen," The Estate of Martin Luther King Jr, April 12, 1963, https://kinginstitute.stanford.edu/sites/mlk/files/lesson-activities/clergybirmingham1963.pdf.

7 Jennifer De Pinto, "Most View Kneeling during Anthem as Acceptable Form of Protest," *CBS News*, July 29, 2020, www.cbsnews.com/news/kneeling-athletes-anthem-opinion-poll-28-07-2020/.

8 These critiques are not only from those that tacitly or otherwise support the status quo, who as King put it prefer order over justice. It also comes from activists that see property destruction, self-defense loosely defined and insurrectionary violence as true radical action. King wondered here about the balance of being both a militant and a moderate of having a "tough mind" and a "tender heart".

9 Martin L. King, "I Have a Dream," Speech presented at the March on Washington for Jobs and Freedom, Washington, DC, August 1968, https://avalon.law.yale.edu/20th_century/mlk01.asp.

10 Martin Luther King, *Pilgrimage to Nonviolence* (Chicago, IL: Fellowship Publications, 1960).

11 Martin Luther King, Jr., *A Gift of Love: Sermons from Strength to Love and Other Preachings* (Boston, MA: Beacon Press, 2012), 20.

12 Ron Large, "Martin Luther King, Jr.: Ethics, Nonviolence, and Moral Character," *Journal of Religious Thought* 48, no. 1 (1991): 51.

13 "The notion of dignity is where the social significance of Martin Luther King's nonviolent theory begins; it is the realization that social change, the vision of justice, lies within the transformation of character from an abject passivity to a sense of worth. A major portion of King's involvement in the struggle for civil rights was the effort to alter the elements of character, to develop a moral character that is capable of rejecting violence".

14 Martin Luther King Jr., "Nobel Peace Prize Acceptance Speech" (Speech, Oslo, Norway. December 10, 1964), www.nobelprize.org/prizes/peace/1964/king/26142-martin-luther-king-jr-acceptance-speech-1964/.

15 Lester R. Kurtz and Lee A. Smithey, *The Paradox of Repression and Nonviolent Movements.* Syracuse (New York: Syracuse University Press, 2018).

16 Martin Luther King Jr., *Speech at Illinois Wesleyan University* (Bloomington, IL, February 10, 1966), www.iwu.edu/mlk/.

17 "US Crisis Monitor Releases Full Data for 2020," *ACLED*, February 2021, https://acleddata.com/acleddatanew/wp-content/uploads/2021/02/ACLED_BDI_USCM 2020Release_2021.pdf and Crowd Counting Consortium https://sites.google.com/view/crowdcountingconsortium/home.

18 Martin Luther King Jr, "Address at the Thirty-fourth Annual Convention of the National Bar Association," 20 August 1959; Wisconsin Milwaukee, *The Papers of Martin Luther King, Jr.: Threshold of a New Decade, January 1959 5* (1960).

19 David Rasmey, *Righteous Martin Luther King Was Slandered as a Communist | David Ramsey* (Colorado Springs Gazette), accessed March 19, 2021, https://gazette.com/news/righteous-martin-luther-king-was-slandered-as-a-communist-david-ramsey/article_aeeb29ac-c3ad-11ea-956e-e7ccd4fb0784.html.

20 Bob Fitch, "Billboard Depicting Martin Luther King Jr. at Highlander Folk School, Labeled a Communist Training School," *Photograph*, June 1966, https://exhibits.stanford.edu/fitch/catalog/hd306zh7365.

21 For example, consistent work by activists during and after Ferguson compelled the media to take a look at their own reportorial bias during BLM protests and to focus on issues of systemic racism in policing and the criminal justice system. In fact, even with the violence, competing narratives and complexities of the protests, a Washington Post – George Mason survey in 2020 found that "more than 2 in 3 Americans – a whopping 69 percent – said that Floyd's killing represents a broader problem in law enforcement, while just 29 percent say it's an isolated incident". This differed greatly from six years earlier, when "43 percent described those deaths as indicative of broader problems in policing while 51 percent saw those killings as isolated incidents". This speaks to the power of sustaining social justice beyond highly visible flashpoint moments and of the ongoing sacrifice that comes from lobbying, developing policy and nurturing activist networks. See, Jacqueline Alemany, "Power Up: There's Been a Dramatic Shift in Public Opinion about Police Treatment of Black Americans,"

Washington Post, June 9, 2020, www.washingtonpost.com/news/powerpost/paloma/powerup/2020/06/09/powerup-there-s-been-a-dramatic-shift-in-public-opinion-over-police-treatment-of-black.

22 For an excellent resource on LaFayette and Selma, see the book "In peace and Freedom" Bernard LaFayette and Kathryn Lee Johnson, *In Peace and Freedom: My Journey in Selma* (Lexington, KY: The University Press of Kentucky, 2013).

23 To learn more about Amelia Boynton, here are several excellent resources: https://snccdigital.org/people/amelia-boynton/ and www.nps.gov/people/amelia-boynton-robinson.htm.

24 "Montgomery Bus Boycott," In the Martin Luther King, Jr., Research and Education Institute, April 26, 2017, https://kinginstitute.stanford.edu/encyclopedia/montgomery-bus-boycott.

25 "Montgomery Bus Boycott," in *HISTORY*, www.history.com/topics/black-history/montgomery-bus-boycott.

26 Mayo Clinic, "Recognize the Signs of Domestic Violence against Women," accessed May 6, 2021, www.mayoclinic.org/healthy-lifestyle/adult-health/in-depth/domestic-violence/art-20048397.

27 Martin Luther King Jr, "Letter from Birmingham Jail," *UC Davis Law Review* 26 (1992): 835.

28 On December 14, 2012, 20 children between the ages of 6 and 7, and six school employees were shot and killed.

29 Newtown, Connecticut is just 48 miles from Hartford. The median household income level of Newtown is $127,602 and only 11.5% of residents are minorities. [Census Data for Newtown, CT, 2019, www.census.gov/quickfacts/newtowntownfairfieldcountyconnecticut]

30 Patrick R. Grzanka, Keri A. Frantell, and Ruth E. Fassinger, "The White Racial Affect Scale (WRAS): A Measure of White Guilt, Shame, and Negation," *The Counseling Psychologist* 48, no. 1 (January 1, 2020): 47–77, https://doi.org/10.1177/0011000019878808.

31 Martin L. King Jr, "The Role of the Behavioral Scientist in the Civil Rights Movement," *American Psychologist* 23, no. 3 (1968): 180.

32 Shanique J. Lee, Portia Marie York, John A. Williams, Sonyia C. Richardson, Alicia W. Davis, Brian Keith Williams, and Chance W. Lewis, "Teachers' Psychological Distress in North Carolina: An Analysis of Urban versus Non-Urban School Districts," *Urban Education*, August 14, 2020, 0042085920948955, https://doi.org/10.1177/0042085920948955.

33 Daniel Mendoza-Castejon, Javier Fraile-García, Montaña Diaz-Manzano, Juan Pedro Fuentes-Garcia, and Vicente Javier Clemente-Suárez, "Differences in the Autonomic Nervous System Stress Status of Urban and Rural School Teachers," *Physiology & Behavior* 222 (August 1, 2020): 112925, https://doi.org/10.1016/j.physbeh.2020.112925.

34 Moral injury is a term developed to describe the "damage done to one's conscience or moral compass when that person perpetrates, witnesses, or fails to prevent acts that transgress one's own moral beliefs, values, or ethical codes of conduct". While these dynamics of the wounds to the spirit occur during war, the terms were developed originally in order to better understand the experiences that Vietnam veterans reported after having come back from the war. This can be an interesting accompanying teaching tool to explore moral injury https://moralinjuryproject.syr.edu/about-moral-injury/.

35 King, *A Gift of Love*, 159.

5 Avoid Internal Violence of the Spirit as Well as External Physical Violence

Cherell Banks is a 43-year-old Black woman with locs that fall below her shoulders and one of the core community educators who work mostly with youth at CTCN. Cherell was born and raised in the Northend of Hartford and knows the city like the back of her hand. At CTCN, she teaches in a variety of settings – the Hartford Public Library, YMCA and at public schools in Hartford and New Haven – and works closely with Victoria Christgau. When you come to know Ms. Banks (as the youth call her), you see that her presence is playful, self-assured and calm. She has a vital knack for making youth in the community comfortable in her workshops and for supporting students who are feeling stressed or going through tough times that make it hard to focus or even be present in an educational setting.

I ask Cherell if she always had these skills and the compassion and internal discipline to handle the challenges of youth work. She replies, "I was very happy, I danced and smiled a lot when I was little".

But as she got older things changed and she became angrier. She wasn't "tearing and burning up stuff; it's just, I was thinking more selfishly, like "Don't bother me. Don't talk to me. Don't touch me".

Cherell had a mother and father at home and was also the oldest of five children and took on the extra pressures, responsibilities and expectations of being the oldest and negating life in the city. When she left the house, she says, those experiences "made me into a bottom-line person. I didn't understand what that bottom-line person looked like. I just knew that if I wanted something, I wanted it and it needed to happen then – and you was going to know that I wanted it and it needed to happen then".

Cherell laughs and tells me, "I was the enforcer".

When I asked Cherell if she got into fights she told me, "if I needed to, yes". She grew up roughhousing with mostly male cousins.

> It wasn't like I did it because I felt bad, or I really wanted to hurt somebody. I did it [at home] because it was fun . . . I thought that all of that was normal. It was just a part of life. I didn't know that it added trauma to other people.

DOI: 10.4324/9781003243915-6

After she signed up with CTCN in 2014 did Cherell question the effects of fighting. "Some things, if you let it continue, it'll continue unhealthy more consistently questioned the effects. I started trying to implement – no, not trying, I did – implement some of the exercises we did [on] types and levels of conflict".

When Cherell first got certified as a community nonviolence trainer, she applied her lessons that year to the family's Thanksgiving dinner. At past gatherings, toward the end of dinner, "the fun would break out" – family arguments and fights. But this year, Cherell made a different decision; "Instead of partaking in it that year, I chose to use my nonviolence training and step back and look at what was happening".

She didn't get involved in the fighting and arguing, and instead used other skills to keep the levels down. Although she didn't think her family noticed, they did. Cherell recalled them asking her, "What's going on with you? You're not so aggressive. You're not fighting no more. You're not so quick to yell and argue, or be in the middle or in the mix of the rah-rah?"

Cherell told her family,

One, people change over time. Two, let me tell you about this nonviolence training. Let me tell you about this superpower [of] *not becoming part of somebody's entertainment.* Let's talk about when you want to talk about something and get your point across. How about getting your point across effectively . . . versus putting your hands on somebody?

Cherell's mom and kids noticed the difference, and so did her old friends. Some of the youth she worked with would go home and talk to their parents about "Miss Banks". The parent might meet Cherell and remember her from their own school days and tell their kids, "This really must be working, because we know what she used to be like . . . You got a real one in front of you talking to you right now. I can tell you she wasn't always like this".

At first, Cherell worried about the youth hearing this about her past but ultimately decided it lent value to the example she was trying to set. "Being nonviolent, it takes work every day", she reflects. "Trust me, I get tried every day. I can imagine what they go through". Her most important mission, she says, is that youth have "knowledge, have the power while they're using their voices . . . and for them not to become part of the distraction".

The fights, the interpersonal "beef" – all of that masks the deeper, systemic problems in a society where racial inequality creates numerous, daily and intense forms of stress that people are responding to and, more personally, anger often masks the pain and the hidden effects of violence on the psyche.

Cherell knows personally what is at stake for so many of these youth. In addition to trying to support these young people through her work, she has dedicated much of her time to advocating with different city and state offices for her son, who has been in prison for most of the time that I've known her. The majority of Connecticut's prison population comes from just five cities

(Hartford, New Haven, Bridgeport, Stamford and Waterbury).[1] Most of the young men and women of color living in Hartford and New Haven live below the poverty line,[2] and Connecticut ranks as one of the worst states in terms of disproportionally incarcerating Black and Latino citizens.[3] Although this is beginning to change, it's still true today that most are incarcerated for nonviolent drug-related offenses. And many of the violent offenses are drug related. As the well-known Chicago community organizer Edward "Buzz" Palmer explains, "Everyone promised us jobs and income, but only one industry delivered, at far too high a price: the illegal drug industry".[4]

It is absolutely exhausting work to stand up to the criminal justice system and other institutions. Cherell advocated and worked with the mayor's office, Family and Youth Services, local mentoring programs Blue Hills Civic Association Youth Development Services and many other groups for those with incarcerated family members and at-risk youth. Eventually, her son was finally released – she beams when she tells me this, that he is "home and free. Free, innocent" – but Cherell didn't fully realize the enormous struggle that would follow.

"I thought that him coming home would be like a breath of fresh air", she remembers.

> I thought I was ready, I thought I had everything lined up, I talked to the right people, I made sure I connected to the right resources [for when he got out] and that they were active resources. I used everything that I teach and train in the community [about nonviolence], and talk to others about [what] I went through, and I made sure I went through the walk myself.

Even with all of this, Cherell "wasn't ready for the transition literally and mentally" and she "tried to use all of my nonviolence training. It's like they was ready to just give me trouble". When she pushed for more support and tried to problem-solve with them asking what they could do to help, the halfway house suspected that Cherell might be a "plant", sent undercover to evaluate their work, and then they set up a lot of "blockades", a lot of, "Oh, no. That's not how it is".

She saw "all kinds of opportunities to practice nonviolence" in the halfway house and remembered principle number three, "Attack the evil, not the person. I'm looking at evil," she says. "I'm trying to look past them [and attack the problem]. They're constantly trying to shut me down, or create a situation that would allow them to put me off the premises. They're also, in turn, doing this to the people inside the halfway house. I'm like, 'Oh, no. Oh, no'. They didn't like that."

Cherell wrote an op-ed in Hartford's longest-running newspaper, the *Northend Agent*,[5] "My Not So Golden Ticket: My Experience Navigating the Criminal Justice System with My Son". After reading her article, the group of Hartford residents that were meeting to discuss criminal justice reform with the Katal Center for Equity, Health and Justice planned to go to the legislature to talk about mental health resources for community members in halfway houses, more services for newly freed incarcerated people and a shift of resources toward re-entry.

All of this work requires a lot of emotional awareness and fortitude because, as Cherell points out, when you challenge institutions while treating people with dignity, and are not easily emotionally thrown off balance – when you don't become part of the "distraction" of violent conflict – the institutional response is not always positive. Cherell explains that her struggle with resistant institutions is "like a battle because, really, the satisfaction is being able to not fall into that distraction" and thereby more effectively fighting for changes.

I comment on how much commitment that takes, and she agrees.

"A lot of people go in that place [of] hopelessness. I'm thinking especially for anybody, Black folks or anybody, who's had to deal with this shit their whole lives, it's easy to go to [that] place", she trails off.

After a while, Cherell continues, confiding,

> I do a lot of praying, Arthur. I do a lot of praying. I do a lot of, in my car yelling. What you call it? I let it out. I let it out. I do a lot of dancing. Sometimes you might find me somewhere randomly just turning circles, with my arms out – [just letting it go].

Photo 5.1 Cherell Banks enjoys a relaxed moment with mentor Bernard LaFayette, Jr. in PA 2018 © CTCN

Photo 5.2 Ms. Cherell Banks at the MLK Day Celebrations 2018 at the Wadsworth Atheneum Museum of Art, Hartford, CT © CTCN

Key Concepts

Cherell as well as other community educators working and living in violence-affected neighborhoods work to maintain internal peace and prevent "internal violence of the spirit" even as they live and work in the midst of systemic racism and violence. This principle provokes vital questions that make this material relevant, and lively, when it's taught today:

- Does "avoiding" internal violence mean that we just accept the world as it is when it is so unfair?
- Why, according to Dr. King, is awareness and control of emotions so important?
- How can one shift or avoid internal violence?

On April 17, 1960, in one of the most pivotal media appearances of his life, Dr. King was interviewed on *Meet the Press* – the longest-running show on television, and arguably the most influential news program of its time. The White hosts of *Meet the Press* – then Ned Brooks, Lawrence Spivak and Linus Pauling – asked questions that revealed a distrust and fear of both King and the civil rights movement that many White people doubtless shared. For 20 minutes, they implied that lunch counter sit-ins and other nonviolent direct actions were unnecessary and excessively radical,[6] and that King and his associates were likely inciting violence. In one such exchange, Spivak rebuked the Nashville sit-ins:

> But wouldn't you be on stronger grounds, though, if you refused to buy at those stores and if you called upon the white people of the country to follow you because of both your moral and your legal right not to buy [and called off the sit-ins]?[7]

King made clear the first reason, that nonviolent discipline – the ability (and practice) to control fear and anger in the midst of nonviolent direct action – is critically important. It holds up "a mirror" for people (White folks especially, in this case) who are not impacted by that violence to see its brutality and injustice. Furthermore, Black people see other Black people and their allies not backing down from this injustice and even from physical violence. Bystanders not only see the immediate drama of these public actions (the standoff on the Edmund Pettus bridge, or violence against Freedom Riders or those sitting in) but also feel moral culpability and responsibility for supporting the side of justice. On *Meet the Press* King described it this way:

> I think, Mr. Spivak, sometimes it is necessary to dramatize an issue because many people are not aware of what's happening. And I think the sit-ins serve to dramatize the indignities and the injustices which Negro people are facing all over the nation. And I think another reason why they are necessary, and they are vitally important at this point, is the fact that they give an eternal refutation to the idea that the Negro is satisfied with segregation. If you didn't have the sit-ins, you wouldn't have this dramatic, and not only this dramatic but this mass demonstration of the dissatisfaction of the Negro with the whole system of segregation.[8]

Importantly for educators teaching about nonviolence, one easily missed component of nonviolent direct action is what psychologists refer to as *emotional regulation* – especially the regulation of fear, anger and hatred.[9] This discipline (regulation) allows nonviolent practitioners to be more effective while they are resisting in terms of both sticking to a plan and innovating when the plan fails while avoiding both external and internal violence.

Emotional regulation – avoiding or at least controlling internal violence – can be taught and is not an attribute of personality or disposition alone.[10] It is not spontaneous, but planned, and can be practiced. This is why education played such a key yet largely overlooked role in the civil rights movement. The film *A Force More Powerful* includes some of the most vivid images of that preparation. A young James Lawson is seen leading a workshop of mostly college students who are preparing to face an angry mob as they engage in sit-ins at lunch counters in Nashville, Tennessee. In this simple but powerful role play, Black activists take their seats at the lunch counter, and a group of White activists, playing in turn the role of locals, begin to use racial epithets, calling the college students "jungle bunny" and "Nigger" while attempting to put cigarettes out in their hair as they simulate physically attacking them, dragging each out of their chairs and to the ground.

Dr. LaFayette was one of the young people in those workshops, and he faced these attacks from White people on numerous occasions during nonviolent actions. He even went so far as to write his will before he joined the Freedom Riders in response to the very real possibility of death.[11] LaFayette, who developed a reputation among activists for his fearlessness,[12] recalls how essential it was to prepare, both mentally and physically, for such intense violence. Discussing the possibility of violence and what might happen would not provide enough preparation, however, as activists would face intense physical violence, threats and insults that required additional training and support. Instead, they needed to simulate these moments in advance, as best they could, to learn experientially about the limits of their self-discipline in these situations and how they would be able to perform under great stress. Some advance exposure to violence helped them learn to avoid or at least control internal violence and to practice nonviolent resistance in the midst of intense fear, anger and rage.[13]

These workshops had another important function: some people discovered that they could, in fact, control their fear and anger and their desire to retaliate or flee, even under intense circumstances. They hadn't realized this entirely before, and they became more confident because of these simulations and conversations with fellow participants. Seasoned nonviolence practitioner George Lakey makes an important observation based on his years of engaged research in social movements: By planning and testing strategies in advance, participants can develop a sense of familiarity, and even control, in inherently unpredictable, chaotic and frightening moments.[14] Lakey's insights align with broader research findings that experiential education helps people perform in the midst of conflict.[15] Training and education provide opportunities to ask questions and "replay" key dynamics – participants get a "do over" that they do not get in real life. Participants can also stop, pause the action and discuss things if they are overwhelmed without putting others at greater risk, as could happen during actual events. In practice, some movements may adopt an attitude of bravado that does not allow for this kind of acknowledgment of fear, yet this dialogue and reflection is a key component of nonviolence education at CTCN and in Dr. LaFayette's approach.

Researchers in psychology have extensively studied two major strategies for emotion regulation: cognitive reappraisal and expressive suppression.[16,17,18] Expressive suppression refers to "the attempt to hide, inhibit, or reduce ongoing emotion-expressive behavior",[19] and cognitive reappraisal means that we reinterpret an emotion-eliciting situation so that we alter its meaning and change its emotional impact.[20] One of the major misunderstandings of nonviolence is that avoiding internal violence equates to suppressing our emotions.

Instead, Lawson relied, as do many movements today, on reappraisal: Look again at the context, see it in a new light and reinterpret it.

This is an important point for educators teaching the fifth principle of non-violence, in terms of both understanding the psychological implications of King's teachings and considering how to respond to injustice today. Students usefully begin to situate the suffering they will face as a result of their activism along a much broader historical arc – a wider movement against enslavement, colonization and dehumanization that spans centuries – and perhaps even, as the next chapter highlights, a moral arc toward justice by which God is on their side. In King's time, this broader perspective fostered greater emotional control and awareness – a critical skill to challenge systemic racism without resorting to physical violence.

Expressive suppression is a far less effective way to regulate emotion. Suppression is difficult to sustain and has many negative effects. As Debora Cutuli explains in her research, emotional suppression is a strategy that occurs after strong and unwieldy emotions are already present. While suppression may prevent destructive behaviors, the subjective and physiological experience of negative emotion can "continue to linger and accumulate unresolved". This approach is not only late in terms of the emotions generated but also takes a great deal of individual effort to maintain.[21]

Some activists made a very different, and important, discovery in workshops during the civil rights movement, namely, that this kind of role, on the front lines, was not for them. They realized during these simulations and preparations for emotional control that they simply would not be able, or did not see it as acceptable, to endure such vile hatred and maintain that kind of nonviolent discipline in the throes of direct racist attacks. This point is often missed in discussions of Kingian nonviolence, which tends to present him as a martyr who paid the "ultimate price", and puts a premium on others who are able to engage with the same level of visibility or willingness to take risks.

The discovery and realization of people's emotional limits is an important part of nonviolence preparation, too, so rather than get belittled or devalued, those who didn't feel emotionally able to stand on the frontlines made important contributions, nonetheless. Community members in Nashville, for example, played many other roles. *A Force More Powerful* shows a team organizing behind the scenes so that as people were arrested for sitting in, another group would arrive to take their seats. It required a great deal of coordination and support to arrange the logistics of "shifts" for frontline activists. These activists prepared meticulously and in great detail, going so far as to ensure that all protestors had coins to make calls from the payphone if needed. Victoria echoes this sentiment when she says that those activists in the direct line of violence do not represent a "gold standard" in terms of physical risk or the toll that all people were willing to take.[22] Rather, it took the efforts of many people and those people were on a spectrum in terms of the risks they could take and the degree of emotional regulation they had.

Applying the Concepts, and Lessons Learned

Youth in Hartford and New Haven most often deal with systemic racism in the form of persistent everyday risk, indignity, inequality and even violence that interfere with their education and impact their mental and physical health. For these participants in CTCN nonviolence programs at the public library or the YMCA in Hartford or New Haven, the most pressing challenges are not to prepare to sit in at the lunch counter or weather attacks from police dogs while crossing the bridge in Selma but to get to and from school safely without being profiled by the police or caught up in neighborhood violence, and then avoid discrimination again once they get to school. Educator and scholar Shawn Ginwright explains,

> Young people in urban settings who have fallen prey to . . . discriminatory practices often have few opportunities to address the psychosocial harm resulting from persistent exposure to an "ecosystem of violence". Their experiences are not only traumatizing, but often have a profound negative impact on their sense of efficacy and agency.[23]

Cherell knows this dynamic well. When I ask her if she hears about these issues of violence and other challenges in the community during nonviolence workshops and afterschool programs, she quickly replies:

> I was hearing a lot of it. It was a lot of shooting going on. It seemed somebody in my class had a friend who died every week. I think one week, we had at least three shootings. In one week! If there wasn't a shooting, there was a car accident where they were in a car and something happened. It was a lot of it going on to the point where they would try to talk about it but it was getting too much for them [to discuss], where now they want to joke around about it. They want to joke around, they want to laugh.

While laughter may seem like an unusual response, it is a fairly common way to deal with trauma. Cherell explains,

> Yes, [it is a] a coping skill. How are they dealing with that internal violence? I know one girl, she is in the middle school – sometimes they will come and just sit for lunch and talk. She got up and she was like, "I'm tired of crying. I just got finished crying last week. I got to cry again this week." She was like, "Enough with that. Enough with that. I'm mad." I was like, "That's good. That's good, but what you going to do with your madness? What you going to do with your madness?"

When teaching this principle, Cherell, Tremayne, Victoria and other community nonviolence educators emphasize the importance of cultivating everyday awareness of one's emotions – to observe how stressful situations affect one's mental, emotional, physical and spiritual health and, as Cherell points out, to do something about it – to engage in action. Social Psychologist Carol Tavris says, "The question is not, 'Should I express anger or should I suppress it?' It is, 'What can we do to solve the problem?'"[24]

During workshops, Cherell, Pastor Lane, Victoria and YFs like Tremayne and Paris cultivate emotional awareness. They regularly ask participants to brainstorm a list of things they do to shift their emotional state when things get difficult. Within a few short minutes, participants in both youth and adult workshops can generate a variety of strategies that typically include working out, listening to music, making art, prayer and meditation and connecting with friends to cultivate emotional balance in a violent world.

The language of the fifth principle is to avoid internal violence, which in practice means being able to consciously shift or regulate one's internal world. Community members already have some of these skills, and there is no one-size-fits-all approach for educators at CTCN for how best to do this. Instead, they emphasize that it is important to experiment with and expand the tools that work for you in terms of transforming, controlling and redirecting fear, anger, shame and other emotions that, if left unchecked, can lead to destructive outcomes for yourself as well as the people you may see as your adversaries.[25] Kingian trainers make a point, especially in working with the youth, that they shouldn't have to do this processing alone, and that many other people are dealing with these kinds of emotions as a result of America's deep history of systemic racism. Generations of people, especially Black people, have worked together to survive and challenge everyday racism, from attacks on their character and looks to institutions that serve to exclude them from equal opportunities.

Awareness of the body also often comes up as a theme when discussing this principle – that in intense situations, especially when facing perceived threats, our breathing becomes hurried and short, our bodies tense up and our thinking and ability to process complex choices can be compromised.[26] Pastor John Lewis practices martial arts and teaches that we need to slow down when situations speed up and to use breathing and breathing awareness to calm down. Pastor James Lane was an athlete in high school and many of the youth he works with play sports, so he often encourages young people to think about how they have developed physical calm even when they are nervous (for example, shooting a basketball free throw under pressure or putting in golf).

Nonviolence educators in Connecticut have discussions about the fifth principle that anecdotally mesh with some of the latest research, which describes how the early recognition of physical signs of anger and fear can allow us to take hold of them before they spiral out of control.[27,28,29] Importantly, people who increase their ability to respond to their anger constructively – for example, by working to solve the problem that made them angry – "have lower resting blood pressure than people with fewer coping skills".[30,31] This effect applies not only to moments of peak nonviolence (such as during a protest) but also to people's everyday experiences, especially when they are trying to survive, thrive and resist in a violent world.

Conversely, emotions that linger, fester and go untended can have serious negative repercussions. King had some of these effects in mind when he spoke of internal violence. Many in the field of psychology refer to these as "destructive emotions", and they can cause a host of problems even before the affected person lashes out physically. As health editor Michael Schroader points out, "chronic anger can lead to increased anxiety, insomnia, mental or brain fog and fatigue, and it can reduce the immune system's ability to fend off threats".[32] Exposure to violence and inequality can affect one's general disposition. John Schinnerer, an expert on anger management, writes, "Irritability is like low-level intensity anger sort of stretched thin over time. And moods don't necessarily need a cause; they just are – they kind of come and go like waves".[33] Regarding people who seem to be hostile by nature, Schinnerer explains

> Hostility has been shown to be a personality trait of some people, and it's a longstanding trait that involves beliefs that others are unworthy or likely to be sources of frustration. So they tend to be suspicious, cynical, jealous, bitter, and that's been linked to anger and aggression. So these people tend to evaluate others more harshly, and they're slower to positive judgment.[34]

King agreed noting especially that hate had a way of twisting one's moral character yet he also pointed out that anger, especially righteous indignation was grounded in a valid way of seeing injustice in the world and could be a powerful force for good. Awareness of emotional states in nonviolence then has wider benefits and implications for community health, and this is a key lesson that arises in the community-led nonviolence workshops.

Each of the CTCN's educators has developed tools for discussing and cultivating awareness of internal emotional states. Warren Hardy, for example, uses a color-coded system. Green is for someone who is feeling really good, had a great day, is grateful, is feeling really connected to people and perhaps hopeful. Yellow is where things are alright – good but not great. Orange is a lot of anger, sadness, even rage – feeling alone – and red is ready to explode. Regarding this system, Warren explains:

> I do my color-coded check-in [every time I facilitate]. And if a person is walking' around on orange or red, you know? It's a matter of time, you know what I'm saying, before he explodes.

Warren knows that in the US, where people have easy access to firearms, unaddressed emotions can be deadly, and it is a national problem. He brings the importance of this inner awareness back to Dr. King's own words:

Injustice, you know what I'm saying, anywhere is a threat to justice everywhere.

> When [the Sandy Hook mass shooting] first happened, I was shocked, but I wasn't shocked . . . because I've had plenty of conversations with individuals who are as clean as a whistle, smile every day, and internally are just stressed the hell out. Literally, like, they [are] just like overwhelmed, stressed, just any second they're ready to explode. So I was not shocked. But again, when I speak, I always tell people, "How do we get involved before it gets to that point?" You know, if you don't – do you have to wait, literally wait, until it's your son, your daughter, or husband or wife get taken away before you do something preventative?

In the profoundly tragic aftermath of Sandy Hook, Warren has supported and lobbied in Washington, DC, with activists affiliated with the Everytown project,[35] but Warren knows that we also need to acknowledge that we are losing beautiful, promising kids right down the road in his neighborhood and throughout Hartford and that for many years, this loss of Black lives was not a concern for many people in Newtown. The lives of these kids in Hartford are not any less valuable than those in Newtown, and though it happens more slowly than a mass shooting, violence is happening to Black and Brown youth right under our noses every day across the country.[36]

Internal violence, then, is not simply a matter of cultivating and building on resilience in Black communities. Like Warren, Dr. King knew that these issues of complicity and internal violence in White communities are a pressing issue for America:

> White America needs to understand that it is poisoned to its soul by racism and the understanding needs to be carefully documented and consequently more difficult to reject. The present crisis arises because although it is historically imperative that our society take the next step to equality, we find ourselves psychologically and socially imprisoned. All too many white Americans are horrified not with conditions of Negro life but with the product of these conditions-the Negro himself.
>
> White America is seeking to keep the walls of segregation substantially intact while the evolution of society and the Negro's desperation is causing them to crumble. The White majority, unprepared and unwilling to accept radical structural change, is resisting and producing chaos while complaining that if there were no chaos orderly change would come.[37]

King is reflecting on the dynamics that keep racist systems in place and, by extension, he, like Warren, was imploring White Americans to think about the psychological and emotional scaffolding underpinnings of that status quo. Black Lives Matter activists today make the same observation, questioning not only why police so often kill unarmed black people but also why so many people are willing to accept injustice simply because their children are not directly affected. They also make the point that deep racial inequalities in education, housing and employment are part of the same system that devalue black life and are highlighted in those moments of police violence.

I talk with Victoria about this work of looking at the emotions of guilt and shame in White people when we recognize that we've benefited from racism or other forms of inequality and have been complicit in the reinforcement of those systems. This is a kind of "inner violence" that racism inflicts on the more privileged. Victoria says that nonviolence requires a lifelong commitment to reflection and to consistent action to influence change. This is a central part of the practice of nonviolence for White people – developing emotional fortitude. Victoria shares, "I think a warrior is willing to feel the pain and to acknowledge joy. That's a real warrior".[38] Pastor Lane agrees and points out that this kind of honest self-reflection is where work across race lines and even reconciliation can begin. This work needs to be done, but it requires that White folks not distance themselves from this pain. As he puts it,

> in light of what most people, white people, would say, well you know I'm not like that; maybe my ancestors [were involved in racism but not me]. I've always said, "if you buy a house that was built 90 years ago and it needs to be repaired, you know you repair the House because you live in it now".

When Cherell talked about laughter as a coping mechanism, she also mentioned that many participants in the workshops *shut down as a result of trauma*. She recalled a conversation with a high school student in New Haven who had said all the violence doesn't matter to them that they just live their lives and don't worry about it. Cherell replied,

> Sometimes you are quick to say this doesn't matter. It doesn't matter because it has nothing to do with you all. You don't live like that [engaging in violence or selling drugs], but how about your friends that live around you? The ones that's dying? Why are they dying?

The young woman responded. "Miss, I don't know why they're dying. They're hardheaded. They got no money. They're hungry". Cherell was taken aback by her analysis of the complexity of violence. Understandably, this young person was overwhelmed by the prospects of trying to influence change and desensitized to the violence – it's a set of problems that she knows well.

This young person is not alone. The research literature on youth violence clearly shows that trying to navigate the indignities of poverty, community violence, racial discrimination in employment and unreported police brutality often results in unresolved rage, aggression, depression and, as in this example, fatalism.[39] This dynamic of shutting down is a key component in discussions of principle five and an important element of Dr. King's legacy. King and the many other women and men who laid their lives on the line to end injustice contended with a wide range of emotions, and this emotional complexity – a part of the inner world of their work – is too often flattened out into a caricature of the martyr or the saint. The conversation really comes alive when participants talk honestly about the emotional impacts of trauma and the complex forms and meanings of violence and engage with the living legacy of nonviolence.

Cherell shares the story of another student in the same high school:

> I said to him, "I heard that you are an A student. You are an honor student, like high honors." I was like, "Do you think this behavior right now that you're displaying, like you don't give a F, matches up to high honors?" He was like, [I] do what I'm going to do."
>
> "Why you doing it?" He said, "I'm doing it for my sister." I'm like, "You're doing it for your sister? You want me to go talk to your sister?" He was like, "No, Miss."
>
> I said, "You just told me about your sister. Your sister around you. You're sitting here because you doing things that don't match up to your high honor roll. This behavior doesn't match," I said, "I got to talk to you because you're around her. I need you to do better around her. If you ain't doing it for you, you're going to do it for her, but you got to watch what you're doing.
>
> You got to be mindful for what you're doing." He like, "Yes. It sound good, Miss. It sound good." I'm happy to report that I see him this school year and he looked like a different guy. He looks very focused. . . . He was like, "Miss, thank you, thank you." I was like, "Thank you for what? Going to talk to your sister?" [laughs] He was like, "You funny, you funny." I was like, "That's just what I do, that's just what I do." They talk about it [violence in the community]. It's just having that moment, seizing that moment when they're sharing it. It does get tiresome, it does weigh down on their brain, it does cause internal violence.

Cherell's approach with young people is not to push these conversations too far but to create an environment, as do other community educators, where students feel comfortable reflecting on and talking about their emotions. For example, with this student, she didn't lecture him about his actions but got him thinking and sitting with his feelings and rationales. Dr. King also struggled with these issues and experienced many "dark nights of the soul", wondering what it would take to transform the brutality of racism. People become desensitized over time, numb, give up hope and feel they have little they can contribute to influencing change.[40,41,42,43,44,45]

What's more, the negative impacts of trauma can develop slowly over time. Some researchers now theorize that it's not just getting angry but also the physical stress of being angry or fearful for longer periods of time that damages cardiovascular health.[46] Elevated rates of depression, sustained despair and an erosion of perceptions of trust all negatively impact one's emotional and physical health and ability to meaningfully connect with others.[47,48] This emotional work to practice nonviolence is not only about developing the discipline to face down police dogs at a Black Lives Matter protest but also to be able to feel again, to live more fully. It includes finding ways to cultivate and share joy, be vulnerable and reach out to others.[49,50,51] This vulnerability builds solidarity and a sense of connectedness which helps people feel more emboldened to resist injustice in their everyday lives. This same capacity and networks of affinity help to create and sustain longer episodes of protest and resistance.

Adult facilitators, Cherell points out, also carry a heavy weight. They work long hours, do not have professional training in counseling and are themselves vulnerable. Most of the facilitators deal with economic insecurity, which in practical terms means they lack reliable transportation (and they drive from site to site all the time), have limited access to health care, eat meals on the run and have worries about stable housing. It is hard work to try to change a toxic system while you are submerged within it. And yet this real talk about the emotional impacts of that system shows intimately what is at stake and some of the ways that people are connected, not only to each other but also to the legacy of the civil rights movement and the living philosophy of nonviolence.

The trauma and emotional violence extend to perpetrators as well. Rachel MacNair's far-reaching work on perpetrators of violence finds a host of negative consequences from what she calls perpetrator-induced traumatic stress (PITS),[52] and others have called moral injury.[53] Importantly, in cases of direct participation in violence, and potentially for those who witness this violence without taking action to disrupt it, PITS can induce many of the same symptoms as PTSD. Sufferers may struggle with re-experiencing, avoiding reminders of specific events, negative thinking and moods, sleep disturbances, outbursts of anger and defensiveness, alcohol and substance abuse and even workaholism. For people who work within systems that directly reproduce racial inequality and especially for those whose jobs involve more direct forms of repression or coercion toward Black people (prison guards, teachers, police, social service workers and healthcare workers) that "privilege" can come with numerous negative consequences.

"How does one avoid the internal chatter and the noise and end the discomfort that is very much part of the human experience. . . [Is it] really feasible that one could ever avoid it?" This is the question Victoria asks when I interview her about the connections between CTCN's *use of the arts and avoiding internal violence* of the spirit. She and other community educators have found that "one could certainly learn to discipline their restlessness and their turbulence if they have more ways to express themselves rather than it . . . eventually blow[ing] up and becom[ing] outer violence".

Victoria explains,

> So one of the best ways to do that is to sing or dance or sit and write in your journal or create . . . You start to utilize a different part of your brain. And it also helps you to just touch something that you may not be able to verbalize but you can articulate through a piece of art.

For learners who have experienced violence and injustice, the arts can be particularly useful in teaching about nonviolence and have indeed been used successfully in peace education around the world.[54,55] Dr. LaFayette likes to say that violence is the language of the inarticulate. Refining that expression and connecting with one's emotional states require more than just dialogue, as many of the educators I interviewed emphasized. The research backs this up, especially in cases of trauma as alternative forms of expression can be powerful pathways to access one's inner world.

When individuals attempt to gain control and protect themselves, they often rely on repetitive patterns of thinking or get stuck in their feelings.[56] Flexibility is linked to resilience and coping, and the arts can help by allowing subtle or unrecognized experiences to be processed and the integration of new and more complex points of view.[57] In other words, this shifting of our inner stories, about self-worth, about how we fit into the world (or do not) and the possibilities for alternative futures are all critically important to internal healing and change and to using nonviolence to resist and change your neighborhood or the wider society.

Victoria, a Certified "Master Teaching Artist" for the state of Connecticut, frequently improvises to introduce smaller arts interventions into larger conversations. For example, on a summer day in a small room with a lot of fidgety students (conditions not that conducive to balance or calm), she assigned a simple activity: Draw circles. Next, Victoria says, she asked students

> to start drawing multiple circles on the page and any pattern that they wanted to. And then I asked them once they saw that to describe to me what a circle is – now bear in mind that I had never taught this lesson before and it became a regular lesson that grew over the next 6 or 7 years as a permanent lesson to teach.

Victoria reported that this immediately shifted the rhythm in the classroom as students became quiet and very focused. The activity also gave them something that even if they weren't artistically skilled, they would feel that they could accomplish. Victoria then asked them to describe what a circle was and numerous people said it's something that has no beginning and no end. She explains, "And I saw that directly related to agape love and also our connection to the Beloved Community and the power of unifying people through nonviolence". This inspired her to build on the activity at the moment as she asked the students to make a list of at least 10 circles that they could see in the room they were in or in another room they are familiar with. The instructions were simple, she explains:

I gave him an example like a tire wheel. But I know if you're all just take the time to t think of 10 things in this room that have a circle, you'll find them. So then they start writing them down. Everybody's quiet and they're just writing and writing . . . And then I have them start to compare lists and if two people say the clock on the wall. I have them like SNAP or pound on the table or say "that's me".

After they generated their lists, Victoria offered a glimpse into how she improvised, what the youth educators call freestyling,

And now I say pay attention to your circles of influence, they are circles that you're a part of. Maybe you go to gym, you know, maybe you're part of a sports team. Maybe you're part of a dance team. Those are circles that you belong to. And now I have them make their own circle map on the page. Like, who they are and what's close by to them.

Yeah, in their circle and whose circles are influencing them. I said a circle can draw you in or it can keep you out. Are there circles that you would like to be a part of that you're not a part of yet? Are there circles that you know you shouldn't participate in, but that they are part of your life and how do you get yourself into a circle that is healthy and all that? . . . So we wound up having the circle maps of the student's lives and they're really beautiful and using this exercise has become a regular thing we do. . . . Pastor (Lane) goes really deep into it [in the activity to explore connections] between the spirit mind, body.

Activities like this can shift learners' emotional experiences and help them see connections between their inner and outer worlds and between inner states and social spaces, even built spaces we inhabit. This was the same process that Cherell was guiding her students through when they were shut down and engaging in potentially destructive activities. Importantly, as Victoria points out, this is an opportunity to recognize that we are profoundly interconnected. She brings up agape love because that is a sense of goodwill that comes from a recognition of these deep connections, that as King says, "We love men not because we like them, not because their attitudes and ways appeal to us, but we love them because God loves them [they are deserving of human dignity]".[58]

Community educators use the arts in other ways, often using drumming or rhythm activities and songs. Victoria is an improvisational vocalist, and her students learn to play a variety of rhythms. She works with local drummers as well, like Gambi Moses from New Haven – a certified community nonviolence educator who drums to reconnect people. Victoria often distributes simple wooden rhythm sticks, easily transported to various locations. "It's a way to really get the room to be quiet and reflective", she says, "and yet do something fun and, yeah, with the sticks, we've adapted other rhythmic lessons that I've learned from different drum workshops . . . I am not officially a drummer, but I love rhythm". She explains,

> I would start with a simple rhythm and pass out rhythm sticks and students would be encouraged to respond. And they normally really do get lost in them. There is a real desire for that. And there's even times where students think it's really corny and they don't want to deal with it. And then before too long they're really playing with them on a regular basis [and they start to ask for it or initiate it]. One student [for example] in recent years, who had never really explored rhythm or drumming just became completely absorbed in a plastic bucket drum to the point where [he] was carrying that bucket drum with them all over the high school like that was his signature. He just couldn't get enough of playing on his bucket drum. You know, It's just, it's language that there are so many ways to express yourself. And if you don't have exposure to these variations it's such an injustice to our children because they are capable or they're likely to be very gifted in something that they wouldn't know unless they're exposed to this and repeatedly teachers say things to me, in my many years of being a teaching artist, "I never knew that Manuel or somebody else could [do these things]".

Learning civil rights songs is a critical component of their programs as well. Dr. LaFayette and Christgau like to point out that music, and especially singing, can help lift people's spirits and shift perspective by forging tangible connections to past activists and to each other.

"We sing all the time when we're together", she says, and almost always when she is with LaFayette. Teaching the freedom songs connects into the soil and root of American history, Victoria explains, and the songs are "birthed from struggles". The songs have spirit, even if they are secular, and they captivate the imagination and draw students into connections with each other. Victoria has found that some students are embarrassed or intimidated by singing acapella, but if those students don't want to sing, then

> they've got a big piece of art paper and markers in front of them. They might be drawing while we're singing or they might, you know, be building something else. "I've had students, you know, mock me from the beginning when I'm singing – like laughing and chuckling – to where by the sixth or seventh week" they are urging her to sing those songs. Some of her students have modernized the songs [and improvise or put it to new beats].

One danger with the fifth principle that we avoid internal violence is the possible implication that those who are oppressed are somehow violent for not maintaining Zen-like calm in the midst of that violence. In Hartford and New Haven, educators cannot focus on emotional states without linking that discussion to the context they live in and the series of issues community members are navigating. This came clearly into view with a high school student in one of Victoria's groups:

> A student raises her hand: Miss Victoria. My mother saw my brother get shot when she was pregnant with me. I don't think she avoided internal violence of the spirit. I think she was really upset, she felt that violence. If feeling those feeling are bad for us, do you think that was bad for her and me when I was in her belly?

Victoria scrambled to explain that neither the student nor her mother did anything wrong. She tells the high schooler that Dr. King and many other people in the movement, including powerful women like Ella Baker, Claudette Colvin and Rosa Parks, even the children and people in the church who survived the bombing, all experienced strong feelings when they saw violence. She described that "this is normal and natural. This shouldn't be happening, we should be upset when those things happen but we also need to find ways to heal over time and to play a role in healing our communities". In this example, the principle to avoid internal violence is misleading and may be impossible, so the challenge is not to avoid those feelings but to find the best ways to engage with them.

The psychological literature and the experiences of community educators show that it is important to be aware of one's emotions but also to engage in activities that release that energy constructively. According to James Averill, in a functioning society, "if the anger is justified and the response is appropriate, usually the misunderstanding is corrected". Anger can also be constructive "when people frame it in terms of solving a mutual problem rather than as a chance [solely] to vent their feelings".[59]

When speaking to the American Psychological Association, Dr. King challenged them not to pathologize oppressed people who have strong emotional responses to deplorable and unacceptable social conditions: "You who are in the field of psychology", he said,

> have given us a great word. It is the word "maladjusted." This word is probably used more than any other word in psychology . . . I am sure that we will recognize that there are some things in our society, some things in our world, to which we should never be adjusted . . . there are some things concerning which we must always be maladjusted if we are to be people of good will. We must never adjust ourselves to racial discrimination and racial segregation. We must never adjust ourselves to religious bigotry. We must never adjust ourselves to economic conditions that take necessities from the many to give luxuries to the few. We must never adjust ourselves to the madness of militarism, and the self-defeating effects of physical violence.[60]

King's point that we must *keep fighting and remain maladjusted* to injustice departs somewhat from psychological approaches that people should adjust to or cope with the world as it is. Rather, as he points out, anger, shame and fear illuminate the wrongs in our environment, especially when it comes to the abuse of power and attacks on human dignity.[61] King was bolstered by the fact that during his lifetime, as now, so many Black people were taking to the streets and challenging injustice in all corners of society. As he put it,

> The slashing blows of backlash and frontlash have hurt the Negro, but they have also awakened him and revealed the nature of the oppressor. To lose illusions is to gain truth and Negroes today are experiencing an inner transformation that is liberating them from ideological dependence on the white majority.[62]

King understood that because the emotional landscape and what people experience are shaped differently according to our social identities, White and Black people do different emotional work in response to systemic racism. He also understood that successful nonviolent action required emotional discipline and destructive emotions, while helpfully alerting us to injustice, can also have a wide variety of negative consequences on people's physical health and ability to respond to problems. Kingian nonviolence educators seek to avoid this by controlling and transforming those feelings while remaining usefully maladjusted to an unjust system. In King's time, they used the term, "I am a man" as a reminder of basic human dignity and protest, and today "Black Lives Matter" similarly is an affirmative response – a call to demand human rights without passivity or apology.

Anger is an interesting emotion; it is fundamentally negative yet classified as an "approach" emotion – [an emotion that can be managed] – that carries the potential for motivation and can help shift challenging circumstances.[63,64] Anger can easily be destructive and there are many good reasons to avoid getting angry. Not only does anger make you feel bad, but it can also make you do stupid and self-destructive things and ignore risks. However, anger – especially what King called righteous indignation – is critically important to improving one's self-worth and capacity for effectively resisting racism and inequality. As Psychologist Ricardo Williams explains, anger can benefit relationships, promote optimism and be a useful motivating force to challenge violence.[65]

When teaching the underlying ideas about nonviolence that animated Martin Luther King, Jr.'s life, it is important to grapple with one of his central contributions. The nonviolent resister not only refuses to shoot his opponent but also refuses to hate him. At the center of nonviolence, stands the principle of love.[66] In King's view, injustice twists the inner worlds of those who oppress others as it also harms those denied their human rights. Dr. King made this larger picture clear in one of his most important and overlooked pieces of writing, The

World House, a chapter in his last book, *Where Do We Go from Here: Chaos or Community?* He adapted this chapter from his Noble Prize Lecture at the University of Oslo on December 11, 1964. He pored over the ideas and words for over a month, as he prepared to use his platform on a global stage to make a call for a radical new world.

The metaphor of the "World House" came to King when he read a newspaper article about a famous novelist who had died. "Among his papers was found a list of suggested plots for future stories, the most prominently underscored being this one: 'A widely separated family inherits a house in which they have to live together,'" King wrote.

> This is the great new problem of mankind. We have inherited a large house, a great "world house" in which we have to live together – Black and white, easterner and westerner, gentile and Jew, Catholic and Protestant, Muslim and Hindu – a family unduly separated in ideas, culture and interest, who, because we can never again live apart, must learn somehow to live with each other in peace.[67]

King's writing came with a promise: we could be on the edge of an important philosophical and systemic breakthrough, where the understanding, vulnerability and solidarity of a more connected world leads us to build systems that satisfy the full human needs of all. It also came with a warning: if we do not dismantle White supremacy and systemic racism, if we continue to invest in the military at far greater rates than we invest in the poor and other vulnerable people, if we fail to take seriously the wealth gap at home and between the richest nations and our neighbors we will, like so many before us, descend into the "junk heaps" of history, not from external threats but from our own "internal decay".[68] When psychologists talk about transforming destructive emotions, they cite the importance of "reappraising" those emotions and the context in which they arise. Nonviolence provides a framework for doing so that can be actively and experientially engaged with by educators in ways that can contribute to personal empowerment and the capacity to resist injustice and imagine and build more equalitarian systems.

Tips for Educators and Peacebuilders

- *Create supportive spaces to explore internal violence* where students feel heard and comfortable sharing. Community nonviolence educators demonstrate that especially when engaging with people that carry trauma and direct experiences of violence, there is a delicate balancing act between allowing people multiple opportunities to express themselves without prying. A key component of these supportive spaces is to have educators who have lived through similar experiences and dedicated themselves to nonviolence education. Teaching about Dr. King is not a simple activity or learning about a historical figure it touches on deep collective wounds about racism and inequality and requires the emotional and psychological dimension of nonviolent resistance be taken seriously if nonviolence is to be presented as a living legacy. Engage with/identify emotional discomfort so that you can address it and work through it.

- *Engage with shared experiences/traumas happening in other communities.* This chapter offers an example of how people with very different backgrounds in terms of race and class in Hartford and Newtown experienced the loss of young people's lives to violence and how they both were struggling to find the best ways to respond. These shared experiences, however, do not erase other differences and so avoiding internal violence of the spirit is in part about expanding the emotional capacity to ask: What does genuine solidarity look like? What does it mean to be an ally across lines of difference? Over time, this work requires developing relationships strong enough to hold shared trauma without assuming people's overall experiences are the same.
- *Rehearse for difficult moments.* Nonviolent action can be or feel chaotic, whether it is a protest or a difficult conversation with a parent. Role play, practice with a friend and imagine different scenarios and how you can remain calm or cultivate the emotions that are most useful in those situations. Expressing intense emotions in productive ways is a key to everyday resistance and that expression may be spoken or expressed through the use of the arts or even by withdrawing consent by leaving a destructive situation.
- *Explore complicity.* What is it? What emotions come up for you when you are complicit in injustice? What can you do to shift those emotional states? One answer is not only to examine the problem but also to take action. External action shifts internal emotional states as well it is not purely an individual reflective activity. Sometimes people get stuck in that solo reflection.
- *Time matters.* Nonviolent activists gain greater emotional control and stay committed over the long run partly by recognizing that they are part of a long history and global nonviolent movements for change. They are in a social justice relay race, and others are relying on them. There are clear connections between emotion awareness, control, expression and health and well-being over the long haul and a shift in perspective can help. "I am not the first person to feel this way. I don't have to do this alone. Other people are searching for solutions and feeling these emotions as well".
- *The arts are an effective medium for getting in touch with and re-evaluating one's inner life.* Educators do not need to be artists to lead this work, though it can be highly effective to partner with artists. *Start small*, even simple activities like the drawing circles one can ease students into larger, heavier concepts with a greater sense of control. Obviously, this depends on the audience, but the arts are a productive way to access internal responses to the difficult terrain of violence and inequality.

Notes

1 "Imported 'Constituents': Incarcerated People a & Political Clout in Connecticut," *Prison Policy Initiative*, April 2013, www.prisonersofthecensus.org/ct/report_2013.pdf.

2 Mary Buchanan and Mark Abraham, "Concentrated Wealth and Poverty in Connecticut's Neighborhoods," *DataHaven*, August 8, 2015, https://datahaven.carto.com/viz/923322b6-e446-11e4-8d59-0e018d66dc29/embed_map.

3 "Smart Justice," *ACLU CT*, May 16, 2018, www.acluct.org/en/issues/smart-justice.

4 Richard Rubenstein, "The Police May Pull the Trigger, but It's the System That Kills," *Human Wrongs Watch* (blog), June 19, 2020, https://human-wrongs-watch.net/2020/06/19/the-police-may-pull-the-trigger-but-its-the-system-that-kills/.

5 "Weekly Update," *Katal Center for Equity, Health, and Justice*, May 8, 2019, www.katal center.org/update_may_8_2019.

6 When I show this footage to students, they are taken aback by the ways the hosts insinuate that King and others in the movement are going to engage in mass violence. They have been raised to revere King as a man of peace and my White students can't fathom how this could happen when the protests consistently used nonviolent tactics. This opens up avenues to discuss coverage of BLM protests which also have been overwhelmingly nonviolent but also framed in terms of violence.

7 The Martin Luther King, Jr., Research and Education Institute, "Interview on 'Meet the Press,'" April 17, 1960, https://kinginstitute.stanford.edu/king-papers/documents/interview-meet-press.

8 Ibid.

9 Noga Cohen and Kevin N Ochsner, "From Surviving to Thriving in the Face of Threats: The Emerging Science of Emotion Regulation Training," *Current Opinion in Behavioral Sciences, Survival Circuits* 24 (December 1, 2018): 143–55, https://doi.org/10.1016/j.cobeha.2018.08.007.

10 Jessica D. Hoffmann et al., "Teaching Emotion Regulation in Schools: Translating Research into Practice with the RULER Approach to Social and Emotional Learning," *Emotion, Fundamental Questions in Emotion Regulation* 20, no. 1 (February 2020): 105–9, https://doi.org/10.1037/emo0000649.

11 It turns out his concerns were not unfounded, as the bus he was on during the freedom rides was set on fire while local Whites held the doors closed in hopes that the activists inside would be burned alive. They would have likely been killed were it not for a tire or something popping, which sent the racist mob running for fear the bus would explode, allowing the nonviolent activists to narrowly escape.

12 Personal conversation with the author. Lawson told me this during the first James Lawson Institute.

13 Bernard LaFayette Jr and Kathryn Lee Johnson, *In Peace and Freedom: My Journey in Selma* (Lexington, KY: University Press of Kentucky, 2013).

14 George Lakey, "Making Meaning of Pain and Fear," in *The Paradox of Repression and Nonviolent Movements* (Syracuse, NY: Syracuse University Press, 2018), 270.

15 Arthur Romano, Susan F. Hirsch, and Agnieszka Paczynska, "Teaching about Global Complexity: Experiential Conflict Resolution Pedagogy in Higher Education Classrooms," *Conflict Resolution Quarterly* 34, no. 3 (2017): 255–79, https://doi.org/10.1002/crq.21174.

16 Maxim Milyavsky et al., "To Reappraise or Not to Reappraise? Emotion Regulation Choice and Cognitive Energetics," *Emotion* 19, no. 6 (2019): 964–81, https://doi.org/10.1037/emo0000498.

17 Yogev Kivity et al., "The Role of Expressive Suppression and Cognitive Reappraisal in Cognitive Behavioral Therapy for Social Anxiety Disorder: A Study of Self-Report, Subjective, and Electrocortical Measures," *Journal of Affective Disorders* 279 (January 15, 2021): 334–42, https://doi.org/10.1016/j.jad.2020.10.021.

18 Allison S. Troy et al., "Cognitive Reappraisal and Acceptance: Effects on Emotion, Physiology, and Perceived Cognitive Costs," *Emotion* 18, no. 1 (2018): 58–74, https://doi.org/10.1037/emo0000371.

19 Debora Cutuli, "Cognitive Reappraisal and Expressive Suppression Strategies Role in the Emotion Regulation: An Overview on Their Modulatory Effects and Neural Correlates," *Frontiers in Systems Neuroscience* 8 (September 19, 2014), https://doi.org/10.3389/fnsys.2014.00175.

20 Allon Vishkin et al., "One Size Does Not Fit All: Tailoring Cognitive Reappraisal to Different Emotions," *Personality and Social Psychology Bulletin* 46, no. 3 (March 1, 2020): 469–84, https://doi.org/10.1177/0146167219861432.

21 Cutuli, "Cognitive Reappraisal and Expressive Suppression Strategies Role in the Emotion Regulation."

22 Nonviolence can involve emotional suppression, but ultimately, it is about transforming the way we see and approach these situations; this is the heart of avoiding internal violence of the spirit. This is especially important when responding to and living in a world with deeply entrenched structural violence and outside of these short episodic phases of resistance. We "avoid" by reframing and refusing to see those that harm us as outside of the beloved community – in other words as deserving of violence and we also refuse to see ourselves as powerless in responding to their harm or changing these deeply entrenched systems.

23 Shawn A. Ginwright, *Hope and Healing in Urban Education: How Urban Activists and Teachers Are Reclaiming Matters of the Heart* (New York, NY: Routledge, 2016), 3.

24 Tori DeAngelis, "When Anger's a Plus," *Monitor on Psychology* 34, no. 3 (March 2003): 44.

25 This is a necessity given the diversity of participants in workshops which include people from various racial, cultural, education and age backgrounds. Where prayer may work for some participants, others are secular and do not find those strategies useful.

26 Brianna Chu et al., "Physiology, Stress Reaction," in *StatPearls* (Treasure Island, FL: StatPearls Publishing, 2021), www.ncbi.nlm.nih.gov/books/NBK541120/.

27 Eric Shuman, Eran Halperin, and Michal Reifen Tagar, "Anger as a Catalyst for Change? Incremental Beliefs and Anger's Constructive Effects in Conflict," *Group Processes & Intergroup Relations* 21, no. 7 (October 1, 2018): 1092–106, https://doi.org/10.1177/1368430217695442.

28 Ibid.

29 Smadar Cohen-Chen, Ruthie Pliskin, and Amit Goldenberg, "Feel Good or Do Good? A Valence – Function Framework for Understanding Emotions," *Current Directions in Psychological Science* 29, no. 4 (August 1, 2020): 388–93, https://doi.org/10.1177/0963721420924770.

30 Deborah Smith, "Angry Thoughts, At-Risk Hearts," *Monitor on Psychology* 34, no. 3 (2003): 46.

31 "We do not have to experience uncontrollable anger in order for this emotion to have an impact on our body. When fear is the trigger to our anger, a multitude of responses affect our body. It can almost be described as the 'domino effect'. First, whatever it is that caused the fear that lead to anger causes our stress hormones, adrenaline and noradrenaline, to surge through our body. This causes an increased hear rate and blood pressure. Secondly, the muscles that are needed to fight or flee become tense and uptight. This can lead to tension headaches, migraines or insomnia. Thirdly, our breathing becomes more rapid because it is trying to get more oxygen to our brain. Anger can also impact circulation, so if there is not enough oxygen flowing to the brain, this can cause chest pains and even cause an artery to burst resulting in a stroke". From: L. Hendricks, Sam Bore, Dean Aslinia, and Guy Morriss, "The Effects of Anger on the Brain and Body," *National Forum Journal of Counseling and Addiction* 2, no. 1 (2013): 2–5.

32 Michael Schroeder, "The Physical and Mental Toll of Being Angry All the Time," *US News & World Report*, https://health.usnews.com/wellness/mind/articles/2017-10-26/the-physical-and-mental-toll-of-being-angry-all-the-time.

33 Ibid.

34 Ibid.

35 Everytown for Gun Safety is a gun violence prevention organization in America, www.everytown.org/about-everytown/.

36 Warren goes to lobby with them in DC where I have met him before just a few miles from my house and supported their efforts Anytown (the org they started) and they have over time developed an interest in issues of urban gun violence and become dedicated advocates. In part because of the efforts of activists like Warren!

37 Martin Luther King, "The Role of the Behavioral Scientist in the Civil Rights Movement," *Journal of Social Issues* 24, no. 1 (1968): 1–12, https://doi.org/10.1111/j.1540-4560.1968.tb01465.x.

38 Discussion of White fragility and privilege often misses this component of emotional fortitude that Victoria points out is critical to doing anti-racist work.

39 Ginwright, *Hope and Healing in Urban Education*, 4.

40 Sylvie Mrug, Anjana Madan, and Michael Windle, "Emotional Desensitization to Violence Contributes to Adolescents' Violent Behavior," *Journal of Abnormal Child Psychology* 44, no. 1 (January 2016): 75–86, https://doi.org/10.1007/s10802-015-9986-x.

41 Pan Chen, Dexter R. Voisin, Phillip L. Marotta, and Kristen C. Jacobson, "Racial and Ethnic Comparison of Ecological Risk Factors and Youth Outcomes: A Test of the Desensitization Hypothesis," *Journal of Child and Family Studies* 29, no. 10 (October 1, 2020): 2722–33, https://doi.org/10.1007/s10826-020-01772-8.

42 Uma Raman, Philip A. Bonanno, Devika Sachdev, Aparna Govindan, Atharva Dhole, Oluwafeyijimi Salako, Jay Patel, et al., "Community Violence, PTSD, Hopelessness, Substance Use, and Perpetuation of Violence in an Urban Environment," *Community Mental Health Journal* 57, no. 4 (May 1, 2021): 622–30, https://doi.org/10.1007/s10597-020-00691-8.

43 Ijeoma Opara, David T. Lardier, Isha Metzger, Andriana Herrera, Leshelle Franklin, Pauline Garcia-Reid, and Robert J. Reid, "'Bullets Have No Names': A Qualitative Exploration of Community Trauma Among Black and Latinx Youth," *Journal of Child and Family Studies* 29, no. 8 (August 1, 2020): 2117–29, https://doi.org/10.1007/s10826-020-01764-8.

44 Sarah R. Robinson, Kristen Ravi, and Rachel J. Voth Schrag, "A Systematic Review of Barriers to Formal Help Seeking for Adult Survivors of IPV in the United States, 2005–2019," *Trauma, Violence, & Abuse*, April 8, 2020, 1524838020916254, https://doi.org/10.1177/1524838020916254.

45 Alison M. Pickover, Jabeene Bhimji, Shufang Sun, Anna Evans, Lucy J. Allbaugh, Sarah E. Dunn, and Nadine J. Kaslow, "Neighborhood Disorder, Social Support, and Outcomes Among Violence-Exposed African American Women," *Journal of Interpersonal Violence* 36, no. 7–8 (April 1, 2021): NP3716–37, https://doi.org/10.1177/0886260518779599.

46 Jerry Suls, "Toxic Affect: Are Anger, Anxiety, and Depression Independent Risk Factors for Cardiovascular Disease?" *Emotion Review* 10, no. 1 (January 1, 2018): 6–17, https://doi.org/10.1177/1754073917692863.

47 Katharina S. Wehebrink et al., "Pupil Mimicry and Trust – Implication for Depression," *Journal of Psychiatric Research* 97 (February 1, 2018): 70–76, https://doi.org/10.1016/j.jpsychires.2017.11.007.

48 Chee-Ruey Hsieh, Siyuan Liu, and Xuezheng Qin, "The Hidden Costs of Mental Depression: Implications on Social Trust and Life Satisfaction," *The Manchester School* 87, no. 2 (2019): 259–96, https://doi.org/10.1111/manc.12251.

49 Jessica H. Lu and Catherine Knight Steele, "'Joy Is Resistance': Cross-Platform Resilience and (Re)Invention of Black Oral Culture Online," *Information, Communication & Society* 22, no. 6 (May 12, 2019): 823–37, https://doi.org/10.1080/1369118X.2019.1575449.

50 Aarron Booker, "Teach Us How: Love, Relationships, Resistance," *McNair Research Journal SJSU* 16, no. 1 (October 2, 2020), https://scholarworks.sjsu.edu/mcnair/vol16/iss1/5.

51 Valerie Bass-Adams and Chonika Coleman-King, "The Guardians of Black Joy," *Black Mother Educators: Advancing Praxis for Access, Equity, and Achievement* (2021): 57.

52 Rachel MacNair, "The Psychology of Agents of Repression: The Paradox of Defection," in *The Paradox of Repression and Nonviolent Movements*, ed. Lester R. Kurtz and Lee A. Smithey (Syracuse University Press, 2018), 74–101, https://doi.org/10.2307/j.ctt20p56zh.10.

53 Brandon J. Griffin, Natalie Purcell, Kristine Burkman, Brett T. Litz, Craig J. Bryan, Martha Schmitz, Claudia Villierme, Jessica Walsh, and Shira Maguen, "Moral Injury: An Integrative Review," *Journal of Traumatic Stress* 32, no. 3 (2019): 350–62, https://doi.org/10.1002/jts.22362.

54 Greis Cifuentes, "The Role of Arts and Culture in the Colombia Peacebuilding Process," *Jornadas de Investigación en Política y Derecho* 147 (2019).

55 Mary Clark, "The Creative Path to Peace: An Exploration of Creative Arts-Based Peacebuilding Projects," *Creative Studies Graduate Student Master's Projects*, May 1, 2019, https://digitalcommons.buffalostate.edu/creativeprojects/293.

56 Debra Kalmanowitz and Rainbow T. H. Ho, "Out of Our Mind. Art Therapy and Mindfulness with Refugees, Political Violence and Trauma," *The Arts in Psychotherapy* 49 (July 1, 2016): 57–65, https://doi.org/10.1016/j.aip.2016.05.012.

57 Kalamanowitz and Rainbow draw on the work of Bonanno, Horenczyk, and Noll, 2011; Punamaki, Qouta, and El-Sarraj, 2001.

58 Martin Luther King et al., *The Papers of Martin Luther King, Jr., Volume VI: Advocate of the Social Gospel, September 1948 March 1963* (Los Angeles, CA: University of California Press, 1992), 325.

59 DeAngelis, "When Anger's a Plus."

60 King, "The Role of the Behavioral Scientist in the Civil Rights Movement."

61 John Leach, "Psychological Factors in Exceptional, Extreme and Torturous Environments," *Extreme Physiology & Medicine* 5, no. 1 (June 1, 2016): 7, https://doi.org/10.1186/s13728-016-0048-y.

62 King, "The Role of the Behavioral Scientist in the Civil Rights Movement."

63 Annette L. Stanton, Sarah J. Sullivan, and Jennifer L. Austenfeld, "Coping Through Emotional Approach: Emerging Evidence for the Utility of Processing and Expressing Emotions in Responding to Stressors," *The Oxford Handbook of Positive Psychology*, July 30, 2009, https://doi.org/10.1093/oxfordhb/9780195187243.013.0021.

64 Eddie Harmon-Jones, "On Motivational Influences, Moving beyond Valence, and Integrating Dimensional and Discrete Views of Emotion," *Cognition and Emotion* 33, no. 1 (January 2, 2019): 101–8, https://doi.org/10.1080/02699931.2018.1514293.

65 Riccardo Williams, "Anger as a Basic Emotion and Its Role in Personality Building and Pathological Growth: The Neuroscientific, Developmental and Clinical Perspectives," *Frontiers in Psychology* 8 (2017), https://doi.org/10.3389/fpsyg.2017.01950.

66 Martin Luther King Jr, "Address at the Thirty-sixth Annual Dinner of the War Resisters League," February 2, 1959, https://kinginstitute.stanford.edu/king-papers/documents/address-thirty-sixth-annual-dinner-war-resisters-league.

67 Martin Luther King Jr, *Where Do We Go from Here: Chaos or Community?* (Boston: Beacon Press, 2010).

68 Arthur Romano, "Martin Luther King's Vision of an Interconnected World Is More Relevant than Ever," *Waging Nonviolence*, January 16, 2021, https://wagingnonviolence.org/2021/01/martin-luther-king-world-house/.

6   The Universe Is on the Side of Justice

In the early morning hours one day in October 2018, CTCN's director Victoria Christgau prepares to leave her house in the rural northwest corner of Connecticut. In preparation, she begins to gather supplies for the day – training booklets, art supplies, flip chart paper and snacks for her workshops hosted by CTCN. On this day, she will need to be especially careful as the nighttime temperatures have dipped far below zero and the roads are covered with black ice. In that 30-mile scenic journey to the city, she will wind her way through dense pine forests, pass by several lakes where the mist rises in the morning to cover the road, and a number of small towns.

She will also traverse very different social domains. She begins her journey from the home she shares with her longtime friend and educational innovator, Debbie DeGuire in a rural county, one of the few counties in the state of Connecticut that voted Donald Trump into the presidency in 2016. Like other towns in this part of the state, Victoria's town is primarily White (over 80%), with a Black population of just over 2% and the income levels of households in this area are at the state average.[1] Victoria comes from a working-class background, does not have a college degree and has been an artist and educator her whole life.

Victoria's work in Connecticut began in this part of the state over 20 years ago when she hosted her first Martin Luther King Day celebration, a tradition that continued for two decades. She recalls times when stores in town would even refuse to put up flyers for the event and event flyers were torn down. Eventually, celebrations grew to such an extent that organizers needed to change venues several times to accommodate more people. In more recent years, her work in this area has evolved, as was the case after the 2014 shooting of Michael Brown in Ferguson, Missouri when she co-hosted a conversation on uprooting racism in her part of Connecticut. At that event, participants discussed their responses to the incident and how they might work to influence change in relation to police violence. Pastor Lewis, who continuously emphasizes the importance of White people actively engaging other White people in difficult conversations about race and racial injustice, had suggested these conversations.

On her drive to her workshops today, Victoria passes through West Hartford, one of the most highly educated and affluent communities in Connecticut.

DOI: 10.4324/9781003243915-7

The median income in West Hartford is twice[2] that of her town[3] and three times that of the north end of Hartford, where CTCN does much of its work in the city.[4] Typically, her route into the city to meet with Pastor Lane and others at the Center takes her past the Whole Foods in West Hartford, where she sees people rush in and out in expensive leisurewear and load their luxury cars with local produce. It is like a different world, she thinks, and she often talks about the segregated "Black and White worlds" in Connecticut. She tells me, "I came into Hartford to be saved from that disconnect".

If you turn out of the Whole Foods parking lot and drive straight down the same road for a few miles, you arrive at the North End Church of Christ, Pastor Lane's church. Victoria first met Pastor Lane in 2009, after working several years as a nonviolence educator in the community and she has attended Lane's church for the last eleven years. His church has designated the CTCN as a ministry, which means that they raise funds and volunteer to support it. Through Victoria's work with CTCN, she has also forged relationships with some of these more affluent White people in West Hartford, who have been moved by the work and supported it by hosting fundraisers on picturesque estates overlooking the city, recruiting board members from the area and engaging with academics interested in urban education.

The Center's work and Victoria's journey since 2007 have been anything but straightforward. Over 10,000 people have participated in the Center's programs, but peace education work is extremely difficult to sustain, and often underfunded and overlooked by policymakers.

I ask Victoria about how and why the Kingian sixth principle that the "universe is on the side of justice" applies to nonviolence. She replies without hesitation that for herself and most other community educators that sense of being part of something larger and more long term is essential, as

> just keeping your car going, working with no office space, or meeting in coffee shops or in the library to plan while teaching in different locations across two cities, all the time, is really challenging, especially in terms of maintaining that effort and commitment over time.

She explains being a nonviolence educator as "counter-cultural" in a society that often has to be convinced to invest in nonviolence, and even then, only does so in a limited capacity.

Victoria recalls,

> We started in a high school in Hartford, and we brought that summer program to the high school and it was extremely well received and then the principal of the school said, you know, I think this should come in during the school year. This was our first program and we got excited about that and then within a month or two as we started planning and investing time, we learned that that principle [Matthew Conway Sr.] was leaving that school. If you know anything about community and education, you know

that when leadership changes initiatives change within the whole school structure. I felt like the wind had been taken out of our sails, and that was at the very beginning, that was all the way back in like 2013. This was very upsetting to me. And I remember my colleague Gabriel Boyd at the time taking to me saying, "it's gonna work out, the universe is on the side of justice, just wait". You'll find out it's going to work out and a year later, even though we weren't in that school, the social studies curriculum was suspended in the Hartford public schools for a period of time, like a year and so we then got hired to come in and fill in for social studies classes [in different schools]. So we did come back in to the same school and start working with the students again. So that's one small victory but it's very trying.

She elaborates that even though they have been working in the community for over a decade, the funding is still sporadic and

naturally [many] people are only going to be there when the money is there, because they have to live. But I remember there is hope, and we keep working and something will come in, [and it has time and again]. Board members turn over, conflicts between players happen, we are . . . all . . . very independent thinkers. They [community educators] are not regimented 9 to 5 folks, and they like to have freedom in their work. And yet somehow even with all this we always find a way.

Key Concepts: Is the Universe on the Side of Justice?

To take the full breadth of King's ideas seriously, we must ask; do we have a cosmic companion in the struggle for a more just and equitable world for people of all backgrounds? Or, as Shakespeare asks, is life, "a tale told by an idiot, full of sound and fury, signifying nothing?"[5] These are existential and metaphysical questions that tend to get overlooked in many nonviolence workshops, and even in discussions about the importance of King's work or the legacy of the Civil Rights movement in the US.

For those who see nonviolence in purely instrumental terms as a way of influencing political change, these discussions about the long arc of human ethics, morality and progress may seem superfluous and unnecessary. However, these questions and the prospect of long-term, sometimes excruciatingly deferred progress are both practical and necessary for some people when it comes to making meaning about sustaining resistance to injustice in the heat of the battle. Those who practice nonviolence often face intense pressures not just in terms of repression and violence from the police, the military, or mobs, but also – and this is the case for the communities that CTCN serves – with the grinding structural violence of what King used to call "the de facto segregation of the north".[6] King knew well the daunting scope of

Photo 6.1 ThinKING Youth Leader, Tyrone Massey with Mentor, Victoria Christgau, celebrating the completion of his senior film project, about the origins of CTCN. Hartford, CT 2017 © CTCN

the challenge, not only politically but also emotionally, and described it in his writing:

> I have the feeling that nonviolence is as applicable and workable in the northern ghetto as it is in the South. Now there's a larger job there, the frustrations at points are much deeper, the bitterness is deeper and I think that's because in the South we can see pockets of progress here and there. We've really made some strides that are very visible and every southern Negro knows that he can do things today that he couldn't do four or five years ago, where and in the North, the Negro sees only retrogress and he doesn't find it as easy to get his vision centered on his target, the target of opposition as he does in the south. Consequently, this has made for despair and in many points cynicism a feeling that you can't win and it simply means that we've got to develop in the North a massive job of organization and mobilizing forces and resources to deal with the problem in the urban ghettos of the north just as we've done it in the south.[7]

Nonviolence social change requires faith in the future and a willingness to keep fighting, often during times of profound stress and hopelessness. When the apparatus of oppression is deeply baked into our institutions and woven into the fabric of society, change can seem impossible. Nonviolence also involves sustaining efforts to influence change by working collaboratively with other community members and probing the human psyche for clues about how to awaken the compassion and outrage in bystanders, or even adversaries, to get involved in one's moral and ethical cause. In other words, nonviolence is a protracted and long-term movement for change that requires an equally long-term perspective to combat the short-term setbacks and obstacles that would otherwise encourage participants to throw up their hands in despair.

Martin Luther King Jr.'s faith played a key role in how he and others in the movement approached these efforts and was evident when he declared, "I am convinced that the universe is under the control of a loving purpose, and that in the struggle for righteousness man has cosmic companionship".[8]

While his deep faith helped ground his work, however, it did not inoculate him from the dark night of the soul that he faced as he struggled against systemic racism and economic exploitation. Education about King often overlooks this vital part of the story that King himself struggled spiritually and existentially. In teaching this sixth principle, it is important first to note that King grappled deeply with questions about human nature, the depths of hatred in people's hearts and our place in the universe. He had good reason to question and struggle; after all, he faced daily death threats, attempts on his life, in-fighting within the movement and the weight of guilt and despair that came with seeing many others who were more vulnerable than he was harassed or killed. Meanwhile, the FBI waged a relentless campaign to demoralize King and derail his movement.[9,10] At one point, engaging in psychological warfare, they sent Dr. King a letter suggesting that he kill himself, with audiotapes that claimed to have been of extramarital affairs.[11]

As early as 1959 – just three years after beginning his work – King was already exhausted. He worried,

> What I have been doing is giving, giving, giving, and not stopping to retreat and meditate like I should – to come back. If the situation is not changed, I will be a physical and psychological wreck. I have to reorganize my personality and reorient my life. I have been too long in the crowd, too long in the forest.[12]

The sixth principle, essentially, invites us to consider how to shift our frames of reference to remain connected to the universe and to the long view of justice that it affords, but even King, who advocated that we remain aware of our connections to something larger than ourselves or even the here and now of the movement, continually struggled to maintain balance and his sense of connection to the sacred. That connection required effort through prayer, meditation and his work for justice. These daily practices demanded that he tend both to his inner world as well as the more tangible, immediate and external work of influencing change.

King's thinking and theology about the "loving purpose" of the universe and the "cosmic companionship" of the struggle for justice were deeply informed by a rich Black American spiritual tradition that fortified Black people as they fought to maintain a sense of dignity while in the violent grip of slavery and long-term racial caste system in the US. That tradition was centered on a well-developed, socially engaged gospel that saw faith and action as intimately connected and required people of faith to challenge the legitimacy of America's original sin of slavery and uproot White supremacy. Religious historian Charles Marsh describes that the sacred in this tradition is conveyed "not in the abstract, formal diction of western white theology, but more down to earth, sometimes coming from stories, poetry, music, drama, dance, or direct action, that is, more attuned to action or performance than words alone".[13]

The development of King's ideas about agape love and the need to radically reorient our values to realize the promise of an egalitarian democracy are well documented in his writing about his pilgrimage to nonviolence. King said explicitly that his beliefs had evolved over time, citing his undergraduate education at Morehouse College in Georgia as a key influence in the development of his views. He recalled,

> my college training, especially the first two years, brought many doubts into my mind. It was then that the shackles of fundamentalism were removed from my body. More and more I could see a gap between what I had learned in Sunday school and what I was learning in college. My studies had made me skeptical.[14]

Dr. King's evolution continued in seminary and his graduate work. His skepticism extended to questions about the applicability of Christian notions of love and redemption to the political domain. Could Jesus' example of radical love work as a transformative force in political affairs? Working through a litany of Christian thinkers, from Paul Tillich to Reinhold Niebuhr, King reaffirmed his commitment to forging a moral approach that could actively counter injustice and promote what he would later call "the beloved community". Through his struggles with Gandhi and Nietzsche, he discovered how nonviolent resistance and *Satyagraha* – a Hindi concept introduced by Gandhi that means holding firmly to the truth – could be used to take down even the most brutal of empires without surrendering one's humanity in the process.

But even these self-reflective accounts of his pilgrimage of nonviolence do not capture the entire breadth of King's spiritual thinking, which was forged in the everyday struggle against the worst aspects of the American "triple evils" of racism, economic exploitation and unending militarism. This was a theology formed in the streets and courtrooms across the country, in nonviolent battles against powerful people and institutions committed to segregation. King bolstered his moral and ethical understanding in conversations not only with other male pastors and faith leaders like himself, or in seminaries, but also with organizers and youth. Many of these activists were women (some, including Ella Baker, challenged him); others, such as Bayard Rustin, who were gay; and still others who lived in poverty all of whom faced different risks than King did. All of these real-world experiences deepened his spiritual understanding of what it meant to align oneself with justice.

During the past decade, Charles Marsh and his colleagues at the University of Virginia have articulated the concept of "lived theology" to describe theological expressions that are human-centered, drawn from personal or communal experience and often from the laity. It is this living theology and "theology of action"[15] that helped ground King's ideas about the world and humanity's place within it. According to theologian James Cone, this evolution, and King's ability to open himself up to learning from the pain of the worst of humanity's faults as well as the strength of everyday people to challenge those injustices, is what made King the most important theologian in American history.[16]

As a "theologian of action", James Cone explains, Dr. King was actively seeking to transform the structures of oppression. King's theology was "dynamic, constantly emerging from the historical circumstances in which he was engaged".[17] Cone shows how King's incipient theology changed from the Montgomery bus boycott to the fateful Memphis strike, centering first on justice, then more on love (agape) and finally on hope and faith, as the black movement faced implosion and peril.

In his book, Stride Towards Freedom, King explained his views:

> In recent months I have also become more and more convinced of the reality of a personal God. True, I have always believed in the personality

of God. But in past years the idea of a personal God was little more than a metaphysical category which I found theologically and philosophically satisfying. Now it is a living reality that has been validated in the experiences of everyday life. Perhaps the suffering, frustration and agonizing moments which I have had to undergo occasionally as a result of my involvement in a difficult struggle have drawn me to God . . . In many instances I have felt the power of God transforming the fatigue of despair into the buoyancy of hope . . . Behind the harsh appearances of the world there is a benign power. . . . It is certainly true that human personality is limited, but personality as such involves no necessary limitations. It simply means self-consciousness and self-direction. So in the truest sense of the word, God is a living God. In him there is feeling and will, responsive to the deepest yearnings of the human heart: this God both evokes and answers prayers.[18]

This final, sixth principle affords nonviolence educators an opportunity to dig more deeply into the role played by faith and hope in King's commitment to nonviolence and his and other activists' commitments to racial justice. And, as we saw in the fourth principle on suffering, the legacy of faith and spirituality is an especially complex one in the US context, because Christianity, God and religion had been used for so long to justify slavery, inequality and violence. King was well aware of this. He was also aware that he was leading a nonviolence movement in a country with a secular state and a separation of church and state, which affected his spiritual evolution and the place of faith in his thinking and activism.

One of the most vital aspects of this part of King's legacy is his ecumenical approach and his desire to embrace a variety of faith backgrounds in his theology. While Dr. King was a Christian minister, he also put a great deal of effort into broadening his message to include a wide range of faith backgrounds. Some of King's deepest insights and relationships, in fact, were inspired by thinkers from other religious denominations. In particular, his friendship with refugee and Vietnamese Buddhist monk Thich Nhat Hanh was of such significance that King recommended him for a Nobel Peace Prize in 1967.[19] King worked consciously and deliberately to make his moral and ethical perspectives accessible to people from diverse backgrounds. As Robert Michael Franklin Jr. writes,

Personally, he embodied the virtues of liberal Christianity, black folk culture, and the American political tradition of human rights and pragmatism. Symbolically, he came to be a man for all seasons and people, creatively combining the particularity of the African- American freedom struggle (sacred music, theology of hope, inspirational preaching) with the universalist rhetoric of America's constitutive documents (Constitution, Declaration of Independence, Emancipation Proclamation) in order to forge for other blacks, and all Americans, an authentic, progressive American identity.[20]

This is clearly reflected in Martin Luther King Jr.'s language – his use of poetic imagery related to the "structure of the world", a wider "garment of destiny", the "moral arc" and other terms that invited people to consider the transpersonal without reference to God. He also was more explicit in his humanist and inter-faith approach to movement building as was the case in (1958) when he contended.

> Whether we call it an unconscious process, an impersonal Brahman, or a Personal Being of matchless power and infinite love, there is a creative force in this universe that works to bring the disconnected aspects of reality into a harmonious whole.[21]

King understood that many White Americans would dismiss his ideas simply because he was African American, and this inspired his ecumenical approach.[22] King kept his rhetoric as open and accommodating of other religious faiths seeking to find pathways for broader movement building and a movement that was global. Even as King would sometimes make appeals to the Hebraic-Christian heritage, he would often frame moral appeals in terms of broader notions of mutual responsibility and care.

King was a strong advocate of the separation of church and state and the importance of the secular state in a pluralistic democracy. He supported the Supreme Court's decisions that struck down government-endorsed prayer in public schools. In a January 1965 interview with *Playboy* magazine, King was asked about one of those rulings. He not only backed the Court's decision but also noted that his frequent nemesis, Governor George Wallace of Alabama, stood on the other side of this important issue.

"I endorse it. I think it was correct", King said, adding,

> In a pluralistic society such as ours, who is to determine what prayer shall be spoken, and by whom? Legally, constitutionally or otherwise, the state certainly has no such right. I am strongly opposed to the efforts that have been made to nullify the decision. . . . When I saw Brother Wallace going up to Washington to testify against the decision at the congressional hearings, it only strengthened my conviction that the decision was right.[23]

Although King was a pastor and recognized the powerful role that churches and other faith communities could play and had played in advancing social justice, he also remained deeply critical of his own church and its leaders when they played more timid and less constructive roles. This willingness to criticize faith leaders and implore them to more meaningful action in the current struggle comes across most vividly in King's *Letter from Birmingham Jail*. As I previously examined in Chapter 3, King had received a letter from "moderate" White clergy that asked him to be less militant. He replied:

> In deep disappointment I have wept over the laxity of the church. But be assured that my tears have been tears of love. There can be no deep disappointment where there is not deep love.

There was a time when the church was very powerful. It was during that period when the early Christians rejoiced at being deemed worthy to suffer for what they believed. In those days the church was not merely a thermometer that recorded the ideas and principles of popular opinion; it was a thermostat that transformed the mores of society. Whenever the early Christians entered a town, the people in power became disturbed and immediately sought to convict the Christians for being "disturbers of the peace" and "outside agitators" "But the Christians pressed on, in the conviction that they were "a colony of heaven," called to obey God rather than man. Small in number, they were big in commitment.

Things are different now. So often the contemporary church is a weak, ineffectual voice with an uncertain sound. So often it is an arch supporter of the status quo. Far from being disturbed by the presence of the church, the power structure of the average community is consoled by the church's silent and often even vocal sanction of things as they are.

But the judgment of God is upon the church as never before. If today's church does not recapture the sacrificial spirit of the early church, it will lose its authenticity, forfeit the loyalty of millions, and be dismissed as an irrelevant social club with no meaning for the twentieth century.[24]

As his searing words in the *Letter from Birmingham Jail* suggest, King may have taken comfort in the notion of the long moral arc of the universe, bending toward justice, but that didn't mean that clergy or others should *wait around passively*, and it didn't excuse fatalism, indifference or complacency. In King's speeches, a clear trend emerges. Before delivering his message that activists had a cosmic companion in their struggles for justice, King talked about the work that needs to be done *right now*! King consistently paired his arc of justice metaphor with an equally vital idea – that we have a critical role in bending it, and just because it is on the side of justice doesn't mean that justice, and victory, is inevitable. He made this point many times:

Human progress is neither automatic nor inevitable. Even a superficial look at history reveals that no social advance rolls in on the wheels of inevitability. Every step towards the goal of justice requires sacrifice, suffering, and struggle, the tireless exertions and passionate concern of dedicated individuals. Without persistent effort, time itself becomes an ally of the insurgent and primitive forces of irrational emotionalism and social destruction. This is no time for apathy or complacency. This is a time for vigorous and positive action.[25]

King had a dual focus on the strength and solace of being part of a deeply embedded and timeless sense of justice and the hard work required immediately to demonstrate that more tangibly. These elements were inseparable. He saw change as the product of

tireless effort and the persistent work of dedicated individuals who are willing to be co-workers with God. And without this hard work, time itself becomes an ally of the primitive forces of social stagnation. So we must help time and realize that the time is always ripe to do right.[26]

It is important to recognize that Martin Luther King Jr. was an existential activist. An existential activist asks, why are we here? Are we alone? What constitutes a meaningful life? What has value? How should we approach our mortality? Or reconciliation and forgiveness? His activism called into question materialistic values, pushed Americans to re-consider the purpose of life or what constitutes a meaningful life and how they were connected to others. He saw the need for radical empathy and to engage in what author and nonviolence educator, Kazu Haga calls "healing resistance".[27]

King sought the solace, strength and consolation of the long view, so memorably conveyed in the key idea of the "moral arc of the universe". This long view can change our perspective. In King's writings on the bending of time, we see this possibility, for a new perspective on what must have often appeared to be insurmountable odds and a hopeless struggle in the here and now for justice. King explained that "although you live in the colony of time, your ultimate allegiance is to the empire of eternity. You have a dual citizenry. You live both in time and eternity; both in heaven and earth".[28]

Applying the Concepts, and Lessons Learned

In some CTCN workshops, participants are asked to prepare questions to be answered by an external panel of nonviolence experts, and this is one of the more powerful learning experiences in the workshops. They are encouraged to consider what they might want to ask King about the particular principle under discussion. When it comes to principle 6, participants ask very consistent questions across all of the groups. They often ask, what is justice? How can the universe be on the side of justice if there is so much inequality and violence in the world? If there is a creator then why would they make such a world? Things seem to be getting worse, not better, so how then is the universe on the side of justice, or the arc bending toward it?

These questions are important if we want to take seriously King's work and understand how people make sense of their sense of agency and their ability to sustain their activism over time. In the workshops, the community educators facilitate conversations, creating opportunities for community members to pair up and talk with each other about ways they see the universe may be on the side of justice and what they see as obstacles. This is also an area where Victoria tends to incorporate songs from the civil rights movement of the 1950s and 1960s which often emphasize having a long-term view and sustaining hope even when justice may seem far-off with lyrics extolling the virtues of keeping your eyes on the prize or to keep marching toward freedom.

These intimate facilitated conversations about the sixth principle invariably come back to some of the most difficult aspects of daily life in the city. During one of the workshops, a new student, 15-year-old Carmen, questions if justice is possible in Hartford. Jonathan, her 16-year-old classmate, is quick to echo her concern.

> "Yeah, the 6th one [principle] . . . I don't think that's true because of how law and 'justice' work [in America]", he asserts. "What we see today! I think the six principle is more like a dream. MLK probably thought of or foresaw it [possibly coming] in his time. It probably happened [then] but now things still haven't changed".

Carmen jumps back into the conversation, agreeing that the sixth principle is aspirational, adding,

> [It's] also about [building] the beloved community. It's about Hartford there is shit like you don't see [positive activities] but I feel the beloved community here [anyway] . . . like after this program, if I do start going out more, um, maybe I'll just try my hardest to stop violence. Without being violent myself.

Both Pastor Lane and Victoria like to point out in the workshops that young people are naturally concerned about issues of fairness and justice. This is a major driver of nonviolent education, building on the internal capacity that young people have to question issues of fairness and a sense of compassion that all people should be treated with dignity.

For Victoria, justice is not just an idea or vision for the future but is part of our own internal structure and moral sense. Reflecting on the workshops, she shares,

> I talk about the fact that when you're a child, around seven years old, you start to become in human development terms, to become much more aware of what's fair and what's not fair. Who's got the pencil or who doesn't. You know who gets to go out and do things and who doesn't and you start as a child to say that's not fair.

Victoria is convinced that

> within each individual is an understanding of fairness or balance or justice, you know and as we get older [we sometimes lose that]. I think like the universe is what we're made up of and so we have innate balance and connectivity to that [justice] and even the rhythms of nature [in our own bodies].

Pastor Lane explains that it should be expected that some of the deepest conversations when preparing youth educators like Paris and Tremayne to facilitate are about this principle as they grapple with why bad things so often are happening in the community and wider world. In the quiet of his home office, he pauses to collect his thoughts and reflects on the last decade of work with new YFs,

Photo 6.2 Victoria Christgau and James Lane sharing the Principles of Nonviolence during a training with AmeriCorps Vista leaders, 2017 © CTCN

"I try to illustrate to them with a story I remember from grade school", the Pastor tells me.

> You know the teacher would put these broken boxes of crayon in cigar boxes before us and we would color. And these girls would always get the new crayons and you know, and I just sit there because I'm saying to

Photo 6.3 ThinKING Youth and Adult Trainers celebrate the completion of a six-week Hartford, CT summer youth development program 2013 © CTCN

myself, I'm not coloring with these broken crayons you know, and I never forget the teacher, saying, well James. "Those crayons are pretty that the two girls got those but those broken crayons, they still can color." You know and I've always used that as an analogy of broken people, you know because we are, we're like crayons we are broken but we still can color you know what I mean?

It's a broken world there is a lot of bad stuff, but still, I still can color [the world] the way it needs to be, the way it should be . . . That's a part of what I share is that I'm personally speaking, I know that the universe is on the side of justice, based upon, who I was [where I have been broken] and attaching myself to the spirit of the universe that is on the side of justice. I mean once you attach yourself to it [justice], it doesn't mean you're going to open up the Red Sea. But there's a sense of purpose that has directed you back to it that you can stay on that path for quite a while.

While we may be "tuned into" issues of justice as a child, Victoria and Pastor Lane suggest we can lose our sensitivity to fairness and an egalitarian ethos over time as we become socialized into inequality and face brutality, humiliation and violence in our own lives. James sees other obstacles as well, and here he echoes King's critique of materialism, as well as racial and economic hierarchies, pulling us away from this sense of intimate connection with others that are in vulnerable positions or are suffering. These elements he says, "disfigure us" and twist our self-concept.

> Really what I'm saying, it's an identification level problem, we identify ourselves based on things like when people introduce themselves, it's what they are, you know, I'm a lawyer. We live, I live in North Harford. You know, it does not fully reflect who we are, but it's just so encultured in our society [to look down on people who live here]. You use the word broken and that's something that I've always accepted that humans are but we can make change and get back to our true selves if we catch on to that spirit of justice.

For community educators, the sixth principle is an invitation for participants to have an existentially vulnerable conversation. Victoria says, "that's the whole beauty of this work . . . You're creating environments for people to really explore thoughts that we don't generally talk about in mixed groups" by race and religion. She describes the workshops as a "soft place to land" in order to create an "inclusive environment for deep probing", beyond the immediate "action point" of social change. This is part of the reason that conversations are interwoven with music, art and sharing food together, Victoria tells me because the dehumanizing realities of systemic racism operate at this more spiritual and abstract level as well as the more tangible and direct physical impacts.

Victoria sees that people react to the sixth principle at their own speed and in radically different ways. Educators should meet people where they are, and this applies to how they are processing the existential questions introduced by this principle. Victoria explains that in workshops, "there are almost always people that just get it and are right there with you", she's seen. "There's some people just nodding their heads and they get it instantly, like they just get it, because maybe they have a belief in a higher power. "And then those who aren't have to chew on it . . . and I welcome the conversation. I welcome them to go and think about it, I welcome them to chew on it, and rebuke" the principle if they disagree. This is especially true because workshops can attract "a lot of wounded people – very, very wounded people who are looking for a place to be".

The recognition that the world is full of injustice that Jonathan raised is part of the creative struggle at the heart of taking nonviolence and King's legacy seriously. Dr. Bernard LaFayette underscores that this principle isn't about convincing people that the world is as it should be nor is it about reinforcing complacency or fatalism. As a young activist, LaFayette recalls, "I wasn't going to do it for my grandchildren [take the long view]. I wanted to do it for my grand*mother*, who didn't have much time [left]".

While CTCN facilitators rely on historical examples from the civil rights era of King's time, Victoria talks about how participants can "grasp the content" of the principle when they think about more recent events. "I use President Barack Obama as an example of the universe is on the side of justice", she says. "You know, for almost 400 years . . . African Americans were part of the United States, and finally at one point he was elected into office . . . And that's where we say" the moral universe bends toward justice. She talks about Rosa Parks and the Montgomery bus boycott that lasted 381 days, "and the whole nation was changed by that, because of that action. So the universe is on the side of justice".

Pastor Lane incorporates this perspective into his mentorship of new community educators.

> Whenever I'm teaching I tell them [new community educators], we all love that quote about the moral arc is sounds good, but we have to bend it (the arc of the universe) to catch the spirit of justice. It is not just from meditations on timeless qualities of the universe, we often catch it from the spirit of the time, the Zeitgeist, from other people. King pulled from Black folks but also from all over the world, Russians, from Habermas and Nietzsche because they had a spirit in them about certain things [related to justice] and so those people, even in the past that the spirit of those virtues I think they are contagious.

Pastor Lane sees this as a make-or-break moment in America and draws inspiration from what young people are doing to address issues of police violence and racism in their schools. He explains, "you don't have to look to the 1960s to see this. I'm seeing these kids you know catch this thing right now".

He sees people catching that spirit at the national level as well.

Even with the Capitol Riots when they certified the vote, you see many people saying I'm not allowing something dark [like those riots] to overshadow democracy that's it, there's that awakening again, and then the reckoning, in terms of civil disobedience when things are not working. But that's still the universe to me and it's bending you know, but you don't necessarily you just don't see it.

> When they do [resist], like Frankl said, that's when people they find their calling, they find their meaning in their lives in this work for justice and that's something important . . . a lot of people go through their years and never find out who they really are what they were supposed to do, and you know. It is wasted years you know. Sometimes in this work people find that sense of what they want to do and commit to.

After one of the workshops, I find a moment to take a walk with one of the YFs, Paris, and ask directly, if he thinks this work helps stop violence? He replied after a brief pause,

> Well, I do think actually we can do that, because with knowing the six principles it really helps. Because the last principle, the universe is on the

side of justice . . . even when Martin Luther King died the universe was on the side of justice and allowed his message to pass forward to us today and even if the universe is on the side of justice all those years ago it will continue to do that because we will be on the just side. And really if this program – well, knowing that this program is on the just side of universe will make it so that this program stretches out of our reaches in ways that we can't see.[29]

This hope that Paris expresses – in the possibilities for the beloved community and for work for social justice to win the day – is refreshing and difficult to maintain. On this journey, King himself had to continually revisit that which anchored his sense of purpose in using nonviolence as a powerful tool for change. In the process, he expanded beyond the limitations of his upbringing and learned from many faiths and secular sources. In time he came to more fully understand that beyond book learning, there was important knowledge to be gained in how everyday people were not willing to wait but instead sought to bend the arc together. He learned from the civil rights movement and the wider community, and it was those efforts, their commitment that informed his spiritual and helped sustain his faith in the possibility of the beloved community. As King put it:

You know, all of this tells us something about the meaning of the universe. It tells something about something that stands in the center of the cosmos, it says something to us about this, that justice eventually rules in this world. This reminds us that the forces of darkness cannot permanently conquer the forces of light and this is the thing that we must live by. This is the hope that all men of goodwill live by, the belief that justice will triumph in the universe and the fact that the old order is passing away and a new order is being born is an eternal reminder of that truth that stands at the center of our faith.[30]

One of the most difficult dimensions of working as a peacebuilder in America's most unequal cities is making meaning in the midst of so much suffering and violence. The everyday work of nonviolence education also involves trying to sustain work in a society where that work is often invisible, underfunded and underappreciated. In thinking about this sixth principle, some of CTCN's community educators look for examples that their work may in some small way be helping to contribute to bending the moral arc of the universe. Those examples surface in unexpected ways and at unexpected times. This happen recently when Victoria picked up the phone to hear a voice of someone that was involved in the earliest days of the work nearly a decade earlier. It was Matt Conway Jr., the son of the principal who was so supportive of CTCN's earliest work at Weaver High School, but soon thereafter took a new job leaving CTCN searching for a home for their fledgling programs with youth. Nearly a decade later, his son reached out to tell Victoria that he was inspired by their work and had linked up with one of CTCN's earliest community youth educators, Gerina Fullwood, who had since graduated from college, returned to

Hartford and had committed to help lead the CT Murals Project. That project will help commission 39 murals, one for every year of King's life, in communities across the state, and they wanted to work with CTCN to deepen the conversation about King's legacy and using nonviolence to engage in the pressing work of racial justice in the state.

Gerina explains,

> Having these murals in different towns we are hoping that this starts conversations and I believe these murals will make a difference in the communities because it is going to bring the community together and have them reflect on what types of systems are in place that oppress people and have the towns look at policies within their own communities that are not demonstrating equity for all.[31]

According to the younger Conway,

> These murals are meant to shed light on the true legacy of Dr. Martin Luther King. A lot of times we were educated that he was a pacifist, that he wasn't out there fighting every single day and that he was color-blind and those things are inaccurate and we want to tell the true story of Dr. King and other civil rights leaders and how they helped change the history of America.

The series aims to show King "as a symbol of bringing light to darkness . . . and for more equal and positive times ahead", Conway said. "While the work will always continue, these Martin Luther King Jr. murals are a reminder that the light is shining in 2021".[32]

In applying the sixth principle to peacebuilding community educators in Connecticut emphasize the ecumenical as well as eclectic sources of King's nonviolence – an idea that Victoria thinks attracts "very innovative thinkers". An easily missed part of the King's work is this existential component which looks at more than the satisfaction of basic physical needs but instead invites an exploration of life purpose and meaning. In Connecticut, the community educators try to create an environment that gives direction to one's growth and increases one's ability to be creative, altruistic, and self-determined. In this container this deeper meaning-making is explored through the arts and in dialogue within a loving and caring community of people, even in the midst of violence. Yet this journey is also deeply personal, and Victoria describes the sixth principle as one of "self-reckoning. You can't escape yourself if you're practicing . . . It's a mirror . . . quite the mirror . . . and you have to look at yourself".

Tips for Educators and Peacebuilders

Remind students King was an eclectic thinker. The sixth Kingian principle is about the place of hope and spirituality in nonviolence, and for the nonviolence educator King's concepts provide rich material. A picture emerges from King's spiritual evolution of someone who drew strength from his faith, but who made a conscious effort to include and learn from a variety of religious and secular sources in his spiritual life as an activist; who embraced a lived, and living, theology that drew lessons from the world around him; who endorsed the secular state and the separation of church and state; who remained vigilantly and constructively critical of his fellow clergy when they faltered in their commitment to social action; who took solace in the long view of time and history; and whose activism and spiritual life alike were informed by a galvanizing hybrid of faith and humanism. A key component of nonviolence education is exploring the eclectic sources of meaning that influence people in developing an ethics of compassion and care even in the face of resistance. Educators can start with creative ways of exploring the question: What sources of meaning inspire you? What aspects of our relationship to the universe or wider world can inspire us to work for justice? What are sources of inspiration in your life? How can those sources of inspiration help you when life is really challenging?

Humans have the capacity to cause great harm or to contribute to the good of others and the wider world. Create opportunities for learners to critically evaluate their views of human nature. Provide examples that help them consider the tendency of humans to abuse power as well as to sacrifice and care for others. How do we strengthen the parts of our nature that are pro-social? What examples are there? How can we cultivate our *spiritual or psychological muscles* that make us willing to be courageous and use nonviolence?

King's activism was grounded in a cosmopolitan and global view. King is rightly, and widely, regarded as an important humanistic thinker who focused on a global ethics of care: "King's conception of the world community was rooted in his own epistemological God- or Christ-centered lens, but his . . . language . . . was meant to include non-Christians"[33] and people from a wide variety of backgrounds. This is very clearly expressed in King's writing on the World House.[34] King thought in terms of the world as a

> neighborhood, and now the challenge confronts us through our moral and spiritual means to make of it a brotherhood. We must live together; we are not independent we are interdependent. We are all involved in a single process. Whatever affects one directly affects all indirectly for we are tied together in a single progress. We are all linked in the great chain of humanity.[35,36]

This opens up excellent questions to explore with students. Why do you think King developed a global view? In what ways are we "woven together" or inter-dependent today? Why is nonviolence important in a profoundly inter-connected world? Why did he not just focus on issues of race or poverty in the US?

The moral arc is long, but we have to help bend it toward justice. Dr. King's concept of a cosmic companion, or that the moral arc of the universe bends toward justice, can be a source of meaning for committing oneself to the long-term work and feeling like we are not alone. Yet he, like the educators in Connecticut, urged us to work for justice *now*. That we need to find our role and purpose in working for justice. Importantly we cannot bend the arc alone as we need to work with others. Nonviolence in Dr. King's view helps us align ourselves with a deep well of meaning as "our lives begin to end the day we become silent about things that matter". Finding meaning and purpose is an important part of what social justice work can give us. Students can explore if they have ever worked for justice or stood up for a cause they felt was larger than themselves. What was this issue you took a stand for? How did you know you were part of something larger? How have people that lived before you were alive worked to address that issue (bent the arc)?

Notes

1 Torrington, CT Census Data, July 2019. US Census, www.census.gov/quickfacts/fact/table/torringtoncityconnecticut/PST040219.
2 West Hartford Median Household Income, July 2019. US Census, www.census.gov/quickfacts/westhartfordcdpconnecticut.
3 Torrington, CT Median Household Income, July 2019. US Census, www.census.gov/quickfacts/fact/table/torringtoncityconnecticut/PST040219.
4 Ibid.
5 William Shakespeare, *Macbeth* (New York, NY: Grosset & Dunlap, 1909).
6 NBC News, "MLK Talks 'New Phase' of Civil Rights Struggle, 11 Months Before His Assassination," *NBC News*, 2018, www.youtube.com/watch?v=2xsbt3a7K-8&ab_channel=NBCNews.
7 Ibid.
8 Martin Luther King, Jr, "Pilgrimage to Nonviolence," The Martin Luther King, Jr., Research and Education Institute, April 13, 1960, https://kinginstitute.stanford.edu/king-papers/documents/pilgrimage-nonviolence.
9 Sam Briger, "Documentary Exposes How the FBI Tried to Destroy MLK With Wire-taps, Blackmail," *NPR.Org*, www.npr.org/2021/01/18/956741992/documentary-exposes-how-the-fbi-tried-to-destroy-mlk-with-wiretaps-blackmail.
10 Deena Zaru, "FBI, Which Conducted Surveillance on MLK, Sees Backlash after Social Media Post," *ABC News*, accessed March 23, 2021, https://abcnews.go.com/Politics/backlash-fbi-post-honoring-martin-luther-king-jr/story?id=68425778.
11 Andrew Prokop, "Read the Letter the FBI Sent MLK to Try to Convince Him to Kill Himself," *Vox*, November 12, 2014, www.vox.com/xpress/2014/11/12/7204453/martin-luther-king-fbi-letter.
12 S. Nassir Ghaemi, *A First-Rate Madness: Uncovering the Links between Leadership and Mental Illness* (New York, NY: Penguin, 2011).
13 Lewis V. Baldwin and Victor Anderson, *Revives My Soul Again: The Spirituality of Martin Luther King Jr* (Minneapolis, MN: Fortress Press, 2011), 114.
14 Clayborne Carson, *The Autobiography of Martin Luther King, Jr* (New York, NY: Grand Central Publishing, 2001).
15 Lewis V. Baldwin and Victor Anderson, *Revives My Soul Again: The Spirituality of Martin Luther King Jr* (Minneapolis, MN: Fortress Press, 2011), 114.
16 James H. Cone, *Risks of Faith: The Emergence of a Black Theology of Liberation, 1968–1998* (Boston, MA: Beacon Press, 2000), 72.
17 Cone, James H., "The Theology of Martin Luther King Jr. *Union Seminary Quarterly Review* (1973)," in *Martin Luther King Jr.: Civil Rights Leader, Theologian, Orator*, ed. David J. Garrow (Brooklyn, NY: Carlson Publishing, 1989), 215.

18 King, Jr, "Pilgrimage to Nonviolence."

19 King had met Hahn two years earlier when he wrote King to urge his support for an end to the war in Vietnam. Explaining the act of monks setting themselves on fire Thich explained, "Sometimes we have to burn ourselves in order to be heard. It is out of compassion that you do that. It is the act of love and not of despair". (1) This idea of sacrifice to try and disrupt social injustice spoke to King's evolving theology.

20 Robert Michael Franklin, *Liberating Visions: Human Fulfillment and Social Justice in African-American Thought* (New York, NY: Fortress Press, 1990), 103.

21 Martin Luther King, Jr, *Stride Toward Freedom: The Montgomery Story* (Boston, MA: Beacon Press, 2010), 88.

22 James M. Patterson, "A Covenant of the Heart: Martin Luther King Jr., Civil Disobedience, and the Beloved Community," *American Political Thought* 7, no. 1 (January 1, 2018): 124–51, https://doi.org/10.1086/695641.

23 Martin Luther King, Jr, "Martin Luther King Jr: Playboy Interview," January 1965, https://scrapsfromtheloft.com/2018/01/01/martin-luther-king-jr-playboy-interview-1965/.

24 Martin Luther King Jr, "Letter from Birmingham City Jail," April 16 (1964): p 1863.

25 King Jr, *Stride Toward Freedom*, 191.

26 Martin Luther King, Jr, *Remaining Awake Through a Great Revolution* (National Cathedral, March 31, 1968), https://kinginstitute.stanford.edu/king-papers/publications/knock-midnight-inspiration-great-sermons-reverend-martin-luther-king-jr-10.

27 Kazu Haga, *Healing Resistance: A Radically Different Response to Harm* (Berkeley, CA: Parallax Press, 2020).

28 Martin Luther King, "Paul's letter to American Christians," *American Baptist Quarterly* 5, no. 1 (1986): 4–11.

29 "You know, all of this tells us something about the meaning of the universe. It tells something about something that stands in the center of the cosmos, it says something to us about this, that justice eventually rules in this world. This reminds us that the forces of darkness cannot permanently conquer the forces of light and this is the thing that we must live by. This is the hope that all men of goodwill live by the belief that justice will triumph in the universe and the fact that the old order is passing away and a new order is being born is an eternal reminder of that truth that stands at the center of our faith". From Martin Luther King, *The Papers of Martin Luther King, Jr., Volume II: Rediscovering Precious Values, July 1951 – November 1955* (Los Angeles, CA: University of California Press, 1992), 344.

30 Martin Luther King Jr, "The Birth of a New Age," Address at the Fiftieth Anniversary of Alpha Phi Alpha, Buffalo, NY, August 11, 1956, https://kinginstitute.stanford.edu/king-papers/documents/birth-new-age-address-delivered-11-august-1956-fiftieth-anniversary-alpha-phi.

31 Quote from a private video shared with the author.

32 S. Dunne, "Martin Luther King Jr. Murals, One for Each Year of His Life, Planned Across Connecticut," *Hartford Courant* [Online] February 16, 2021, www.courant.com/news/connecticut/hc-news-connecticut-murals-mlk-project-20210216-riqndjchpveb3m2csj7stbbpyu-story.html?fbclid=IwAR0-DbaLCtWPDQmPAoIngtVOfSi-Y0eO8LacUjBBw0bWwCTjMTCkBlN0dM8.

33 Roy Whitaker, "'Our Loyalties Must Become Ecumenical': Martin Luther King, Jr., as a Pluralist Theologian," *Journal of Ecumenical Studies* 51, no. 3 (2016): 402–22, https://doi.org/10.1353/ecu.2016.0034.

34 Martin Luther King, Jr, *Where Do We Go from Here: Chaos or Community?* (Boston, MA: Beacon Press, 2010).

35 Martin Luther King, *The Papers of Martin Luther King, Jr., Volume III: Birth of a New Age, December 1955-December 1956* (Los Angeles, CA: University of California Press, 1992), 342.

36 As **Levitt** notes, "King's timing was perfect, even prophetic. His global ministry was birthed during Africa's decolonization period and his transnational advocacy helped

elevate the Black American Civil Rights Movement Richardson observes, King was the first 'modern black leader, subsequent to DuBois to most prominently embody' the unity of the civil rights and international human rights discourses and movements". Levitt, J. I. "Beyond Borders: Martin Luther King, Jr., Africa, and Pan Africanism", *Temp. Int'l & Comp*. LJ, 31 (2017): 301.

Conclusion

The Beloved Community Is a Learning Community

This book has described how a small group of people in two cities deeply impacted by violence and racial inequality in the US have worked to develop a pedagogy and curriculum that takes seriously the use of nonviolence as a way of influencing both personal and wider social change. Over the past decade, these people have touched thousands of lives and supported an intergenerational and multi-racial group of community peace educators committed to applying and realizing Dr. Martin Luther King Jr.'s work in the 21st century.

The CTCN's curriculum is a *fundamentally different and transformative way to teach King. It takes King seriously but not reverentially: it removes him from the pedestal* and the caricatures of supernatural moral courage familiar from MLK Day celebrations. As a result, community members come together to grapple with the complexities, doubts, struggles and rich layers of King's thought and legacy of nonviolence and to create new meaning in relation to struggles for racial justice today. The CTCN curriculum goes beyond popular educational reenactments of King's "I Have a Dream" speech, opting instead to convey King's legacy through the six key principles of Kingian nonviolence. These principles inspire expansive conversations about justice and the necessity for taking action in response to systemic racism today. Each principle is used to raise important and unsettling questions about taking risks to combat oppression and violence, the possibilities for personal and social redemption and the emotional toll of sustaining resistance and peacebuilding over the long haul. It shows how these community members use nonviolence principles as a guide for reflection moving continually back and forth between theory and practice.

This kind of curriculum and education, as shown with the CTCN experience, is a hidden driver of nonviolent social change. Indeed, one of the most exciting things learned through CTCN workshops and community education is that *principles of nonviolence provide a common language for discussing and analyzing challenging situations* with people from diverse, backgrounds. The curriculum allows teachers, teens, janitors, recently incarcerated people, policy makers, cops and others who have been in their workshops to critically discuss issues and have common reference points. Additionally, for some, the curriculum creates a sense of belonging and a new shared identity (as nonviolence educators and advocates) through which participants can disagree and hash

DOI: 10.4324/9781003243915-8

things out. CTCN's workshops are not simply a solitary endeavor in which one reflects on the principles and their importance in one's own life but is, rather, a collective meaning-making process about what it takes to build the beloved community. King opens a door to more deeply understanding the long history of resistance to injustice that includes people from a wide array of backgrounds, straight and gay, black and white, women and children that have played a key role in nonviolent movement both in the US and abroad. Most importantly, community educators teach us that community-led learning is at the center of building the beloved community which is not only an aspirational end goal but also a pedagogical project that requires continuous experimentation with invigorating the values and practices that guide their work.

This process of collective learning and meaning-making is especially significant because alternative educational settings and projects such as we see at CTCN help bridge the country's urban and suburban divide, which is reinforced by formal education and highly segregated school districts. The Center pushes white participants to take more seriously how they can work for change – challenging racism in their communities while leveraging their resources to support urban social justice education. At the same time, educators of color, most often Black and Latino community educators engage their communities in these discussion about building the beloved community amplifying the capacity and resilience of the community to challenge systemic racism and also envision a more positive future.

In the CTCN model, members of different cohorts – for example, teachers or police officers – have opportunities to learn together and meet with other people studying nonviolence. CTCN is a multi-racial and inter-generational group of core supporters and staff, so the use of the six Kingian principles and this shared language does not mean that everyone is on "the same page" or makes meaning out of the principles in the same way. Instead, these common reference points help develop communities of practice over time and conversations are often as much about people's differing social positions, needs, risks and understandings as they are about the common ground that emerges from this shared commitment to nonviolent ways of being.

The CTCN model reconfigures the idea of expertise and *places community members in the position of educators and experts that are part of a city-wide network of peace learners*. It helps communities explore a new spatial imaginary that sees a wider variety of community spaces as the *classroom*. One of the most striking aspects of this work is that community members, many of whom have experienced violence, *become recognized by their peers as educators* and public intellectuals, so in this way, CTCN also challenges existing hierarchical relations in society and supports informal education as an antidote to the top-down approaches especially in relation to violence prevention and social justice. Just as King learned about nonviolence through the civil rights movement on the ground, the CTCN curriculum draws on the lived experiences and expertise of community members who may lack formal educational credentials but have a wealth of knowledge about the problems and systemic racism they encounter each day and what it means to love and care for one another in the midst of oppression.

I believe that this model lays the groundwork for broader urban peacebuilding with a focus on racial justice, which requires that people affected by issues become more involved in shaping solutions to overlapping housing, schooling, and policing crises in their cities. Dr LaFayette likes to talk about integrative change from the "streets to the suites" (as in, office buildings), or what we might call top-down and bottom-up approaches to social change. As there is growing pressure because of social movements to increase federal and state programs that address systemic racism and economic inequality, supporting community-based social justice education and nonviolence education in particular should play an increasingly prominent role. We need to create pathways in which people are given the space they need to articulate and shape the changes that take place in their own communities. This is more than turning people out to vote or participatory spectacles that occur in town halls or listening sessions. This type of community-led education helps pave the way for participatory democracy and shared governance a way to bridge larger governmental initiatives focused on justice and equity and local needs and knowledge. Traditional tools of focus groups and dialogues, short-term civic actions like planting flowers or even participatory budgeting often lack these deeper critical exploratory and community-building elements.

It is clear that sustaining democratic societies requires that people from all backgrounds be supported in developing nonviolent frameworks for analyzing and solving social problems and taking ownership of these processes. King knew a functioning democracy demands an ethical grounding in nonviolence and a willingness to take action on the issues affecting one's community and the wider society. This commitment allows for compassion in the midst of the fight and the ability for marginalized people to implement and drive change without engaging in dehumanization or political violence.

As this book has described, CTCN is doing racial justice work constantly and, often in the background, before and after the crisis points and the major protests such as the country saw in Ferguson, Missouri, and more recently in the wake of the murders of George Floyd and Breonna Taylor. This kind of work, which is behind the scenes and ongoing, is often missed by social movement scholars who focus on the "flashpoint", highly visible protests and *miss the everyday work of nonviolence and principles and ideas that can animate everyday resistance to injustice.* The various journeys of the nonviolence educators featured in this book demonstrate some of the qualities needed in peace educators on the ground in cities across the country.

We can learn from the persistent recognition of interconnectivity that drives Warren Hardy to disrupt violence on the streets of Hartford and push communities in the suburbs to ask questions about their complicity. Pastor Lane's Socratic approach and patience allow youth to grow into community educators prepared to lead groups to take on the most difficult of educational challenges discussing topics ranging from the power of love to influence change to the despair that comes from inter-generational violence. Victoria Christgau's commitment to developing shared models of leadership and integrating the arts creates pathways for connection and expression when conversations reach a roadblock and her dedication brings continuity to a project in flux. Cherell Bank's willingness to meet young people where they are at and delve deep into the emotions they are carrying while also resisting and trying to change institutions that are often indifferent and often hostile to people of color. Pastor Lewis's willingness to use nonviolence education to try and bridge the divide between police and Black communities by teaching about the difficult history of racial violence that has played out through the criminal justice system. Youth educators like Tremayne, Paris and their peers are willing to be courageous by stepping into a leadership role as nonviolence educators and eventually teaching adults about the legacy and relevance of nonviolence today.

From a wider view, community-led nonviolence educators are developing urban informal education that is grounded in a shared language and ethical understanding – nonviolence – that could help engage complex and interdependent social issues in America's cities far more effectively at a time when the country is highly polarized and democratic institutions are stressed. They have created their own kind of diffuse university or, as I would put it, peace learning systems across these cities. King is central to this effort in this case, especially because he is well known and opens a door to think much more deeply about the cross-cutting and entangled problems facing the country today. He was a threat when he challenged racism, but even more so when he pivoted to combine that perspective with an attack on US imperialism and economic inequality (his "triple evils"). Ontologically, King had a sense of radical interconnectivity, and that perspective is deeply relevant to the overlapping problems we contend with globally today, from climate change, racism, gender inequality and violence, to economic inequality.

★★

In a larger sense, the work of CTCN provokes the question of why we should focus on the philosophy and practice of nonviolence at all since the two communities that CTCN serves are besieged by so many immediate, material and tangible problems every day. Don't people have enough to manage in their lives, including the daily indignities of poverty, violence, marginalization and systemic racism – without trying to carve out the time to explore the philosophy and practice of nonviolence? This is a vitally important question that gets to the heart of CTCN's efforts and the role of nonviolence education as a key driver for racial justice. Consider the well-known work of Abraham Maslow and his hierarchy of human needs in light of these questions.

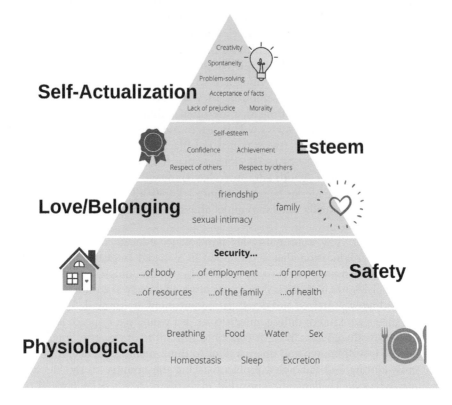

Figure 7.1 Maslow's Hierarchy of Needs

Note: The hierarchy of needs, developed by Abraham Maslow in "A Theory of Human Motivation" (published 1943 in *Psychological Review*) and *Motivation and Personality* (published 1954), is based on the theory that humans have a variety of needs that can be neatly organized into categories. These categories are built one on top of the other, and thus, Maslow argues that humans must be able to meet lower-order needs before they can fully meet higher-order needs.

One may be inclined to think, as this graphic suggests, that the need to make meaning out of one's life, to deeply understand one's context and to live a life of consequence, are "self-actualization" luxuries that sit atop Maslow's pyramid. Perhaps they are issues that are only or mostly of interest – or plausible and accessible – once one has a firm sense of safety and basic security. It would follow, then, that if people's "lower level" needs such as physical safety are not met (and this is most certainly true with many of the participants in CTCN's programs), then they may have little interest, opportunity, ability or need to engage in the lofty work of asking questions about the context of their lives and the value of human life when faced with indignity. As this line of thinking would go, we simply cannot do educational work effectively when more fundamental needs are neglected.

However, the case study presented in this book shows that this assumption is at best a misreading of how people facing violence and material deprivations experience their own lives, and at worst a classist, racist or elitist interpretation of knowledge production.

In fact, as this book illustrates, *people in cities across the country who are experiencing food and housing insecurity and basic needs of safety are actively working to understand why violence is happening in their community and other communities and taking active leadership roles to take education into their own hands.* They are also deeply concerned with what it will take to change these systems. This is not to say that these experiences of deprivation do not have negative effects or make educational work more difficult. However, at the same time, people do not give up on self-actualization or wider collective liberation as they contend with everyday problems, nor do they simply resign themselves to the most dreadful forms of social injustice without seeking to analyze its causes and respond to it.

Even in the direst of circumstances, people seek to make meaning out of their lives and communities. A key and often overlooked driver in violence prevention is this desire to make meaning and influence change. In other words, learning is at the heart of building and sustaining the beloved community. We must ask the community educators in Connecticut: How do we build the beloved community, a community and social structure that reflects our highest values of love, creativity and mutual support, and how do we end systemic racism and other forms of oppression? If we find it hard to motivate students impacted by violence to learn or to care about King or other civil rights activists, especially in Black and Brown communities impacted by violence, then we likely have failed to find ways to make that work relevant to the problems they face and dreams they hold.

Victor Frankl's seminal work on his experiences and observations at the Auschwitz concentration camp powerfully refutes assumptions that people who experience intensive structural violence do not try to make meaning out of it. Speaking of his and others' experiences in German extermination camps, Frankl asserts, "The one thing you can't take away from me is the way I choose to respond to what you do to me. The last of one's freedoms is to choose one's attitude in any given circumstance". Bear in mind that Frankl was speaking of a place where external resistance to violence was virtually impossible – and even in this context, he found some level of agency to make sense out of the world, in an environment strategically designed to strip him of all humanity.

Frankl was certainly not alone in recognizing the importance of meaning-making for people experiencing oppression and for breaking cycles of violence. Harriet Tubman, who knew well the horrors of slavery and the ways that the plantation, like the concentration camp, was designed to take away hope and agency while exacting physical violence, served as an example of psychological as well as physical emancipation. She famously declared, "for no man should take me alive; I should fight for my liberty as long as my strength lasted, and when de time came for me to go, de Lord will let dem take me".[1]

W.E.B. Dubois, too, saw the power of meaning-making and envisioning a better world, highlighting the subversive nature of education. He wrote,

> the South believed an educated Negro to be a dangerous Negro. And the South was not wholly wrong; for education among all kinds of men always has had, and always will have, an element of danger and revolution, of dissatisfaction and discontent.[2]

This book is filled with examples of how people are making meaning out of their experiences in the midst of violence. They do this, in part, by participating in, leading and supporting grassroots nonviolence workshops in their communities. They explore and discuss the six principles of nonviolence and other aspects of Dr. Martin Luther King, Jr.'s work to make meaning out of their own life circumstances, to celebrate and build on the beauty and strength of their communities and to critically examine the oppression and systemic racism they face daily. The stories and cases in this book show that *meaning-making with an ethical grounding in nonviolence can be a key driver of positive change in the US and that this work doesn't have to be done by experts alone but can be led largely by community members* most affected by violence. These are not merely abstract conversations about moral courage, social justice, and the dignity of human life with little connection to hard choices about how to live one's life. The principles are used by participants in nonviolence workshops to reflect on the chaotic and complex undercurrents of destructive conflicts in the US and the possibilities for change. As one of CTCN's 16-year-old nonviolence trainers describes, the principles are "the meat" of the workshops and the place where much of the work comes to life.

But all principles have their limitations and pitfalls. Principles can lead one to focus too much on the ideal, a sense of moving toward a lofty goal. In practice, people may feel as if they are never quite there. Even when making progress, they fall short of all the principles, which can result in shame, inaction, or unwise risk-taking to hasten progress. Principles can similarly be used to glorify people and historical times and struggles – King, for example, is put on a lofty pedestal in formal curricula, so that activists never get to learn about his struggles and evolution as a leader. This can create a sense of inferiority and derail responses to current challenges in pursuit of wrongly perceived necessary preconditions for action. For example, someone might languish with a sense that they simply do not know enough to effectively be part of a social movement. In the case of the six principles of nonviolence, people can fall into a rut, asking: am I courageous enough? Am I too immersed in violence to influence change? Principles can lend themselves to counterproductive purity tests, reduce self-esteem, and make people feel inadequate if they are approached in an overly dogmatic way.

This book shows principles are best seen not only as ideals but as opportunities to bring people together and provide grounding for learning communities in violence-affected environments. Furthermore, principles alone are not enough. Skill, action, and reflection are also critical. Building the beloved community requires sound pedagogy, teaching methods, and committed and skilled educators that can encourage critical thinking and an ethics of care, solidarity and mutual aid in the midst of an unequal world.

★★

I hope that this book has made a case for support of community-led non-violence education, which deserves major funding to sustain these efforts and points toward the central need for supporting learning communities that bring people together from diverse backgrounds in our cities. CTCN like many similar organizations in cities across the country works in the midst of continuous uncertainty because of unreliable funding, the stress of constantly switching offices and headquarters, and staff who work long hours with limited pay and benefits. And yet, CTCN has persisted for over a decade. It has persisted because it works. It has changed many people's lives and created a shared language across barriers of class, education, race and geography. People are consistently drawn to the work and educators remain involved over time.

Although people frequently call for "community engagement" or culturally relevant perspectives to combat systemic racism and violence in America's cities, violence prevention and urban education in reality and practice often rely heavily on external expert-driven approaches.[3] The United States is at a crossroads now, and we need innovative educational approaches that allow for communities to take the lead in examining the complex problems impacting their lives and exploring nonviolent pathways to work together to build more inclusive and equitable systems.

Notes

1 Sarah Elizabeth Bradford (Hopkins), *Harriet Tubman: The Moses of Her People* (Bedford, MA: Applewood Books, 1961), 29.
2 William Edward Burghardt Du Bois, *The Souls of Black Folk* (Chicago, IL: A. C. McClurg, 1904), 32.
3 Kathleen McCallops, Tia Navelene Barnes, Isabel Berte, Jill Fenniman, Isaiah Jones, Randi Navon, and Madison Nelson, "Incorporating Culturally Responsive Pedagogy within Social-Emotional Learning Interventions in Urban Schools: An International Systematic Review," *International Journal of Educational Research* 94 (January 1, 2019): 11–28, https://doi.org/10.1016/j.ijer.2019.02.007.

Index

For Product Safety Concerns and Information please contact our
EU representative GPSR@taylorandfrancis.com Taylor & Francis
Verlag GmbH, Kaufingerstraße 24, 80331 München, Germany